PENGUIN PASSNOTES

Human Biology

Paul Haddlesey was educated at B[illegible] London, and received his Postgraduate Certificate of Education from the Institute of Education at London University. He now teaches in a comprehensive school in north London. He is also co-author of *Biology* in the Penguin Passnotes series.

Trevor Day was educated at Nottingham University, where he obtained a B.Sc. in Zoology. He took his M.Sc. in Marine Biology at the University of North Wales, Bangor. This was followed by a period of research funded by the United Nations Development Programme in Egypt. He has also taught biology at a number of schools in this country.

PENGUIN PASSNOTES

Human Biology

PAUL HADDLESEY AND TREVOR DAY

ADVISORY EDITOR: STEPHEN COOTE, M.A., PH.D.

PENGUIN BOOKS

PENGUIN BOOKS

Published by the Penguin Group
27 Wrights Lane, London W8 5TZ, England
Viking Penguin Inc., 40 West 23rd Street, New York, New York 10010, USA
Penguin Books Australia Ltd, Ringwood, Victoria, Australia
Penguin Books Canada Ltd, 2801 John Street, Markham, Ontario, Canada, L3R 1B4
Penguin Books (NZ) Ltd, 182–190 Wairau Road, Auckland 10, New Zealand

Penguin Books Ltd, Registered Offices: Harmondsworth, Middlesex, England

First published 1988

Made and printed in Great Britain by
Richard Clay Ltd, Bungay, Suffolk
Filmset in Monophoto Times

The publishers are grateful to the following Examination Boards for permission to reproduce questions from examination papers used in individual titles in the Passnotes series:

Associated Examining Board, University of Cambridge Local Examinations Syndicate, Joint Matriculation Board, University of London School Examinations Department, Oxford and Cambridge Schools Examination Board, University of Oxford Delegacy of Local Examinations, Southern Universities' Joint Board.

Contents

1. How to Use This Book

These Passnotes provide a step-by-step guide on how to study, revise and tackle examination questions in Human Biology. Special attention is given to points the examiner is looking for, and common mistakes are pointed out. These Passnotes are not a textbook, but they do contain the basic information needed to gain a good grade. They are best used alongside your class notes when you are revising. With proper use, they should enable you to enter the examination with confidence and achieve success.

The GCSE Human Biology course aims to give the student an understanding of biological principles through the study of humans. The structure and function of parts of the body are studied to appreciate how the human body maintains itself. By studying our relationship with other organisms, and our dependence on plants, it is possible to see how we can exercise control over our surroundings. The course emphasizes health and well-being and aims to contribute to a student's general education and preparation for responsible adulthood.

GCSE Human Biology examinations test a student's ability to:

1. Recall biological knowledge, as applied to humans, and express it in writing or in diagrams.
2. Understand the workings of the human body at a simple level, and appreciate the functional relationship between organs.
3. Appreciate, for cells, tissues and organs, the relationship between structure and function.
4. Understand our relationship with other animals and our dependence on plants.
5. Understand the measures taken by individuals and society to maintain physical and social well-being.
6. Apply biological knowledge to familiar situations in everyday life, e.g. the need to follow good habits of diet, exercise and hygiene.
7. Assess or interpret simple biological experiments and data.

First of all, you need to know through which examination board you are taking your Human Biology examinations. Find out how many papers you will be sitting.

In your revision, you would be unwise to leave out major sections of the syllabus. A proper understanding of biological principles depends on you knowing how the different processes in the body fit together to make a living working unit. Miss out any process, and you do not have the overall picture. For example, how can you understand nutrition properly if you do not know about transport? After all, once food enters the body, it must be transported to where it is needed.

If, because of lack of time, you have to omit certain sections of the syllabus, you are probably wisest to leave Chapter 14 till last, unless you find this section easy to understand. However, you should see your teacher about this.

By now you should know which examination board you are entered with, what type of examination papers you will be set, and you will be aware of which topics you need to know. It is worthwhile at this stage to get a copy of your board's syllabus and some copies of past examination papers. You should ask your teacher about this. With syllabus and papers in hand, you will be clear on the emphasis your board gives to different topics, and you will see for yourself the kind of questions you will be set, as well as the layout of the examination papers.

You can use this book to refer to if you have any points of difficulty during your revision. Perhaps better, the Passnotes can be used alongside your class notes throughout your revision.

Chapters 3 to 16 contain the course contents and each chapter has the following layout:

1. Introduction.
2. The main body of the text, containing numbered topics, and including definitions, examination questions and worked examples.
3. Near the end of the chapter is a checklist of definitions and key words.
4. At the end of the chapter are a number of relevant examination questions.

The checklist of definitions and key words allows you to test yourself on the factual contents of the chapter. The examination questions test your understanding and give you the opportunity to plan examination answers.

The final chapter gives advice and encouragement on what to do just before, and during, your examination.

First of all, however, you should read Chapter 2. This gives a comprehensive guide on how to tackle the different types of examination question you will come across. Learning and revision methods are also included and suggestions are made on how to plan and organize your study.

2. *Working Towards the Exams*

Having worked out which topics you need to know for your syllabus, and what types of question you will be asked, you should then *plan* your study and revision. To do this, follow through the suggested sequence, point by point.

1. First of all make sure your school or college notes are complete.
2. Tidy up your files or notebooks and make sure they include the following:
(a) clear underlined topic titles and sub-titles
(b) underlined 'key words'
(c) clear diagrams with titles
(d) a contents list, referring to numbered pages in your notes.

If you have any notes missing, or have any points of difficulty, see your teacher about these.

3. About three months before the exam, plan how much revision you need to do each week to finish revising your complete course *before* the exam. Break your coursework down into major sections and work out how many sections you need to revise each week in order to finish on time.
4. The use of compulsory short answer questions means that exam questions can be set covering the whole syllabus. You could do well to have a thorough knowledge of all parts of the syllabus. However, if you have particular trouble understanding certain isolated topics, e.g. Genetics (Chapter 14), you might be well advised to 'cut your losses' on some of these topics and concentrate on the rest of the syllabus. Again, you should see your teacher about this. To some extent you can be guided by the topics which have regularly come up in your board's exams in previous years.

2.1. *Revision Technique*

1. To work effectively you need the right surroundings. For most people the ideal situation is a quiet room, by yourself, without obvious distractions.

To work effectively you also need to feel relatively OK in yourself. If anything is worrying you, get it off your chest by taking the appropriate action *before* you start studying. If the problem can't be resolved, write it down. If you are feeling particularly sleepy or have a headache, take an aspirin or have a nap and start work later (but *don't* use this as an excuse for not doing the work).

It is much better to work regularly for a half to one hour a day for five days a week, than to cram all your biology revision into one afternoon a week. These are two important factors to take into account when studying: your *concentration span* and your ability to get information into your *long-term memory* store.

Most people's concentration span is between 30 and 50 minutes; this is the length of time for which they can sit down and study *effectively* without a break.

When you read a passage of text for the first time, most of the material is forgotten within minutes of finishing reading. If you want to remember the facts days or weeks later you need to *review* (look back over) your work at regular intervals. This reviewing reinforces your learning so that the facts enter your long-term memory store and can be remembered later.

So, how can this knowledge about concentration span and long-term memory help in your study:

– first of all, study in half hour spurts with a 5 or 10 minute break in between.

– during your half hour work sessions *concentrate* and work *actively* digging out answers to questions, organizing your work and making notes.

– when you return from your 5–10 minute break, review the work you did in the previous half hour. Remember, regular reviewing aids your memory.

– do not spend more than an hour or two on any one subject. Changing subject after this time will keep your mind fresh and alert.

2. Revise the course topic by topic. You can use the topic headings and sub-headings in this book to help you. Reduce your notes on chapters of this book into topic and sub-topic headings. Write these down on a separate sheet of paper. For example, the notes on pages 199 and 200 concerning the ear can be reduced to the following headings and sub-headings:

Topic: Ear
Sub-topics: Hearing – outer ear
middle ear

inner ear
Balance – utriculus
sacculus
semicircular canals

Read over each topic several times. Make a list of all sub-topics and key facts. Check your understanding of all the biological terms and definitions. At this stage it may be very helpful for you to construct a pattern diagram for each topic (see page 6).

You should be able to reach the stage where you can remember these topics and their contents *without* prompting from the book or your notes. The sub-headings and key words you remember should trigger off a mass of related facts in your memory.

3. Having reached the stage where you can recall topics by remembering headings, sub-headings and key words, do not let your efforts go to waste. Unless you *review* your notes regularly, you will rapidly forget them. Reviewing means quickly re-reading your notes and headings, and this should be done at one or two week intervals. It is only by regular reviewing that your organized knowledge will be retained in your long-term memory.

4. It is sometimes difficult to remember the list of key facts which relate to a particular topic; for example, the functions of blood (page 135) or the functions of the liver (page 100). There are certain techniques to help you do this:

(a) One way is to use a **mnemonic**. These are words, sentences or phrases from everyday language which are simple to remember; these are linked to technical words which are difficult to recall. For example, the seven characteristics of living organisms given on page 19 can be remembered from the following sentence:

Many **f**oolish **r**abbits **e**at **g**reen **r**hubarb **s**hoots.

The first letter of each word can be matched up with the technical word you need to remember:

Movement, **f**eeding, **r**espiration, **e**xcretion, **g**rowth, **r**eproduction, **s**ensitivity.

Wherever possible, make up your own mnemonic. Often ruder ones are easier to remember.

(b) Another way to remember a long list is to group related items together and remember how many there are in each group. For example, the functions of blood (page 135) consist of 11 items which can be grouped into four categories:

1. Formation of tissue fluid (1 function).
2. Transport of substances (5 functions).

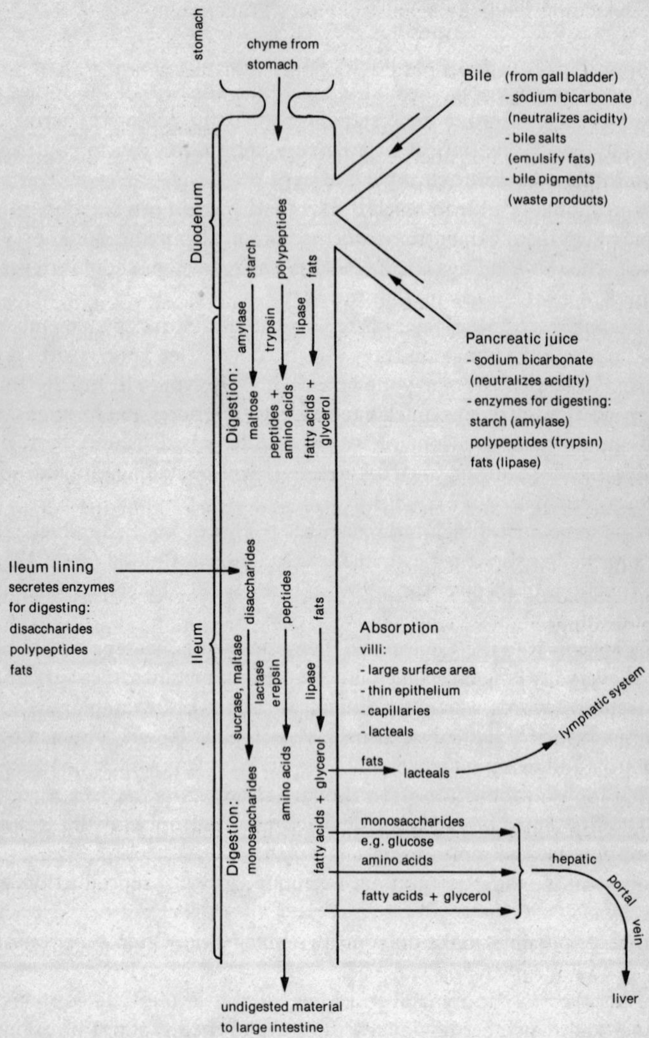

Fig. 2.1. *Pattern diagram for the human small intestine*

3. Regulating body temperature (2 functions).
4. Defending the body against disease (3 functions).

(c) A very important way of remembering key words and their interrelationships is to use a pattern diagram. Start off with the main points which relate to a topic, put these down on paper with plenty of space around them, and then gradually add key words, using arrows to show functional connections between them. For example, what do you know about the structure and functions of blood (see page 135)?

You could start off by writing down headings and sub-headings and very quickly you should be able to build up a pattern diagram linking information from your memory (see Fig. 2.1).

Research has shown that information is best memorized, understood and recalled when built up into pattern diagrams in the mind, rather like the parts of a jigsaw puzzle. When you recall several of the pieces in the puzzle, you can gradually fit the rest together. You will be surprised how much information you will be able to recall. Your own pattern diagram may not be like the one shown; it will be special to you. When you have finished revising a topic always try to summarize it in this way. When you come to the exams you will be able to remember your pattern diagrams and even create new ones when planning answers to essay questions.

5. Now, we will assume that all is going well and that you are keeping to your revision schedule, you are summarizing your notes as headings, sub-headings and key words, and that you are building up pattern diagrams for topics. The next step is to apply your knowledge and understanding to answering examination questions. The questions in the text and at the end of each chapter are there to enable you to do this. To start with you may require prompting from your notes or this book to help you find the answers. Often, you will notice, the answer to a question requires knowledge from different parts of the syllabus. You should reach the stage when you can answer questions without referring to your notes or to the book, and in the time allowed in the examination. Get your answers marked if you can; if not, use your notes and this book to check the answers.

The next section in this chapter looks at the different types of exam question you may be set.

2.2 *Types of Exam Questions*

Short-answer questions

These make up the first part or the whole of certain examination papers.

You are asked to give one-word, one-sentence or short-paragraph answers in spaces provided on the question paper. You can tell how much you need to write by the size of the space provided, and by the mark allocation. Here are two examples. Suitable answers are given.

Q. Fill in the blanks in the following passage.
Plants manufacture carbohydrates by the process called photosynthesis. The process takes place in cell organelles called chloroplasts. During this process carbon dioxide and water, in the presence of chlorophyll and sunlight, are converted to glucose and oxygen.

Protein contains the chemical elements carbon, hydrogen, oxygen and nitrogen.

The latter is obtained by the green plant from the soil in the form of nitrate. [7]

[LON]

Q. (a) What is the normal body temperature?
About 37°C. [1]

(b) Explain concisely the importance of a constant body temperature.
It enables chemical reactions in the body to proceed at their optimum rate irrespective of fluctuations in the outside environment. [2]

[AEB]

In other examples, you may be given a photograph, diagram, table or graph about which you have to answer several short questions or fill in blank spaces. Keep your answers simple, brief and to the point. Be guided by the size of the space provided and by the mark allocation. In general, one mark is given for each part. A definition or brief explanation may be worth two or more marks.

Multiple-choice questions

Normally, you are asked to choose the correct answer from a choice of five. For example:

Q. Which one of the following carries urine from the kidneys to the bladder?
A Renal artery
B Renal vein
C Vas deferens

D Urethra
E Ureter

If you do not know the correct answer right away, you can at least eliminate those which you know to be incorrect. For example, *A* and *B* can be discounted because they are blood vessels. *C*, the vas deferens, is found in the testis and carries sperm. That leaves you with *D* and *E*, and if you blind guess, you have a 50 per cent chance of being right. You may, however by this time, have thought out the correct answer, which is *E* (see page 158). In any case, *D* and *E* are the most likely answers – they both have a *ur* beginning, in common with urine.

Multiple-choice questions ask for *one* correct answer. If you indicate two right answers, you will automatically be marked wrong. If you do not know the answer to a question, you should choose an answer anyway. That way you at least have a chance of getting the answer right and being awarded a mark.

Longer-answer questions

These make up the second part or the whole of an examination paper. There are two types of longer-answer question: the traditional essay-type question and the increasingly popular structured question.

Structured questions are made up of several parts, each of which usually requires a one- or two-paragraph answer. The length of the answer will be governed by the marks allocated to it. For example:

(*a*) *Briefly explain what is meant by the term osmosis.* [5]
(*b*) *How does the process of diffusion differ from osmosis?* [3]
(*c*) *Give an account of the mechanism of excretion in the kidney.* [12]
[OXF]

The answers to sections (*a*) and (*b*) are fairly straightforward. Look carefully at the *meaning* of the question. Part (*a*) is asking you to *briefly explain* . . . So don't write an enormously long answer – you won't gain any extra credit and you will be wasting valuable time. Appropriate key words in your answer would be **selectively permeable membrane**, **water** and **diffusion** (see pages 72–3). A suitable answer to (*a*) would be:

Osmosis is the movement of water from a weak solution to a strong solution through a selectively permeable membrane. A weak solution contains a high concentration of water molecules mixed with a low concentration of dissolved solute molecules. A strong solution contains less water and more solute. This means that osmosis is effectively a form of diffusion. The water molecules move from where they are plentiful to a region where they are scarce.

Part (*b*) is asking you how diffusion *differs* from osmosis. A suitable answer would be:

Diffusion refers to the movement of molecules of *any* substance in a gas or solution from a region of high concentration to one of lower concentration. This need not involve movement of the substance through a membrane. Osmosis, however, is a special form of diffusion involving water diffusing through a semi-permeable membrane.

In part (*c*) key words contained in the question are **kidney** and **mechanism of excretion**. The examiner wants to know how the kidney functions to excrete substances. Section (*c*) leads logically on from sections (*a*) and (*b*); in answering (*c*) you will mention osmosis.

In longer-answer questions it is important to *plan* your answer before writing it out fully. There are a number of reasons for this. In marking your answer, the examiner is looking for a number of key facts, clearly explained and preferably in a logical order. Planning improves your ability to come up with a really clear and complete answer, free of irrelevant information.

A suitable answer plan for (*c*) is:

Simplified drawings of Figs. 10.2 and 10.3 can be used as a starting point.
Key words: **cortex**, **medulla**, **nephron**, **glomerulus**, **Bowman's capsule**, **kidney tubule**, **collecting duct**.
The kidney's excretory mechanism involves two processes:

1. Pressure (ultra) filtration in the Bowman's capsule.
   Key words: **capillaries**, **glomerulus**, **glomerular filtrate**.
2. Selective reabsorption in the kidney tubule and collecting duct.
   Key words: **first convoluted tubule**, **loop of Henle**; **second convoluted tubule**, **collecting duct**
   – **osmosis**, **water**
   – **active transport**, **glucose**, **amino acids**, **salts**, **hydrogen ions**.

By providing a plan, you are not only ordering your thoughts and planning your essay logically, but you are helping yourself to remember the facts you know. Once you have written a fact down on paper, you can concentrate on remembering other facts. Also, without your outline to refer to, key points could easily be left out of your answer.

We can try out this technique on another question:

Q. (*a*) *Make a large labelled diagram to show the structure of the ear.* [10]
(*b*) *Explain how the ear functions when we listen to music.* [11]
(*c*) *What are the other functions of the ear?* [4]
[OXF]

Section (*a*) is straightforward. Fig. 11.16 is a suitable answer. The technique for drawing diagrams is described on page 12.

Section (*b*) is asking about the *functioning* of the ear in *hearing*. We can refer to our diagram in section (*a*) to help explain this. A suitable answer plan for (*b*) might look something like this (refer to pages 198 to 200):

Outer ear – pinna and ear tube collect and channel sound waves
– ear drum caused to vibrate.
Middle ear – vibrations of the ear drum transmitted by the ear ossicles to the oval window
Inner ear – movements of the oval window set up vibrations in the perilymph
– basilar membrane moves and triggers sensory cells in the organ of Corti to generate nerve impulses
– nerve impulses sent to the brain where they are interpreted as 'sound' of distinctive quality, pitch and loudness.

A simplified drawing of Fig. 11.17 could be used to help explain how the inner ear functions.

Part (*c*) is a straightforward factual answer. You would need to mention perception of movement of the head and the position of the head relative to the pull of gravity. This information is used to help achieve balance, posture and muscular coordination in the body.

Part of your revision should consist of preparing essay plans or pattern diagrams for questions likely to come up in the exam. Get hold of past examination papers so that you can map out specimen answers.

Nowadays, essay-type questions are the exception rather than the rule. In general, they are harder to answer than structured questions. You are given few clues in the question and in your answer you may need to piece together information from different parts of the syllabus. For example:

Q. Outline the processes by which energy from the sun is stored in the liver. [25]
[OXF]

This is quite a difficult question. Your answer would need to include an outline of the following processes:
1. Photosynthesis in green plants and the manufacture of carbohydrates and fats.
2. In humans, the digestion of carbohydrates and fats.
3. In humans, the absorption of the products of carbohydrate and fat digestion.
4. The transport of products of digestion to the liver.
5. The storage of carbohydrates and fats in the liver.

In general, if given a choice, you would be wiser to answer a structured question in preference to an essay-type question (but see page 10).

Diagrams

Drawing biological diagrams is a skill you should master. With patience, care and practice almost anyone can draw clear and accurate diagrams. They are a valuable source of marks in examinations.

Diagrams can be used in longer-answer questions whenever they make your answer clearer and save time. Alternatively, diagrams may be specifically asked for in questions, for example, 'Make a large labelled diagram to show . . .' or 'Give an illustrated account of . . .'

In longer-answer questions, diagrams can be used to complement written text. In the text you can freely refer to your diagram, but do not simply repeat information shown in the drawing. Remember, diagrams are supposed to make your answer clearer and save time.

Diagrams are simplified, explanatory drawings. They are not the same as 'true-to-life' drawings done in some practical classes.

When drawing diagrams, take note of the following points:
1. Draw in pencil (that way you can easily rub out mistakes).
2. Your diagram should be large (at least twice the size of those shown in this book).
3. The diagram should be made up of distinct, continuous lines (do not sketch).
4. The diagram should be fully labelled.
5. Label in ink.
6. A straight line should run from the label to the structure to which it refers (do not use curved or branched lines).
7. Label lines should not cross.
8. The diagram should have a specific title.

When drawing, use a sharp pencil – a 1H or HB pencil is best. First, map out the general shape in pencil. Divide up the diagram into its major parts, making sure the proportions are correct. Fill in any detail last of all. There is nothing worse than starting at one end of your diagram, drawing in detail, and getting to the other end and finding it will not fit on the page. Always begin with a general plan, getting the proportions of the major parts right, and then fill in the detail last.

It is well worth copying out the major diagrams from your class notes or from this book. Then try drawing them *without* referring to the original. Be critical when assessing your diagrams. Are they clear, accurate, properly labelled and titled?

In general, you should avoid colouring or shading. This takes time and may make your diagram less clear. In diagrams of the human circulatory system (page 141), blood vessels which carry oxygenated blood can be shown in red, and those carrying deoxygenated blood in blue. If you do this, you should provide an explanatory key.

Always give a title to your drawing.

When drawing a section, always give its orientation. A transverse section (T.S.) is really another name for a cross-section. In a structure which has a long and short axis, a T.S. is a cut *across* the long axis. A longitudinal section (L.S.) is a cut *along* the long axis (see Fig. 2.2).

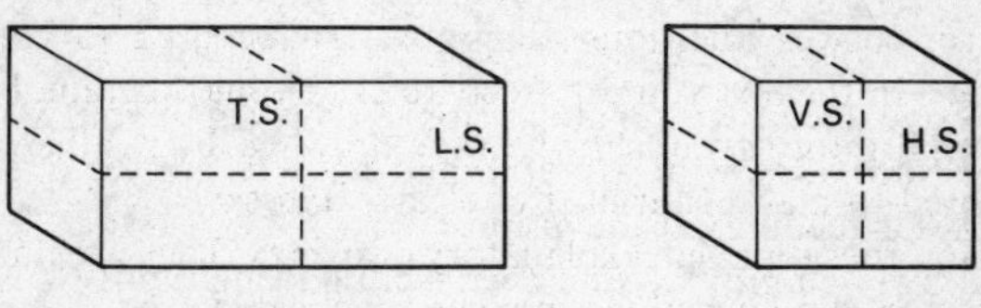

orientation of sections

T.S. = transverse section
L.S. = longitudinal section
V.S. = vertical section
H.S. = horizontal section

Fig. 2.2. *Orientation of sections*

A vertical section (V.S.) is an upright section and is commonly used for describing sections through the kidney, heart and skin. It is used particularly for structures which do not have a noticeable long or short axis.

For the human body (Fig. 2.3) you should be aware which is the ventral (front) and dorsal (back) surface.

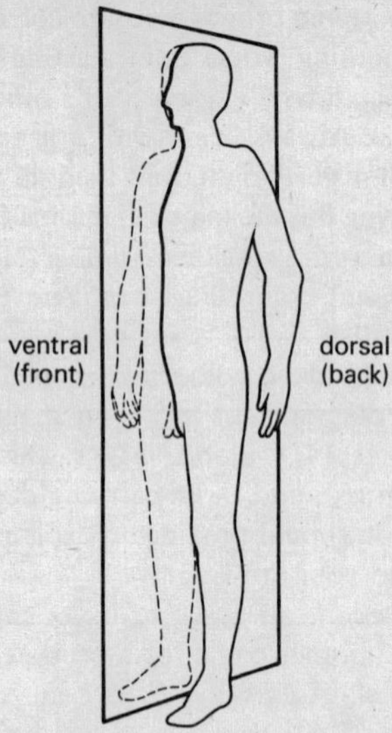

Fig. 2.3. *Orientation of the body*

Graphs

You may have to construct a graph from data given to you. More likely, you will be provided with a graph, and have to answer questions by interpreting or reading off the graph.

When drawing a graph, remember the following points:

1. Plan how you are going to fit the graph on to the paper provided.
2. The horizontal or x-axis is used for the controlled variable – those measurements which are set up and controlled by the experimenter.
3. The vertical or y-axis is used for the uncontrolled variable – those results which the investigator finds out from the experiment.
4. Each axis must be divided into the correct number of units marked off at equal intervals.
5. Each axis must be fully and accurately labelled.
6. Plot each point with a circled dot or with a small cross.
7. Join up the points with a smooth curve or with straight lines drawn with a ruler.
8. The graph should have a title.

Let us work through the following examination question.

Q. The graph below shows average measurements of a foetus from the third to the tenth lunar month of pregnancy (1 lunar month = 28 days)

[LON]

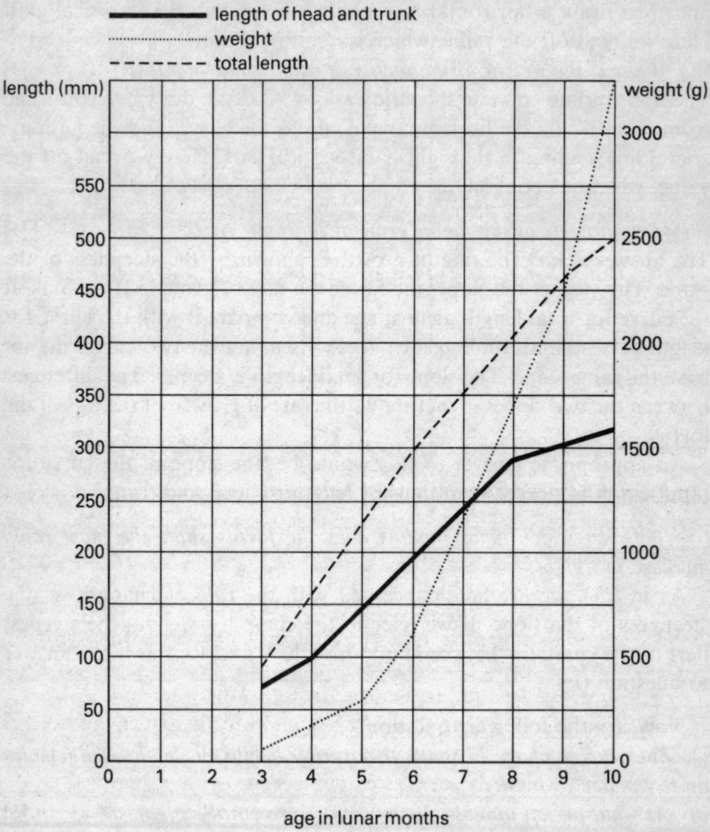

If we look carefully at the graph we see it is slightly unusual. It has *two* vertical axes, one on the left showing length (mm) and one on the right showing weight (g). The graph is really two graphs in one. Both the vertical axes are uncontrolled variables – they are what the investigator is measuring. The horizontal axis shows the controlled variable, age. Three curves are plotted on the graph. Two refer to length and one refers to weight. Now, let us answer the questions that follow.

(*i*) *What is the total length of the foetus at eight lunar months?* [1]
First of all, we need to find the curve which refers to total length. The

appropriate curve shown by --------. Next, we find month 8 on the horizontal axis, draw a vertical line leading up to the total length curve, and then draw a horizontal line leading to the left hand vertical axis. Here we read off the value, which is about 408 mm.

(*ii*) *What is the weight of the foetus at seven lunar months?* [1]

The appropriate curve is shown by ----------. We draw a vertical line from month 7 on the horizontal axis, up to the curve, and then a horizontal line leading to the right hand vertical axis. Here we read off the value, which is about 243 g.

(*iii*) *Do all parts of the foetus grow at the same rate?* [1]

The answer is *no*. The rate of growth is shown by the steepness of the slope. The steeper the slope, the faster the rate of growth. If we look at the curve for total length against age and compare it with the curve for length of head and trunk against age, we see that the two curves do not have the same slope. The slope for total length is steeper. The difference between the two slopes in fact shows the rate of growth of the legs of the foetus.

An appropriate answer to (*iii*) would be 'the slope of the curve for total length is steeper than that for length of head and trunk'.

(*iv*) *Between which lunar months does the foetus show the most rapid increase in weight?*

As in (*iii*), we are here concerned with the *rate* of change, i.e. the steepness of the slope. If we refer to the curve for weight, the steepest part of the curve lies between lunar months 9 and 10; this is the answer to question (*iv*).

Now, try the following question.

Q. The graph on page 17 shows the average heights for males and females up to the age of twenty.

(*a*) *At what period in males is the rate of growth the greatest?* [1]

(*b*) *During which four years do males show the slowest rate of growth?* [1]

(*c*) *What is the average height of the fully grown males?* [1]

(*d*) *What is the average height of females at twelve years of age?* [1]

(*e*) *Name the phase of development which is occurring in girls between 10 and 13 years and in boys between 13 and 16 years, which causes the rapid rate of growth.* [1]

[AEB]

You can check your answers on pages 251–3.

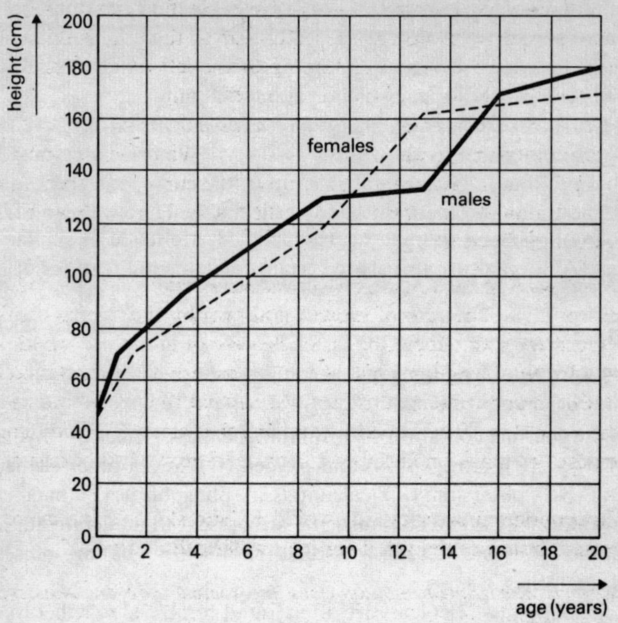
height (cm)
200
180
160
140
120
100
80
60
40
20
0
0 2 4 6 8 10 12 14 16 18 20
age (years)
females
males

3. The Organization of Life

All living organisms, human beings included, are made of similar substances. All organisms also share certain fundamental features of life.

3.1. *The Chemistry of Life*

Living organisms contain four common chemical elements – hydrogen (H), carbon (C), nitrogen (N) and oxygen (O). Seven other elements – sodium (Na), potassium (K), calcium (Ca), phosphorus (P), magnesium (Mg), chlorine (Cl) and sulphur (S) – are present in moderate amounts. A number of elements such as iodine (I) and iron (Fe) are present in small quantities.

In the body these elements are often found combined together to form inorganic or organic molecules.

Inorganic molecules are generally small and simple and consist of two or more elements chemically bonded together. Inorganic molecules are abundant in both living and non-living things. A common example is water (H_2O).

Organic molecules are an important feature of living organisms. These molecules are based on carbon chemically combined with hydrogen and usually other elements notably oxygen. Organic molecules are generally complex. In living organisms four types are important: carbohydrates, proteins, fats and nucleic acids. These are examined in section 3.8.

The average percentage composition of the adult human body is:

Water	58	inorganic (63)
Minerals	5	
Fat	20	organic (37)
Protein	16	
Carbohydrate	1	

As you see, most of the body is water:

1. Water is the *universal solvent*. It is the liquid in which substances in

the body are dissolved. All the body's chemical reactions take place in it.
2. Water itself takes part in certain chemical reactions, for example, digestion (page 96).
3. Water serves as a medium for the transport of materials (page 132).

The commonest minerals in the human body are calcium and phosphorus. They are found in moderate quantities particularly in blood, bones and teeth.

Fat represents the body's long-term energy store (page 100). Proteins control cell chemistry and make up the structural parts of cells (page 99). Carbohydrates are the body's short-term energy store (page 97).

3.2. *The Characteristics of Life*

(NOTE: this is not examined by all boards)

Although it is very difficult, some say impossible, to define what life is, it is possible to describe what characteristics living things share. There are seven such characteristics:

1. **Movement:** all living things move either a part or the whole of their bodies (Chapter 12).
2. **Feeding:** all living things feed. Food is the material from which an organism obtains (i) the energy and (ii) the raw material, to build, repair and maintain itself. The study of food and feeding processes is termed **nutrition** (Chapter 7).
3. **Respiration:** this is the process by which the body obtains energy from organic foods (Chapter 8).
(NOTE: respiration is often confused with breathing, page 110)
4. **Excretion:** this is the removal of waste substances produced by chemical reactions in the body (Chapter 10).
(NOTE: excretion is often confused with egestion or secretion, page 156)
5. **Growth:** a living organism grows, i.e. increases in size. The term growth is usually taken to include increase in complexity as well as size (Chapter 13).
6. **Reproduction:** this is the production of new individuals (offspring) from existing individuals (parents) (Chapter 13).
7. **Sensitivity:** a living organism is sensitive. It has the ability to respond to a stimulus (Chapter 11).

A living organism shows *all* of these characteristics at some time in its life. A convenient way to remember these is given on page 5.

3.3. *Metabolism*

A living organism is an immensely complex arrangement of inorganic and organic molecules. Energy is needed to convert simple substances into the complex organic molecules which form an essential part of the organism. The energy is used in forming chemical bonds within these molecules. Organisms thus need a continual supply of energy in order to maintain themselves.

Metabolism is the word used to describe all the chemical reactions which take place in the body. There are two types of metabolism: **catabolism** and **anabolism**.

Catabolism is the process by which complex substances are broken down into simpler ones, usually with the release of energy. Respiration (page 112) is an important example.

Anabolism is the process by which simpler substances are built up into more complex ones. This type of reaction requires a supply of energy. Examples of anabolism are photosynthesis (page 49) and all cases of growth and repair in the body.

Both catabolic (breaking down) and anabolic (building up) processes occur in the body. Energy released from catabolic reactions is used to drive anabolic reactions.

3.4. *Cells*

In common with most organisms, the human body is made up of cells. A cell consists of a **nucleus** suspended in **cytoplasm** and enclosed in a **cell** (plasma) **membrane**. The living parts of the cell – the nucleus, cytoplasm and cell membrane – are sometimes called **protoplasm**.

Definition: The cell *is the basic unit of living organisms. It consists of a nucleus suspended in cytoplasm and enclosed in a cell membrane.*

The red blood cell is an exception to this definition – it does not have a nucleus (see page 134).

There are over 50 million million (5×10^{13}) cells in the human body. Human cells range in size from 5 μm to 100 μm (1 mm) across; the largest is the human egg or ovum (page 241).

There are good reasons why cells are so small. One reason is that all living parts of the cell must be in close contact with their surroundings. Only then can they obtain supplies and get rid of wastes quickly enough to support life. Movement of substances into and out of the cell is

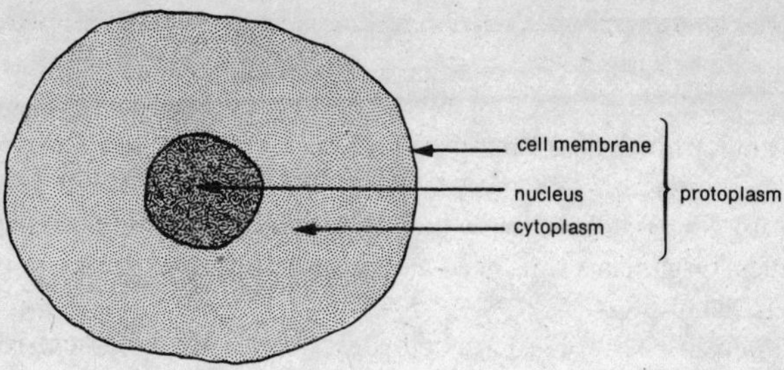

Fig. 3.1. *The chief characteristics of cells*

mainly by diffusion (page 71) and this will only occur rapidly across short distances.

Cells come in different shapes as well as sizes and the appearance of a cell (its structure) is closely linked to its function. For example, a nerve cell (page 176) is usually long and thin. It transmits nerve impulses (electrical messages) from one point in the body to another. This cell has a fixed shape and does not move around. In contrast, there are certain types of white blood cell (page 150) which can move around and change shape. They are *phagocytic*, which means they can take in particles by flowing round and enclosing them. The function of such cells is to ingest foreign organisms which get inside the body. They can feed themselves, whereas the nerve cell needs its food delivered by the blood.

This relationship between structure and function is a very important theme in biology. We will return to it again and again. At all levels of organization within the body (Fig. 3.3), from organic molecule to complete organism, structure is related to function.

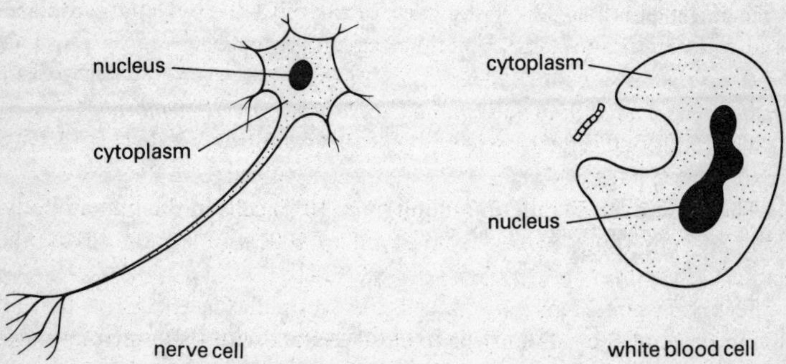

Fig. 3.2. *Comparison between two types of cell* (*not to scale*)

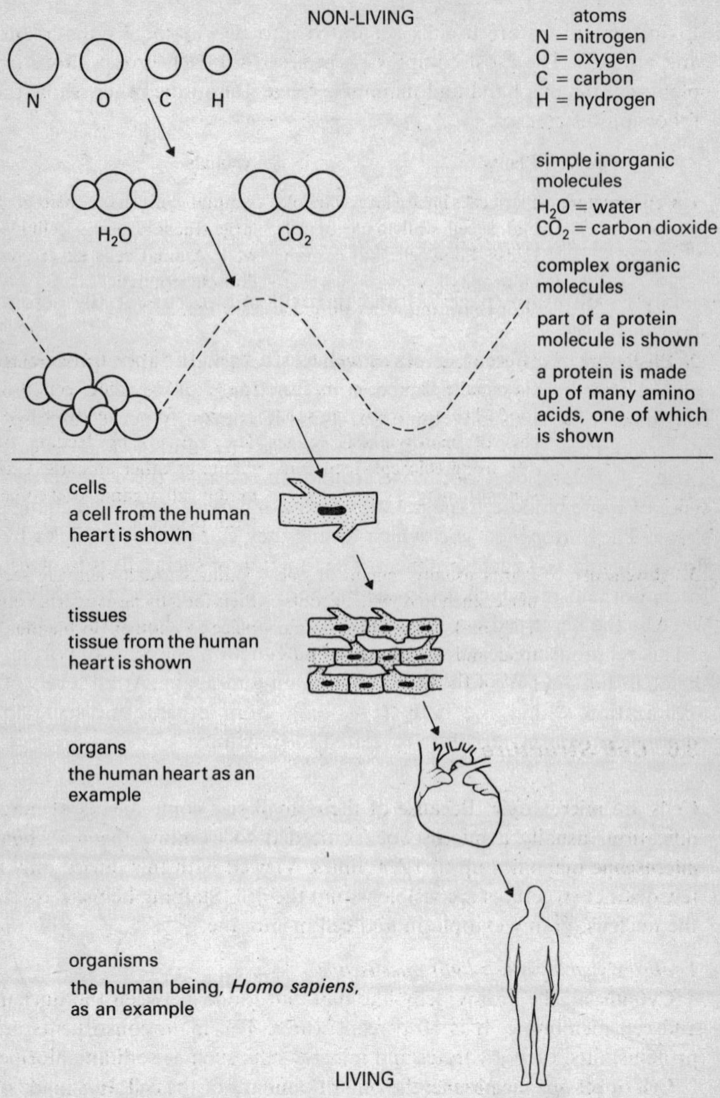

Fig. 3.3. *Levels of organization*

3.5. *Plants and Animals*

Living organisms are usually separated into two major groups: plants and animals. The most complex examples from each group, flowering plants on the one hand and mammals (page 41) on the other, show the following differences:

	Plants	**Animals**
1. Cell structure	Plant cells have a large vacuole and a cell wall made of cellulose. Plant cells may contain chlorophyll.	Animal cells have neither a large vacuole nor a cellulose wall. Animal cells never contain chlorophyll.
	(For these and other differences see Fig. 3.5)	
2. Feeding	Green plants are **autotrophic** – they make their own organic food. They do so by the process of **photosynthesis** (page 49), using **chlorophyll** to trap sunlight energy.	Animals are **heterotrophic** (page 78) – they get their organic food 'ready made'. They do so by feeding on plants or other animals. Ultimately, all organic food comes from plants.
3. Movement	Plants usually remain in one place, anchored by their roots. They bask in the sun to obtain food and usually move only part of the body.	Animals usually actively seek their food by moving from one place to another (**locomotion**).

3.6. *Cell Structure*

Cells are **microscopic**. Because of their small size some means of magnification, usually a microscope, is needed to examine them. A **light microscope** magnifies up to 1,500 times. Viewed with this device only a few distinct structures are visible within the cell. Staining helps to reveal the nucleus, grainy cytoplasm and cell membrane.

Features visible with a light microscope:

Cytoplasm: the grainy, jelly-like material found between the nucleus and cell membrane. It is 80 percent water. The main constituents are proteins, fats, carbohydrates and mineral salts such as sodium chloride.

Cell or **plasma membrane:** the outer boundary of the cell. It is made of protein and fat (page 81) and controls the passage of substances in and out of the cell.

Nucleus: a darkly-staining round structure. It is sometimes called the 'brain' of the cell because it controls activities within the cell. It contains threadlike **chromosomes** which carry instructions for building the cell and controlling how it functions. Chromosomes are not visible except during cell division (page 265). At other times they are unravelled and spread throughout the nucleus as darkly staining **chromatin**.

To examine cells in more detail an **electron microscope** is used. This is an expensive, complex apparatus which can magnify up to 500,000 times. A black and white photographic image is produced. When the cell is viewed in this way many more structures become visible (Fig. 3.4). The cytoplasm ceases to be a grainy mass, but is seen to be made up of compartments. These compartments, together with the nucleus, are called **organelles**.

Definition: An organelle *is a structure within the cell which has a specific function or functions.*

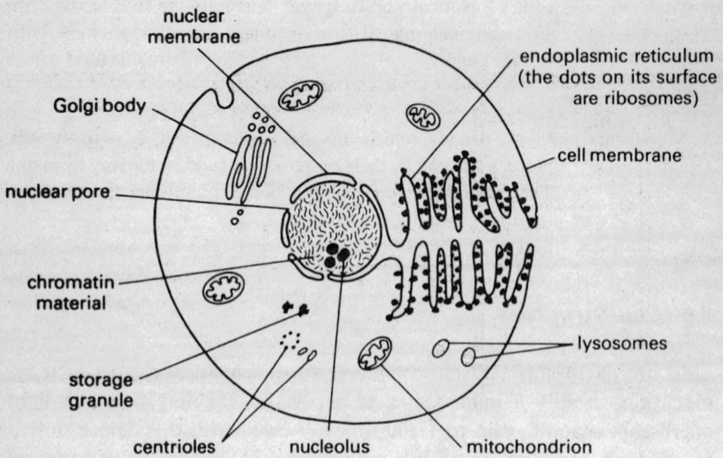

Fig. 3.4. *Generalized diagram of an animal cell: structures visible with an electron microscope*

Features visible only with an electron microscope:

Mitochondria (singular **mitochondrion):** these sausage-shaped organelles are the main sites of respiration (energy release) in the cell. They have a folded inner membrane giving a large surface area for the attachment of enzymes involved in respiration. Mitochondria are the 'power houses' of the cell. Cells which have a high demand for energy, for example, muscle cells and those involved in active transport, have a large number of mitochondria.

Endoplasmic reticulum (E.R.)**:** this is a network of folded membranes arranged to form tubes and sacs throughout the cytoplasm. It is thought to transport substances (particularly proteins) around the cell. On the surface of the E.R. are often found **ribosomes**.

Ribosomes: these are the sites where proteins are made (page 29). They are usually found on the surface of the E.R. but may be scattered throughout the cytoplasm.

Golgi body: this apparatus packages the protein from the E.R. and mixes it with carbohydrate. This material is then carried in small membrane sacs called **vesicles** to the cell membrane, where it is released from the cell.

Lysosomes: these are sacs of powerful digestive enzymes. They are used for breaking down worn-out organelles. If the cell itself is damaged or worn out, they may act as a 'self-destruct' mechanism to destroy the whole cell.

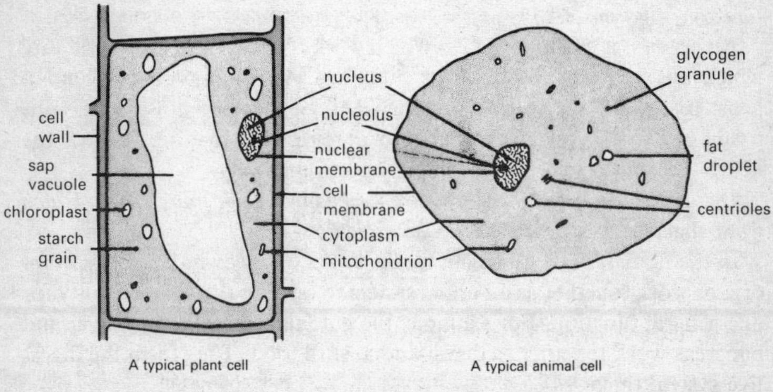

Fig. 3.5. *Comparison between a plant and an animal cell*

The following features are found only in plant cells (see Fig. 3.5)

Cell wall: a rigid wall made of cellulose and surrounding the cell membrane. It gives shape and support to the cell.

Sap vacuole: a large space in the cytoplasm filled with fluid. The vacuole pushes the cytoplasm and cell membrane out against the cell wall.

Chloroplasts: slightly larger than mitochondria, these organelles are the sites of photosynthesis in plant cells. They contain the green pigment **chlorophyll** together with the enzymes needed for the reactions of photosynthesis (NOTE: not all plant cells contain chloroplasts).

Starch: this is the storage carbohydrate in plant cells. It is found as grains in the cytoplasm.

The following features are found only in animal cells (see Fig. 3.5)

Centrioles (centrosomes): these are two small cylindrical structures lying just outside the nucleus. They are visible with an electron microscope. During cell division (page 265) these structures give rise to spindle fibres.

Glycogen: in animal cells glycogen is the storage carbohydrate. It is found as granules in the cytoplasm.

3.7. *Cells, Tissues and Organs*

Most cells in the human body are grouped together to form tissues. In turn, tissues are usually grouped together to form organs.

Definition: A tissue *is a group of cells with a similar structure and function, e.g. muscle.*

An **organ** is a group of tissues which work together to form a structure which has a specific function or functions. An example is the human heart (page 142). It contains epithelial tissue, cardiac muscle, nervous tissue and blood, all organized into a complex structure. One of the heart's functions is to pump blood around the body.

Definition: An organ *is a structure formed by two or more tissues which work together to perform particular functions.*

In the human body an organ rarely works on its own. Usually several organs work together as an **organ system** to take on the responsibility for one general function. For example, the gut (alimentary canal), liver and pancreas work together to digest and absorb food. They form the digestive system (page 90).

Fig. 3.3 (page 22) attempts to show the relationship between chemical substances, cells, tissues and organs, and the body as a whole. Chapter 5 takes a closer look at tissues, organs and organ systems.

3.8. *Organic Molecules*

As mentioned in section 3.1, the principal organic substances found in living organisms are carbohydrates, proteins, fats and nucleic acids.

Carbohydrates

As their name suggests, carbohydrates are hydrates of carbon. They contain the elements carbon, hydrogen and oxygen. Their general chemical formula can be represented as $C(H_2O)_n$.

Carbohydrates are made up of units called six-carbon sugars. The commonest example of a six-carbon sugar is **glucose**. It has the chemical formula $C_6H_{12}O_6$ and its chemical structure is:

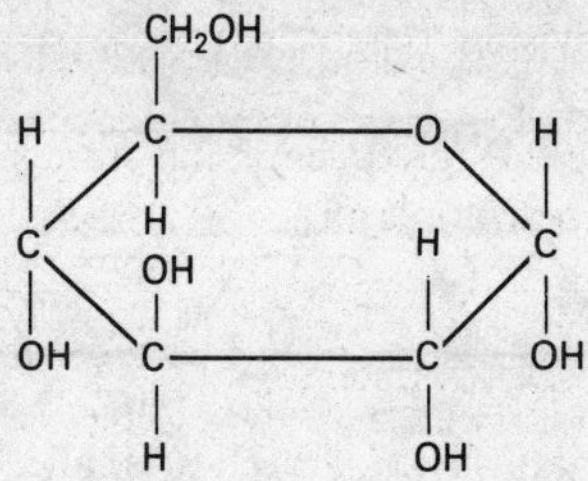

or more simply:

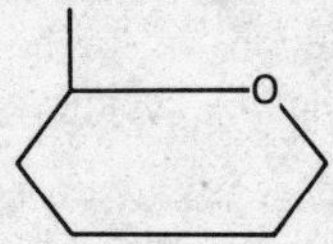

These six-carbon units can be joined together or broken apart, rather like beads on a string. **Monosaccharides** are made up of one unit, **disaccharides** are made up of two, and **polysaccharides** are made up of many.

The smaller carbohydrates are water-soluble, sweet-tasting and are called sugars. Polysaccharides are insoluble and are not sweet-tasting. Within the body, simple sugars can be joined together and stored in the form of polysaccharides. When necessary,the polysaccharide can be broken down to release the simple sugars. Carbohydrates are transported in the bloodstream as monosaccharides but are built up into the polysaccharide glycogen for storage in cells. Being insoluble, glycogen does not generate an osmotic potential (page 75) and so does not create problems of water movement.

When two sugar units are joined together a molecule of water is released; this type of reaction in which water is produced is termed a **condensation** reaction.

When two sugar units are separated a molecule of water is used in

Type of Carbohydrate	*Chemical Formula*	*Solubility in Water*	*Examples*
Monosaccharides (one sugar unit) 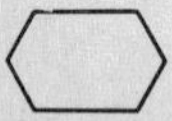	$C_6H_{12}O_6$	Soluble	Glucose Fructose Galactose
Disaccharides (two sugar units) 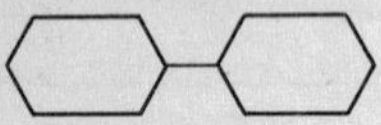	$C_{12}H_{22}O_{11}$	Soluble	Maltose (malt sugar) Sucrose (table sugar)
Polysaccharides (many sugar units) 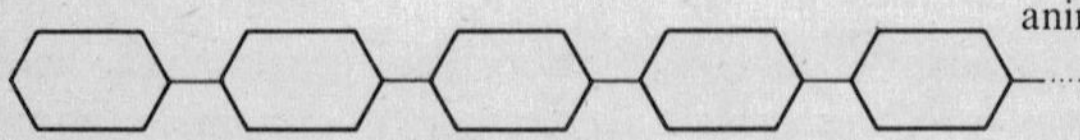	$(C_{12}H_{22}O_{11})_n$	Insoluble	Starch and cellulose in plants. Glycogen in animals.

breaking the two apart; this type of reaction is called a **hydrolysis** reaction (Greek **hydro** = water, **lysis** = breakdown). Hydrolysis is the reverse of condensation. Digestion (page 96) is a hydrolysis reaction.

As with all chemical reactions in the body, hydrolysis and condensation reactions are controlled by chemicals called **enzymes** (page 33).

The building up and breaking down of carbohydrates

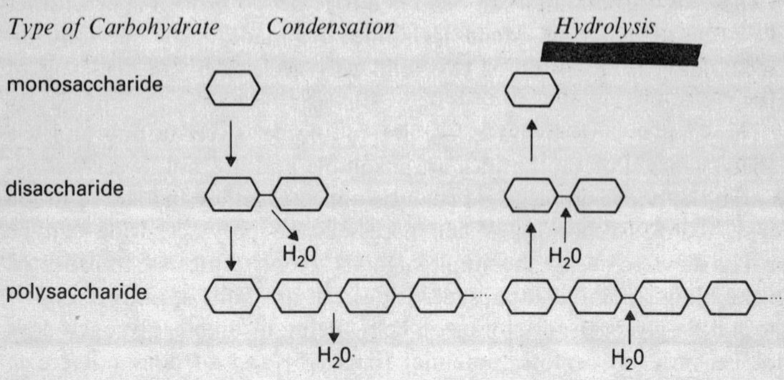

The role of carbohydrates in the body

Carbohydrates in the diet provide the body's main source of energy. This energy is released by respiration (page 112). Complex carbohydrates must be broken down (digested) to monosaccharides before they can be absorbed into the body (see page 97). Any monosaccharides surplus to requirements can be converted into glycogen and stored. If there is a large excess of sugars these can be converted into fats and stored.

Proteins

In addition to the elements carbon, hydrogen and oxygen, proteins contain nitrogen and often sulphur.

Proteins are made up of units called **amino acids**. An amino acid contains an amine (NH_2) group and a carboxylic acid (COOH) group. In a protein you can find up to 20 different types of amino acid. These can be joined in any order to form a chain tens or hundreds of units long, called a **polypeptide**. The arrangement, or sequence, of amino acids in the chain varies from one protein to another. For example, in one protein we may have

and in another

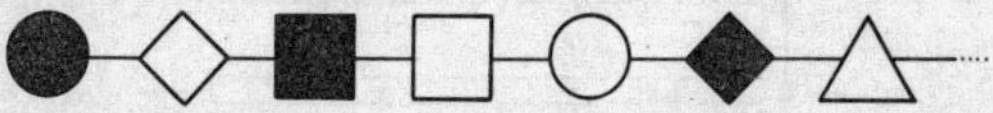

where each symbol represents a different amino acid.

The result is that it is possible to have an almost limitless number of different proteins. In the human body alone there are estimated to be over 10,000 different ones. The immense variety of life is largely due to the enormous number of different proteins that exist.

Many protein molecules are made up of two, three or four chains bonded together.

As with polysaccharides, proteins can be broken down by hydrolysis into their constituent units (amino acids) and then built up again by condensation. Amino acids are transported round the body in the bloodstream. They then pass into body tissues where they are built up into proteins as required.

The role of proteins in the body

Proteins make up most of the structural parts of the cell and so are needed in the growth, repair and maintenance of all living cells. The plasma membrane and the membranes surrounding cell organelles are made of protein combined with fat. Muscle and bone, in particular, contain a high proportion of protein. Enzymes, the chemicals which control cell chemistry (page 33), are made of protein; so are antibodies (page 150) and certain hormones (page 202).

Proteins in the diet must be broken down (digested) to amino acids before they can be absorbed into the body (see page 98). Within the body, cells manufacture proteins using amino acids transported by the bloodstream. Amino acids cannot be stored in the body, so a steady supply of them must be supplied by the diet. Surplus amino acids are broken down by the liver (page 101), where the amine (NH_2) part of the molecule is converted to **urea** and the remainder used in cell respiration.

Fats

Fats, like carbohydrates, contain only carbon, hydrogen and oxygen. In fats, however, the proportion of oxygen is lower. Tristearin, $C_{57}H_{110}O_6$, is an example of a fat.

The most common type of fat molecule has four parts, one part derived from glycerol and three parts from fatty acids:

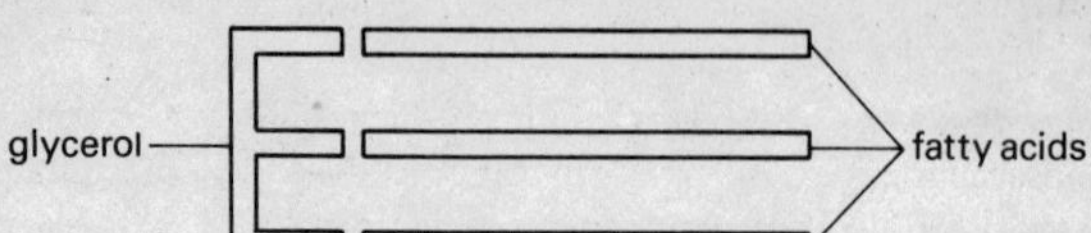

When a fat molecule is broken down by hydrolysis, the glycerol part is separated from the three fatty acids. The original fat, or a different one, can be built up by condensation:

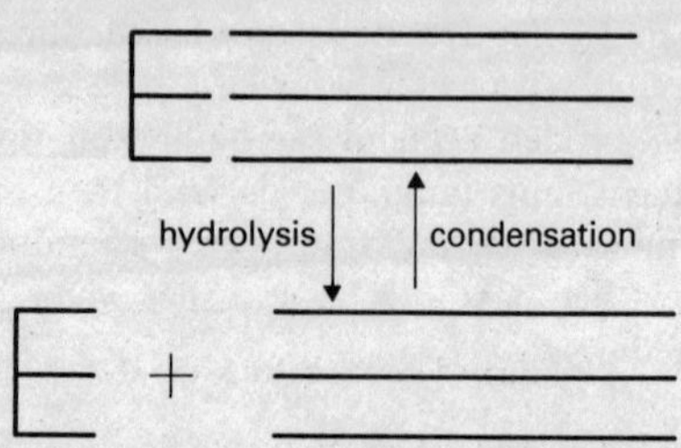

Liquid fats are usually called **oils**. Oils usually contain short-chain fatty acids. A fat containing long-chain fatty acids is usually a solid at room temperature.

Together, fats and oils, as well as waxes, are called **lipids**.

The role of fats in the body

Fats, like carbohydrates, represent a usable source of energy. Fats are energy-rich and in respiration yield twice as much energy per gram as carbohydrates or proteins. Fat in the diet is broken down (digested) into glycerol and fatty acids before absorption into the blood. These constituents are either broken down in respiration (page 112) or reconverted into fats and stored. Fat stored under the skin (page 163) acts as heat insulation, and fat stored around certain internal organs cushions them against damage.

Fats in combination with proteins are a structural part of the membranes in cells.

Fats in the diet are also essential for the fat-soluble vitamins they contain (page 82).

Carbohydrates, **proteins** and **fats** are classed as foods (page 81). Their presence in organic material can be determined using food tests. These

Table 3.1. *Food tests*

Food	*Test*	*Positive result*
1. CARBOHYDRATES		
(a) *Reducing sugars:* monosaccharides and the disaccharide maltose	Make a solution of the test substance in water. Add an equal quantity of **Benedict's Reagent**. Gently bring to the boil	An orange or green precipitate
(b) *Non-reducing sugars:* disaccharides other than maltose (NOTE: this test should only be used after test (a) has given a negative result)	Dilute hydrochloric acid is added to the test sample and the resulting solution boiled. If a non-reducing sugar is present it will be hydrolysed to a reducing sugar. The solution is then neutralized with sodium carbonate and the test for a reducing sugar carried out as before	An orange or green precipitate
(c) *Polysaccharides*	Add iodine solution to the test substance	For starch, a blue-black colour forms; for cellulose, blue; for glycogen, reddish-brown

2. PROTEINS	Use either of these tests:	
	1. Place test substance in a test tube. Add twice the volume of **Milton's Reagent** and heat gently	The test substance turns red on warming
	2. **Biuret test** for dissolved proteins. To the test solution add an equal volume of sodium hydroxide and one or two drops of copper sulphate solution	On shaking, a mauve coloration appears
3. FATS AND OILS	Use any of the following tests:	
	1. Rub test solid on to filter paper	Grease spot forms on paper
	2. Shake test substance with ethanol. Pour ethanol into water	Milky suspension
	3. Add few drops of red dye Sudan III to the test substance in water. Shake. Allow to stand	Red oil layer floats on surface

tests are shown in Table 3.1. A positive result indicates that the substance being tested for is present. Questions on food tests are fairly popular in exams (see, for example, *Q3* on page 39).

Nucleic acids

These are the fourth type of organic molecule important in the body. They are made up of the elements carbon, hydrogen, oxygen, nitrogen and phosphorus. They are large, complex molecules built up of units called **nucleotides** joined together in long chains. Their main function is to provide instructions for making proteins in the cell.

There are two types of nucleic acid: deoxyribonucleic acid (**DNA**) and ribonucleic acid (**RNA**). DNA is found in the chromosomes (page 24) within the nucleus of the cell. DNA carries a coded message for manufacturing proteins. The message is carried from the nucleus to the cytoplasm by RNA. At the ribosomes (page 25) within the cytoplasm, proteins are made under instructions from the RNA.

Both the structural part of the cell and the enzymes which control cell metabolism are made of protein. Thus the functioning of a cell is determined by the proteins it contains. The DNA, by controlling which proteins are made in a cell, controls the functioning of the cell. This is what we mean when we say the nucleus controls the cell's activities (Fig. 3.6).

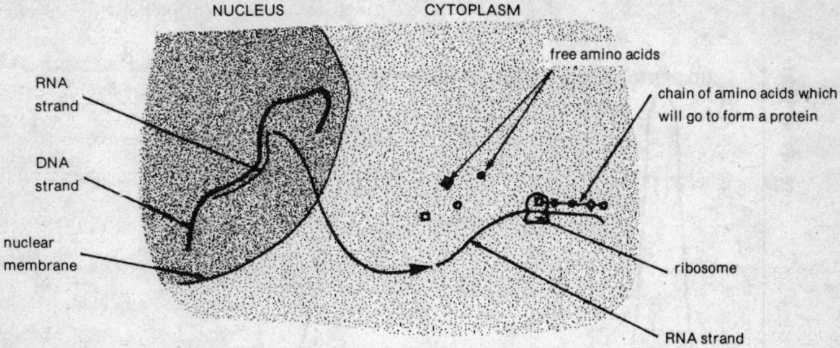

Fig. 3.6. *How the nucleus controls the cell*

3.9. *Enzymes*

Enzymes are **biological catalysts.** Catalysts are chemicals which alter the speed of chemical reactions. The catalyst itself remains unchanged at the end of the reaction.

Unlike the inorganic catalysts used in the chemical industry, enzymes are made of protein. Without enzymes, chemical reactions in the body would be too slow to support life.

Enzymes, just like other proteins, are manufactured within cells. The properties of enzymes can be summarized as follows:

1. They are proteins made by living cells (they sometimes incorporate vitamins).
2. They are catalysts.
3. They are specific – one type of enzyme catalyses one type of reaction.
4. An enzyme works best at a particular temperature (the optimum temperature). As with other proteins, they are destroyed (denatured) by heating above about 50°C.
5. Each enzyme works best at a certain degree of acidity or alkalinity (the optimum pH).

Outside its optimum temperature and pH an enzyme may cease to work or may even be destroyed (we normally say 'denatured' to indicate that its chemical nature has been lost). The optimum temperature for most enzymes in the body is around normal body temperature, 37°C. The optimum pH for enzymes varies. Those enzymes which work inside cells have an optimum pH of about 7.0 (neutral). For those enzymes which work outside cells in the gut the pH optimum varies, e.g. pepsin (page 93) pH 2 (very acid) and salivary amylase (page 92) pH 7.5 (nearly neutral). Curves of enzyme activity against pH are shown in Fig. 3.7.

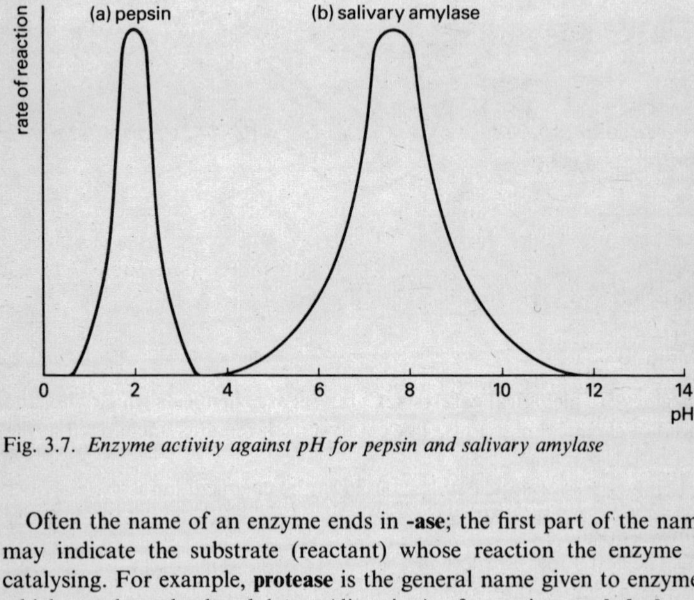

Fig. 3.7. *Enzyme activity against pH for pepsin and salivary amylase*

Often the name of an enzyme ends in **-ase**; the first part of the name may indicate the substrate (reactant) whose reaction the enzyme is catalysing. For example, **protease** is the general name given to enzymes which catalyse the breakdown (digestion) of proteins; **carbohydrases** catalyse the breakdown of carbohydrates; and **lipases** catalyse the breakdown of lipids. Individual enzymes, however, may not follow this rule. **Pepsin** (page 93) is an example of a protease. **Salivary amylase** (page 92) is a carbohydrase which catalyses the digestion of starch.

Enzymes catalyse *all* chemical reactions in the body. However, the enzymes you are probably most familiar with are digestive enzymes (pages 92–4). These are secreted into the gut and are, in fact, unusual enzymes because they are **extracellular** (work outside cells). Most enzymes are not secreted but are **intracellular** (work inside cells). An example of an intracellular enzyme is **carbonic anhydrase** (page 134) found in red blood cells.

Questions on the effect of temperature and pH on enzyme activity are popular with examiners. For example:

Q. (a) What are the effects of a change in
(i) temperature
(ii) pH upon the rate of any named *enzyme* [7]
(b) Describe with full experimental details how you would investigate either of these effects. [12]
[OXF]

In such questions it is usual to use a digestive enzyme as the named example.

Investigating the effect of temperature on the digestion of starch by salivary amylase

This experiment investigates how rapidly starch is digested at different temperatures under the action of salivary amylase. When a starch solution no longer gives a positive test with iodine (see Table 3.1) it is assumed that the starch has been digested.

Method

1. A 1 per cent starch solution is made up and 5 cm³ added to each of five test tubes.
2. 1 cm³ of freshly collected saliva is added to each of four other test tubes.
3. The test tubes are placed in water baths at various temperatures as shown in Fig. 3.8.
4. The test tubes are left in their respective water baths to reach the required temperature, and then the solutions in the two tubes are mixed.

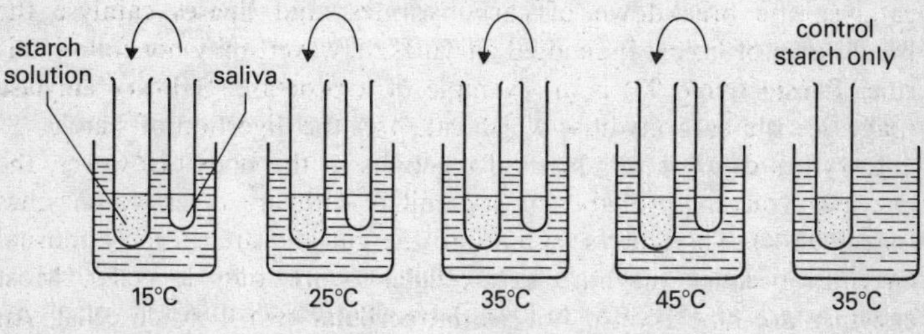

Fig. 3.8. *Apparatus for investigating the effect of temperature on starch digestion*

5. At timed two-minute intervals a drop of each mixture is removed by dropper pipette and tested for starch, using iodine. (NOTE: iodine is *not* added directly to the mixture – this would affect the reaction.)
6. For each mixture, the time is recorded when a drop of the solution no longer turns the iodine blue-black, i.e. starch has been digested. The experiment is stopped after 20 minutes.

Results

Typical results are as follows:
A. Starch test negative after 18 minutes.
B. Starch test negative after 10 minutes.
C. Starch test negative after 4 minutes.
D. Starch test negative after 12 minutes.
E. Starch test still positive after 20 minutes.

The results when plotted give the following curve:

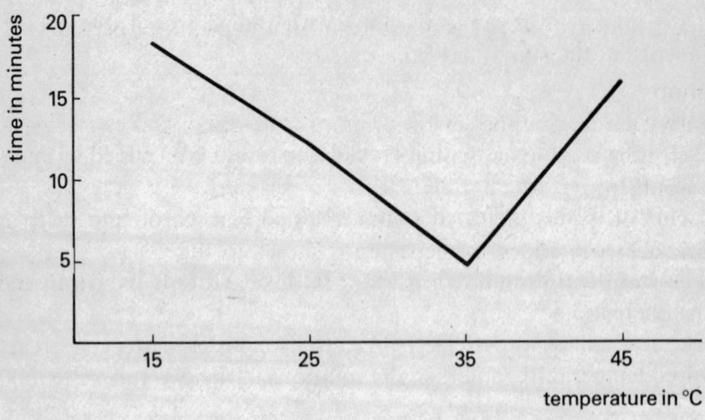

Fig. 3.9. *Reaction time against temperature for salivary amylase*

The *rate* of reaction can be plotted by dividing the volume of starch by the digestion time. This type of curve is shown in Fig. 3.10.

Conclusions

The results taken as a whole indicate that the enzyme works best (digests starch fastest) at 35°C, and at lower or higher temperatures the reaction is slower. The control shows that starch does not break down of its own accord.

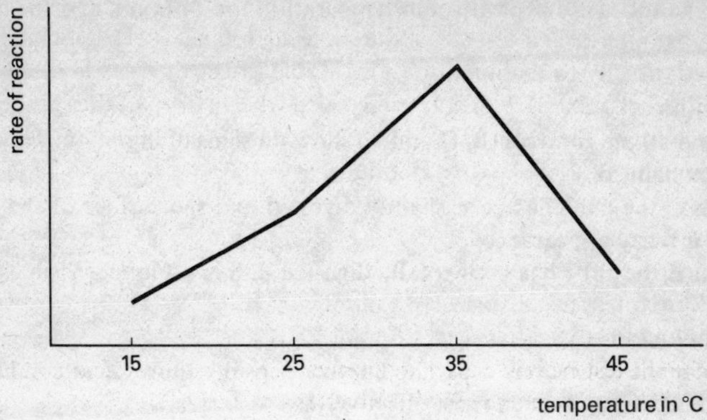

Fig. 3.10. *Rate of reaction against temperature for salivary amylase*

Investigating the effect of pH on the digestion of albumen by pepsin

This experiment investigates how rapidly cooked egg albumen (a protein) is digested at various pH conditions under the action of pepsin.

Method

1. Into each of six tubes is put a 5 mm cube of cooked egg white and to each tube is added a thymol crystal to prevent bacteria digesting the egg albumen.
2. 2 cm³ of water, or 0.1 m solutions of sodium carbonate or hydrochloric acid, are added to the tubes as shown in Fig. 3.11.
3. 2 cm³ of pepsin solution are added to A, C and E. Tubes B, D and F act as controls.

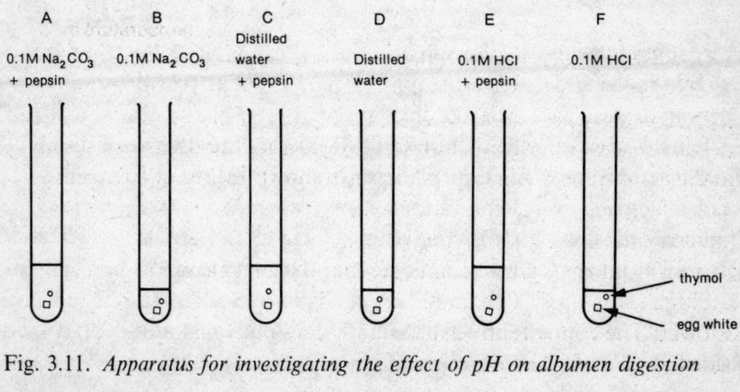

Fig. 3.11. *Apparatus for investigating the effect of pH on albumen digestion*

4. The tubes are kept at room temperature for 24 hours and the cubes then examined.

Results

A and all the controls (B, D and F) show no signs of digestion. The cube is unchanged.

In C the cube has been slightly digested and the surface of the cube has a fuzzy appearance.

In E the cube has been totally digested and is no longer visible.

Conclusion

Under the conditions used, the enzyme pepsin requires acid conditions to digest egg albumen most effectively.

Here are two final points regarding enzymes:

1. Students sometimes write of enzymes being 'killed'. Enzymes cannot be killed because they are not alive. They can, however, be denatured.
2. Enzymes catalyse *all* the chemical reactions of metabolism, not just those concerned with digestion.

Definitions

Cell
Organelle
Tissue
Organ

Key Words

Inorganic molecules	Chlorophyll	Glycerol
Organic molecules	Heterotrophic	Fatty acids
Carbohydrates	Microscopic	Oils
Proteins	Mitochondria	Lipids
Fats	Endoplasmic reticulum	Benedict's reagent
Nucleic acids	Ribosomes	Millon's reagent
Universal solvent	Golgi body	Biuret test
Movement	Lysosomes	Ethanol
Feeding	Cell wall	Sudan III
Respiration	Sap vacuole	Nucleotides
Excretion	Chloroplasts	DNA

Growth
Reproduction
Sensitivity
Metabolism
Catabolism
Anabolism
Nucleus
Cytoplasm
Cell (plasma) membrane
Protoplasm
Phagocytic
Autotrophic
Photosynthesis

Starch
Centrioles (centrosomes)
Glycogen
Six-carbon sugar
Monosaccharides
Disaccharides
Polysaccharides
Condensation
Hydrolysis
Enzymes
Amino acids
Polypeptide
Urea

RNA
Biological catalysts
Optimum temperature
Optimum pH
Denatured
Protease
Carbohydrase
Lipase
Pepsin
Salivary amylase
Extracellular
Intracellular
Carbonic anhydrase

Exam Questions

1. (*a*) *Make a large labelled diagram to show the structure of a typical animal cell and give one function of each of the parts you name.* [12]
(*b*) *Name* three *ways in which a typical photosynthetic plant cell differs from such an animal cell.* [3]

[OXF]

NOTE: the mark allocation in section (*a*) indicates that a detailed drawing, such as that shown in Fig. 3.4, is required.

2. (*a*) *What is a cell organelle?* [2]
(*b*) *Name the part of the cell concerned with:*
(*i*) *transmitting inherited information*
(*ii*) *formation of proteins*
(*iii*) *increasing the interior cell surface*
(*iv*) *respiration*
(*v*) *separating the cell from its surroundings* [5]
(*c*) *Name the structures within the nucleus where deoxyribonucleic acid* (*DNA*) *is concentrated.* [1]

[LON]

3. A, B and C are solutions of three different food substances. Samples of each were taken and tested with iodine and other samples were boiled with Fehling's/Benedict's solution. The results are shown in the table where √ *indicates a positive result and* × *indicates no change in the reagent.*

	A	B	C
Iodine	√	×	×
Fehling's/Benedict's	×	√	×

(*a*) (*i*) *Describe the change which indicates a positive result with iodine.* [2]

(*ii*) *Describe the change which indicates a positive result with Fehling's/Benedict's solution* [2]

(*b*) (*i*) *What is the nature of the substance in A?* [1]

(*ii*) *What is the nature of the substance in B?* [1]

(*c*) *Describe* three *tests that could be used to determine the nature of the substance in C.* [8]

[JMB]

4. (*a*) *Describe how you would carry out an experiment to find out how the rate of activity of salivary amylase varies between 15°C and 40°C. Draw the apparatus that you would use.* [12]

(*b*)

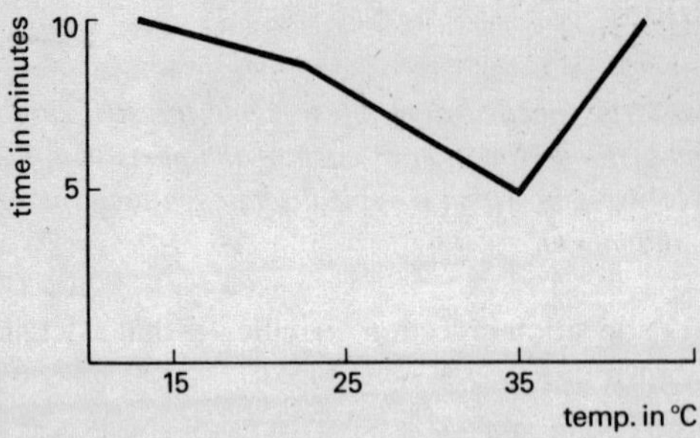

The graph shows the results obtained by a student doing such an experiment. What does the graph tell you about the effect of temperature on the action of salivary amylase on starch? [3]

[CAM]

4. *The Place of Humans in Nature*

4.1. *The Classification of Living Things*

Living things are divided into two main groups, the **plant kingdom** and the **animal kingdom**. The differences between plants and animals have been described in Chapter 3.

The animal kingdom is further divided into two more groups. Animals that do not have a backbone are **invertebrates**. Animals that do have a backbone are **vertebrates**.

The vertebrates are divided into five classes.

1. Fish
2. Amphibians (frogs, toads, newts, salamanders)
3. Reptiles (lizards, snakes, crocodiles)
4. Birds
5. Mammals

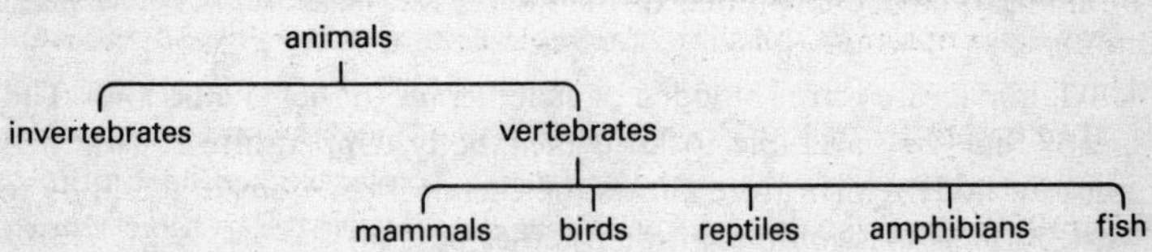

Fig. 4.1. *Divisions of the animal kingdom*

Humans are mammals, so it is this group we are most concerned with. The class of mammals is arranged into a number of **orders**, the chief ones of which are:

1. Monotremes – these mammals lay eggs. The only two types are the duck-billed platypus and the spiny anteater.
2. Marsupials – these are the mammals that carry their young in pouches e.g. kangaroo, wallaby, opossum, koala bear.

The remaining orders of mammals feed their young through a placenta (see Chapter 13).

3. Edentates e.g. sloth, giant anteater, armadillo.

4. Ungulates – hoofed mammals e.g. horse, sheep, cow, goat, deer.
5. Cetaceans – mammals that live and breed in the sea e.g. whales, dolphins, porpoises.
6. Carnivores – meat eaters e.g. dog, cat, weasel.
7. Rodents – mammals with gnawing teeth e.g. rat, mouse, squirrels, porcupine.
8. Chiroptera – flying mammals i.e. bats.
9. Insectivores – insect-eating mammals e.g. shrew, mole, hedgehog.
10. Primates e.g. bushbabies, lemurs, monkeys, apes and humans.

All mammals share certain characteristics that are not found in any other organisms, that is, they are mammalian characteristics. These are listed below:

1. Hair on the body.
2. The young are fed on milk that is produced in **mammary glands** (hence the name 'mammals').
3. External ears.
4. Sweat glands.
5. The thorax and abdomen are separated by a **diaphragm** (see Chapter 8).
6. There are four types of teeth i.e. incisors, canines, premolars and molars (see Chapter 7).

Mammals also have features which, though shared with other groups of animals, have contributed to their success. These are:

1. Mammals are warm-blooded or **endothermic** (or **homoiothermic**). This means that they are able to keep their body temperature constant. A constant body temperature allows the chemical reactions in the body to work at their maximum (optimum) efficiency.
2. A four-chambered heart and double circulation provides efficient transport of substances around the body (see Chapter 9).
3. The mouth and nasal cavities are separated by a **hard palate** which allows mammals to breathe at the same time as they are feeding.
4. The brain is well developed which allows mammals to learn quickly.
5. The young are usually born live (except monotremes). Consequently the young mammal is protected by being inside the mother during its early, vulnerable stages.
6. Most mammals care for their young for some time after birth. This provides protection and gives the young an opportunity to learn from the adults.

The Primates

Humans are primates and this order has characteristics that distinguish the primates from the other orders of mammals:

1. The skeleton is more flexible than that of other mammals, especially at the wrist and often at the ankle.
2. They have fingernails and toenails instead of claws.
3. The thumb of a primate can touch the fingers of the same hand (an **opposable** thumb). Many primates, including humans, can hold very small objects between fingers and thumb (**precision grip**).
4. The teeth are not specialized for a particular diet but can be used to eat a variety of foods.
5. There are four incisors in both the upper and lower jaws.
6. In monkeys, apes and humans the eyes face forward and vision is **stereoscopic** (they can see depth).
7. Associated with the stereoscopic vision is a shortening of the snout.
8. The sense of smell is not as good as that of most other mammals.
9. Facial expressions are used for communication and the muscles in the face are well developed to allow this.
10. Many primates also use sound to communicate and they have well-developed vocal chords. This skill has reached its peak in humans.
11. The frontal lobes of the brain are enlarged in primates, compared to other mammals. This is associated with the ability of primates to learn quickly.
12. Most primates live in social groups, which provides certain benefits. A group of animals is better able to defend itself against predators than an animal on its own. Young primates within a social group are able to learn from the adults in the group.

Humans are apes, along with gibbons, orang-utans, gorillas and chimpanzees. Apes are easy to tell from other primates because they do not have a tail. Also their shoulder blades are at the back of their body rather than at the sides.

4.2. *The Human Primate*

Humans share the characteristics above with other primates but have special features that make them unique among the primates:

1. Humans are bipedal, that is they walk on two legs (except for a short crawling phase during infancy). The resulting upright stance has led to other structural changes, the spine has an S-shaped curve and there have also been changes in the pelvic girdle.

2. The cranium of humans is larger, relative to body size, than that of other primates. This is associated with the use of speech, tools and the ability to write.

In general, humans are less specialized than other primates so they are able to carry out a wider variety of activities and can adapt to changes in their surroundings more easily than other primates.

Evolution

The study of evolution is not required by all of the syllabuses, so check before learning about it. Some people find that their religious beliefs do not allow them to believe in evolution but this need not be a problem. The important thing is that you know what the theory of evolution is.

Before thinking about how humans have evolved we must look at the theory of evolution.

Until about the middle of the nineteenth century people believed that all species had been created and had remained unchanged. At about this time, however, scientists were beginning to think that there might be another explanation for the wide variety of living organisms. Their ideas became known as the theory of evolution.

The best known of these scientists was **Charles Darwin**. Darwin pointed out that all organisms need to be able to find food and shelter to survive. If they did not survive they would not produce any young. Therefore only those organisms **adapted** to survive in their **environment** were able to produce offspring. Darwin had noticed that certain characteristics were passed from one generation to the next and he suggested that the characteristics that allowed an organism to survive were passed on to its offspring. He called this the **survival of the fittest**. Darwin's ideas are known as the **theory of natural selection**.

Human Evolution

Within the order primates, humans are classified in the sub-order Anthropoidea. This sub-order is divided into four families:

1. Cercopithecidae – monkeys.
2. Hylobatidae – gibbons.
3. Pongidae – orang-utans, chimpanzees, gorillas.
4. Hominidae – humans.

It is now generally accepted that all four of these families had a **common ancestor** which lived many millions of years ago. It is thought that separate populations of this common ancestor evolved in different ways because they lived in different conditions.

The only surviving species of the family Hominidae is *Homo sapiens* (that's us) but fossils show that in the past there have been other species of **hominid**. The earliest hominids are thought to have evolved about 2.5 million years ago (not very long ago in evolutionary terms).

The ancestor of the hominids probably lived in forests and was adapted to living in trees. It has been suggested that a change in climate many millions of years ago led to the loss of some of these forests. Therefore our ancestors were forced to live on the plains and over many generations, helped along by natural selection, changes took place in the structure of these animals. The feet became flatter and more rigid to help them move around. Their posture became more upright, possibly helping them to see over the top of long grass on the plains. The legs became longer so that they could run faster. Walking upright meant that the hands were free to do other things and hand movements became more versatile. There were also changes in the shape of the head. The cranium became larger and more rounded, the eyebrow ridges became less prominent and the lower jaw became smaller. Fig. 4.13 shows the skulls of four primates.

It was once thought that the early hominids were the direct ancestors of humans. We now believe that *Homo sapiens* is descended directly from the hominid ancestors and that the other hominid species were offshoots of this line. This relationship is shown in Fig. 4.2.

The earliest known hominids are in the genus *Australopithecus*. These walked upright but were much smaller than modern humans (about 1.2 metres tall) and had an ape-like skull. They lived about 1.5 million years ago.

Homo erectus lived about 1 million years ago and had a larger brain than *Australopithecus* but still had many ape characteristics.

The neanderthals (*Homo sapiens neanderthalensis*) walked upright and buried their dead. They used a wide variety of tools and are considered to be close enough to modern humans that they are placed in the same species. The brain was smaller than that of modern humans and the eyebrow ridges were more pronounced. Neanderthals lived at the same time as our early ancestors but died out about one hundred thousand years ago.

It is important to remember that there are many theories about the evolution of humans. If your syllabus contains a section on human evolution make sure you know what theory you are expected to know.

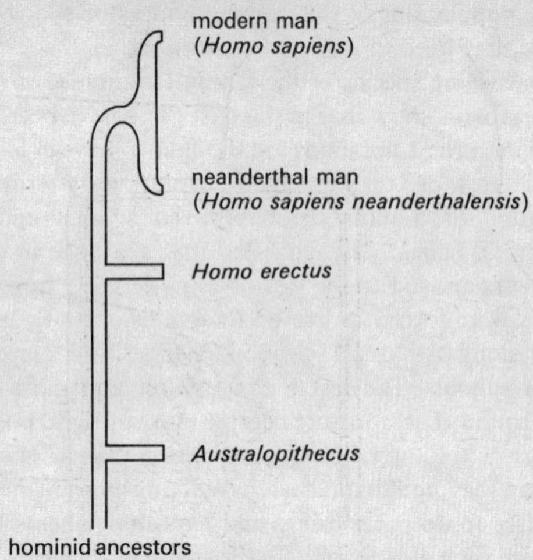

Fig. 4.2. *The main stages in human evolution*

4.3. *Organisms Associated with Humans*

Although, as humans, we are one species we are not isolated from other species and we come into contact with a wide variety of other organisms. The most important of these are described in the following pages and some will be discussed in more detail in later chapters.

Viruses

Viruses are very small, simple organisms. They do not have a nucleus or cytoplasm and so are described as **non-cellular**. Their average size is 100 nanometres. They are totally parasitic, causing disease in a wide variety of other organisms. Viruses that cause disease in humans will be discussed further in Chapter 16.

Bacteria

Bacteria are made of one cell, i.e. they are **unicellular**. The typical structure of a bacterium is shown in Fig. 4.3.

Bacteria are usually classified as plants because they have a cell wall (some also contain chlorophyll). However they do not have a nucleus.

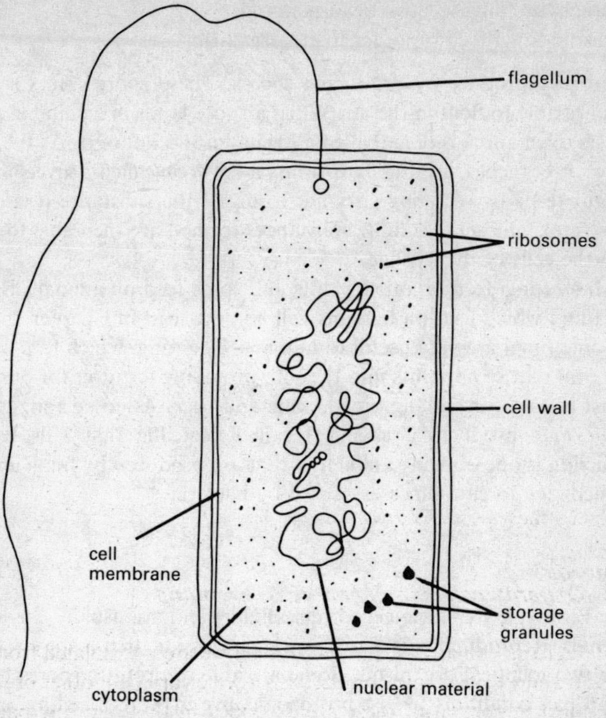

Fig. 4.3. *A generalized bacterium*

Some bacteria are able to form a protective capsule around themselves to withstand adverse conditions.

Some bacteria cause disease (see Chapter 16) but most are harmless. The bacteria involved in the nitrogen cycle (see page 59) are essential to the survival of most other organisms, including humans. Humans have also been able to make use of bacteria in the manufacture of yoghurt, some cheeses, vinegar, leather and many other items.

Fungi

The cells of fungi also have cell walls so they are usually classified as plants. None of the fungi contain chlorophyll and they are not able to make their own food, unlike other plants. There are two ways in which they may obtain food:

Saprophytic fungi feed on dead material.
Parasitic fungi feed on other living organisms.

Fungi reproduce by producing **spores**. These spores are very small and are able to float in the air. When a spore lands in a suitable place it bursts open and a thread (called a **hypha**) grows out of it. As the thread grows it branches, eventually forming a network called a **mycelium**. The fungus feeds by secreting enzymes to digest the substance it is on (the **substrate**). The small soluble substances formed are then able to diffuse into the cells of the hyphae.

Many fungi feed on other plants and some feed on animals. Some of the fungi which feed on humans will be described in Chapter 16.

Some fungi are very useful to humans. The fungi which feed on dead material release nutrients into the soil, providing fertilizer for our crops. **Yeast** is used for making bread, wine and beer. A mould fungus called *Penicillium* produces a chemical called **penicillin** that kills bacteria. Penicillin is one of many **antibiotics** that are produced by fungi and used in medicine to cure illnesses caused by bacteria.

Protozoa

The Protozoa are single-celled (**unicellular**) and are usually classified as animals. Reproduction is usually by **binary fission**, that is the cell divides into two identical organisms. Some are able to produce spores to withstand bad conditions. Most protozoans live in water, feeding on small food particles. A few cause disease and these are described in Chapter 16.

Nematoda

Nematodes are flatworms made of many cells (**multicellular**). The sexes are different and reproduction is sexual. Most nematodes are free-living but some cause disease (see Chapter 16).

Arthropoda

The arthropods are the largest group of animals. The body has a hard covering (**exoskeleton**) and is divided into segments. The limbs are jointed with muscles inside them that produce movement. The arthropods are divided into four groups:

1. Crustacea – crabs, lobsters, shrimps, woodlice.
2. Arachnids – spiders, ticks, mites, scorpions.

3. Myriapoda – centipedes and millipedes.
4. Insecta – flies, bees, ants, cockroaches, butterflies.

The insects are the group we are most familiar with and for a variety of reasons. Most of the fruit we eat is produced as a result of pollination of flowers by insects, so they are very useful in this respect. Some insects like the same food as we do and a great deal of money is spent trying to control these insects to protect our food supply. Predatory insects that eat these pest species are therefore very useful to us. Some insects spread diseases and these will be discussed later (see Chapter 16).

4.4. *Photosynthesis*

Green plants are green because they contain a pigment called **chlorophyll** which is used to trap the energy in sunlight in order to make food. This process is called **photosynthesis**. In photosynthesis carbon dioxide and water are combined to make simple sugars. The formula for this reaction is:

$$6CO_2 + 6H_2O \rightarrow C_6H_{12}O_6 + 6O_2$$

The sugars made during photosynthesis may be used for making energy (**respiration**) or they may be combined to form larger carbohydrate molecules (**polysaccharides**) such as starch or cellulose. Starch is used by many plants as a food store. Cellulose is used to make the cell walls. Sugars may also be converted into fats or proteins.

Your syllabus may require you to know about experiments to determine the conditions necessary for photosynthesis. These experiments are described below.

Photosynthesis experiments

For photosynthesis to take place plants need an adequate supply of carbon dioxide, water, light and chlorophyll. The temperature also affects the rate of photosynthesis.

In experiments concerned with photosynthesis the presence of starch is usually taken to show that photosynthesis has taken place. This is because the sugars formed by photosynthesis are usually converted to starch. Consequently it is important to know how to test for starch.

Testing for starch

A green leaf is removed from a plant and the following steps are taken:

1. The leaf is placed in boiling water for five minutes to fix (kill) the leaf tissue and break down the waxy cuticle.
2. The leaf is then transferred to boiling ethanol (alcohol) heated in a water bath to reduce the danger of fire. The ethanol removes the chlorophyll. This decolourizes the leaf so that colour changes used in the starch test are not masked by the green colour of the chlorophyll.
3. The decolourized leaf is put in hot water to soften it.
4. The softened leaf is spread out on a white tile.
5. It is covered for one minute with dilute iodine solution.
6. The iodine is then rinsed off with water.

A blue-black colouration indicates the presence of starch. If the brown colour of the iodine persists, the test for starch is negative.

Destarching plants

If a plant is to be used to indicate photosynthesis it should not contain starch before the experiment. Any starch found after the experiment must have been formed during it. A plant can be destarched by keeping it in darkness for 48 hours. If you have to describe such an experiment it is important to mention that a destarched plant was used.

An experiment to show that light is needed for photosynthesis

Method

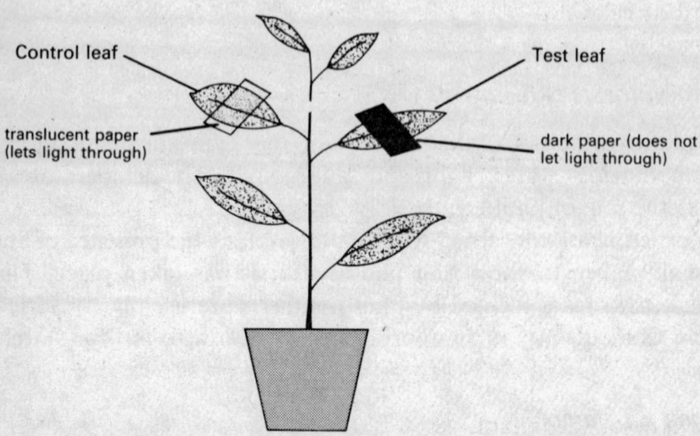

Fig. 4.4. *Apparatus testing the need for light in photosynthesis*

1. Use a destarched plant.
2. Set up control and test leaves as shown in Fig. 4.4. For the test, the leaf is sandwiched between two sheets of dark paper, so that both top and bottom surfaces of the leaf are covered. For the control, transparent or translucent paper is used.
3. Give the plant water and leave in daylight or artificial light for six hours.
4. Remove the test and control leaves and test them for starch (see starch test above).

Results
1. The covered strip on the control leaf turns blue-black with iodine (positive for starch test).
2. The covered strip on the test leaf does not turn blue-black (negative for starch test).

Conclusion
The absence of starch in the covered strip of the test leaf indicates that in the absence of light photosynthesis does not take place.

Light is needed for photosynthesis to occur.

An experiment to show that carbon dioxide is needed for photosynthesis

Method

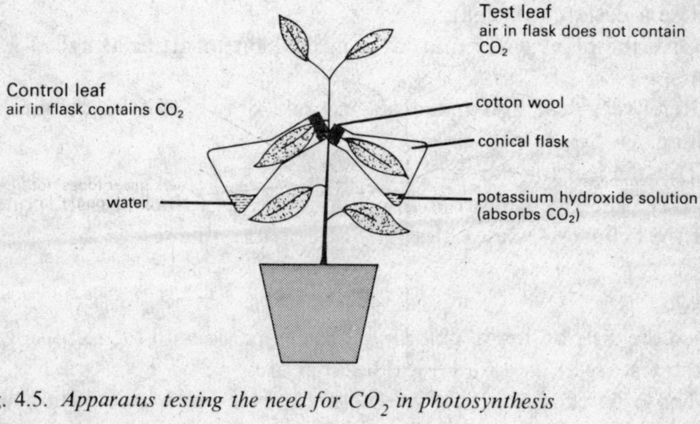

Fig. 4.5. *Apparatus testing the need for CO_2 in photosynthesis*

1. Use a destarched plant.
2. Set up the control and test leaves as shown in Fig. 4.5.

3. Give the plant water and leave in daylight or artificial light for six hours.
4. Remove the test and control leaves and test them for starch (see starch test above).

Results

1. The control leaf turns blue-black with iodine (positive for starch test).
2. The test leaf does not turn blue-black (negative for starch test).

Conclusion

The absence of starch in the test leaf indicates that in the absence of carbon dioxide photosynthesis does not take place.

Carbon dioxide is needed for photosynthesis to occur.

An experiment to show that chlorophyll is needed for photosynthesis

In this experiment part of a leaf containing chlorophyll is compared with part of the same leaf that does not contain chlorophyll. The easiest way to do this is to use a plant that has variegated leaves. These are leaves that have chlorophyll-free patches on them, usually coloured white or yellow.

Method

1. Use a destarched plant.
2. Give the plant water and leave in daylight or artificial light for six hours.
3. Remove a leaf and make an accurate drawing of its colour patterning.
4. Test the leaf for starch.

NOTE: The green chlorophyll-containing part of the leaf is the control and the yellow or white chlorophyll-free part is the test.

Results

When the distribution of chlorophyll is compared with the results of the starch test (see Fig. 4.6), typical findings are:

1. Those patches originally green give a blue-black colouration with iodine (positive for starch test).
2. Those patches originally white or yellow do not turn blue-black with iodine (negative for starch test).

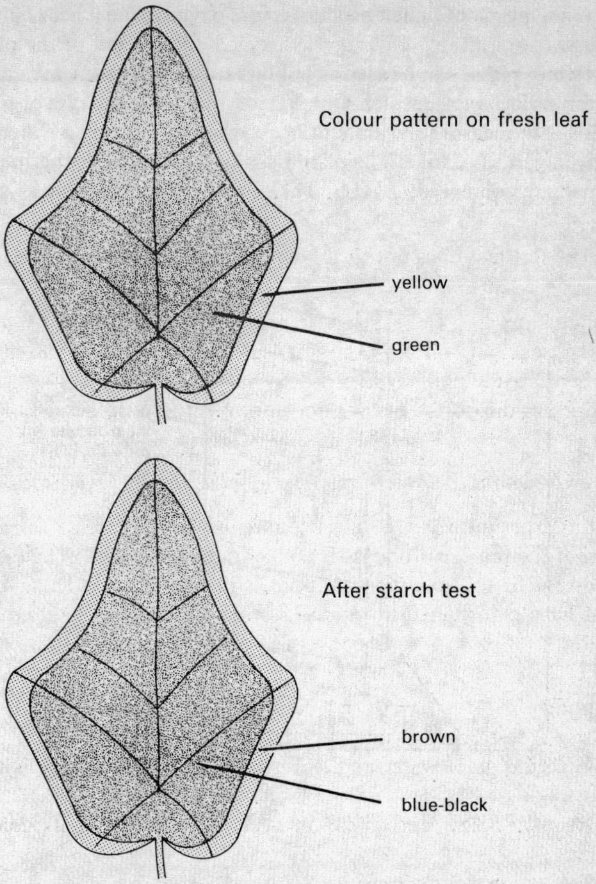

Fig. 4.6. *Variegated ivy leaf before and after testing for starch*

Conclusion

The absence of starch in the chlorophyll-free part of the leaf indicates that in the absence of chlorophyll, photosynthesis does not take place.

Chlorophyll is needed for photosynthesis to occur.

An experiment to show that temperature affects the rate of photosynthesis

One of the products of photosynthesis is oxygen and when the plant is receiving plenty of light it produces more oxygen than it needs for making energy (respiration). This surplus oxygen diffuses out of the plant and, in a water plant, can be seen as bubbles forming on the leaves and rising to the surface of the water. One way of measuring the rate of photosynthesis is to measure the amount of oxygen given off by a water plant in a given period of time. The plant usually used for this experiment is the Canadian pondweed, *Elodea*. The apparatus is arranged as shown in Fig. 4.7.

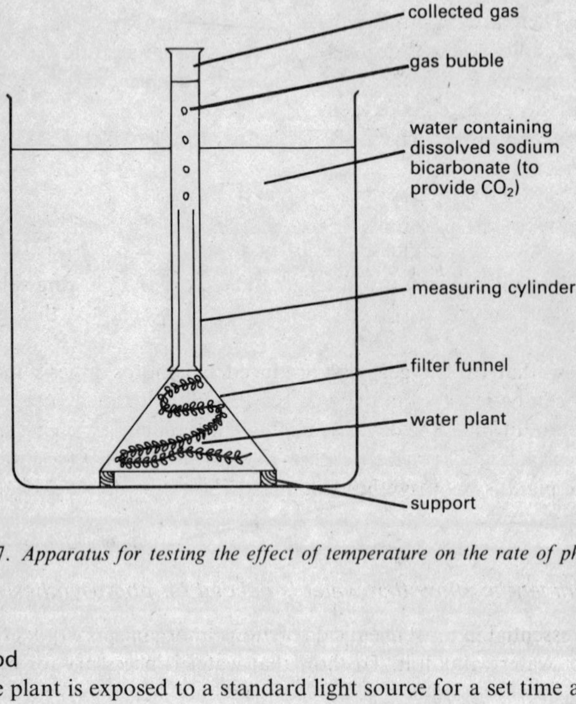

Fig. 4.7. *Apparatus for testing the effect of temperature on the rate of photosynthesis*

Method

1. The plant is exposed to a standard light source for a set time and the bubbles of gas given off in this time are collected in a measuring cylinder. The total volume of collected gas is recorded.
2. The experiment is conducted at different temperatures, starting at 15°C and repeated at 10°C intervals up to 45°C. The apparatus is kept in a water bath to minimize temperature fluctuations.

Results

The rate of photosynthesis (as measured by the volume of gas given off per hour or minute) increases with temperature up to 35°C. At 45°C very little gas is collected.

Conclusions

Rate of photosynthesis, as measured by gas evolved, is influenced by temperature. Between 15°C and 35°C, a rise in temperature increases the rate of photosynthesis. This is typical of reactions involving enzymes. At 45°C, photosynthesis is inhibited because the enzymes involved are being denatured (see page 33).

NOTE: There are certain complications with this experiment:

1. The solubility of gases decreases with rise in temperature.
2. Gases increase in volume with rise in temperature.
3. Not all gas collected is oxygen.
4. Some of the oxygen given off in photosynthesis will be used up in respiration.

In the above experiment a test for oxygen can verify that the gas given off was oxygen. If a splint is lit and then blown out and placed into oxygen while still glowing it will relight. Therefore if a glowing splint is put into the gas collected from the *Elodea* it will relight if that gas is oxygen.

To show that the oxygen was produced by photosynthesis the experiment can be repeated in the dark. In this case there will also be gas collected but it will not be oxygen and it will not relight a glowing splint. The gas, in fact, will be mainly carbon dioxide produced by respiration. When the plant is photosynthesizing this carbon dioxide would be used up in this process.

An experiment to show that water is needed for photosynthesis

Water is essential in most chemical reactions in organisms, so depriving a plant of water will kill it. To show that water is necessary for photosynthesis therefore requires a different method. Most oxygen has an atomic weight of 16 but some atoms have an atomic weight of 18, which can be detected using special techniques. If a plant is given water containing ^{18}O the fate of that ^{18}O can be followed in the plant. In such experiments the ^{18}O is found to be used in the manufacture of glucose and, subsequently, starch. This shows that water is used in photosynthesis to make starch.

This type of experiment is called a **labelling** experiment because the oxygen (in this case) has been 'labelled'.

4.5. *The Importance of Photosynthesis to Humans*

Animals are unable to photosynthesize and so they depend on plants or other animals for their food. Ultimately, therefore, all life depends on the sun as a source of energy.

Green plants are **producers** of organic material. Animals that eat the plants are **consumers**.

This arrangement of consumers eating producers is called a **food chain**. Two such foods chains are shown below:

grass → cow → human
cabbage → caterpillar → bird → cat

In most food chains there is more than one consumer. The first consumer in the chain is called the **primary consumer** (e.g. cow, caterpillar). Next comes the **secondary consumer** (e.g. human, bird). The cat in the second example is a **tertiary consumer.**

In a food chain energy passes from one link to the next. Thus energy, stored as food, in the cabbage is passed to the caterpillar. Energy stored in the caterpillar passes to the bird when the caterpillar is eaten. Each of these organisms, however, uses some of the energy it gets from its food for its day-to-day activities. Each organism, then, has less energy to pass on than it received and there is an overall loss of energy along the food chain. Because of this there are nearly always fewer organisms in one level than in the level before. For example, there have to be more caterpillars than birds if the birds are to get enough to eat. This arrangement can be represented in **a pyramid of numbers** as shown in Fig. 4.8.

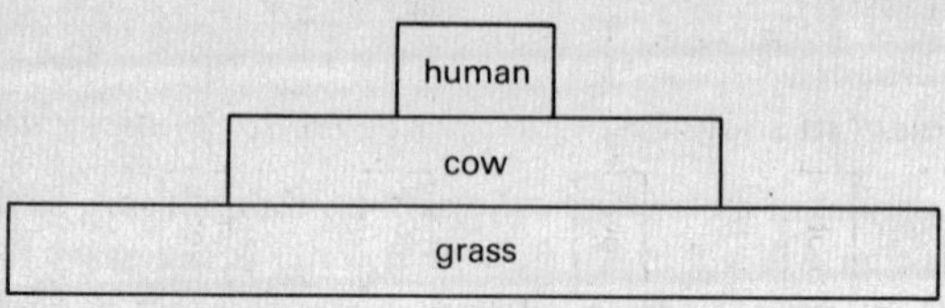

Fig. 4.8. *A pyramid of numbers*

Food chains are very simplified ways of looking at feeding relationships because most consumers eat more than one type of food (humans do not just eat cows for example). In reality food chains are joined together to form **food webs**. An example of part of a food web is shown in Fig. 4.9.

All the organisms in a food web eventually die and their remains are

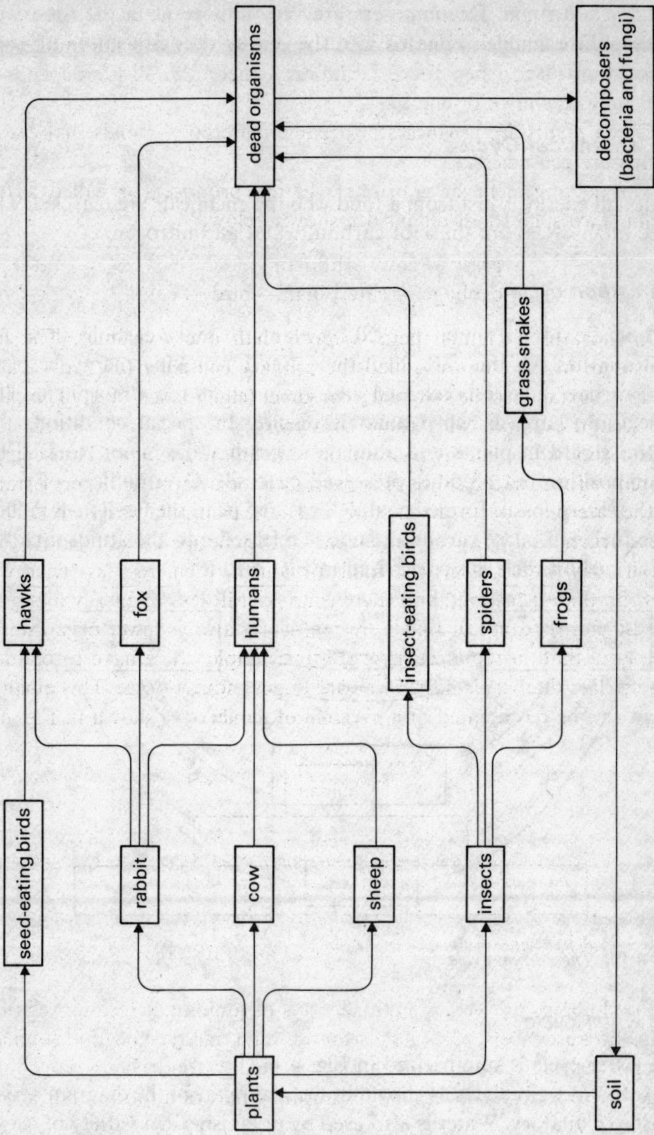

Fig. 4.9. *Part of a food web*

broken down into small molecules by **decomposers** which are mainly bacteria and fungi. Decomposers are very important in the food web because the chemicals released into the soil by decomposition are used again by plants.

4.6. *Chemical Cycles*

Although energy is lost from a food web the chemicals are recycled. The three main cycles are those of carbon, water and nitrogen.

The carbon cycle

Carbon dioxide in the air is used by plants to make carbohydrates by photosynthesis. If this carbohydrate is used for making energy (respiration) carbon dioxide is released and again enters the atmosphere. The same thing happens when animals respire. In special conditions the carbon stored in plants and animals when they die is not released by decomposition but becomes preserved in fossils. Over millions of years some of these fossils formed coal, oil, gas and peat, the **fossil fuels**. When these fuels are burnt carbon dioxide is released into the atmosphere.

The carbon cycle is summarized in Fig. 4.10.

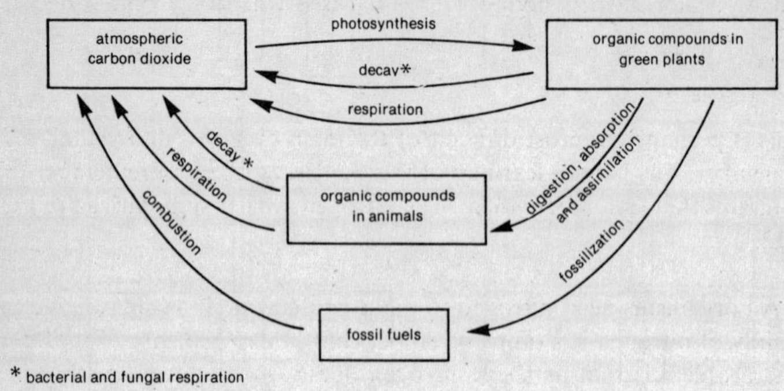

Fig. 4.10. *The carbon cycle*

The water cycle

The water cycle is summarized in Fig. 4.11.

Most water circulates as shown in the main part of the diagram which is self-explanatory. Water is also used by organisms in a variety of ways. Plants take up water through their roots and use it for photosynthesis.

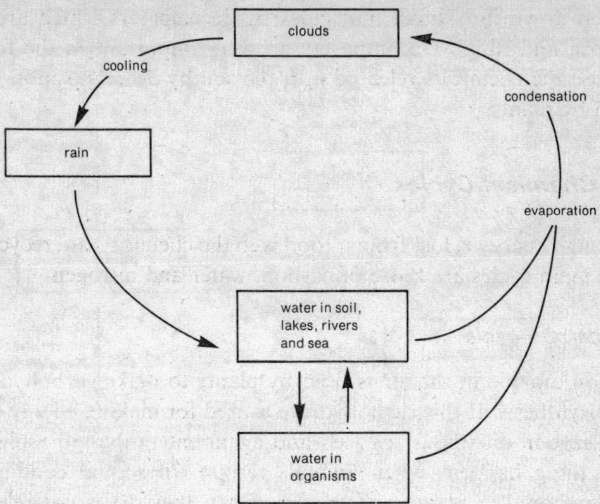

Fig. 4.11. *The water cycle*

The respiration of plants and animals produces water which may be used in other reactions or be released into the atmosphere. When organisms die any water in their bodies will be released when their bodies decay.

The nitrogen cycle

This is perhaps the most difficult of the main cycles to understand and remember. The way to learn all of these cycles is to try to remember the diagrams that summarize them. The nitrogen cycle is summarized in Fig. 4.12.

All organisms need nitrogen to make proteins and, as air is made up mainly of nitrogen gas (approx. 80 per cent), there is plenty of it about. The problem is that as a gas nitrogen does not react easily with other chemicals and most organisms cannot use it in this form. There are some organisms, however, that are able to convert nitrogen gas to **nitrate** which other organisms can use. Some of these **nitrogen-fixing bacteria** live on their own in the soil (e.g. *Azotobacter*) where they 'fix' atmospheric nitrogen and release the nitrates formed into the soil where they are then available for plants to use. Better known are the bacteria, such as *Rhizobium*, which live in swellings **(nodules)** on the roots of **leguminous** plants such as peas and beans. The nitrates formed by these bacteria

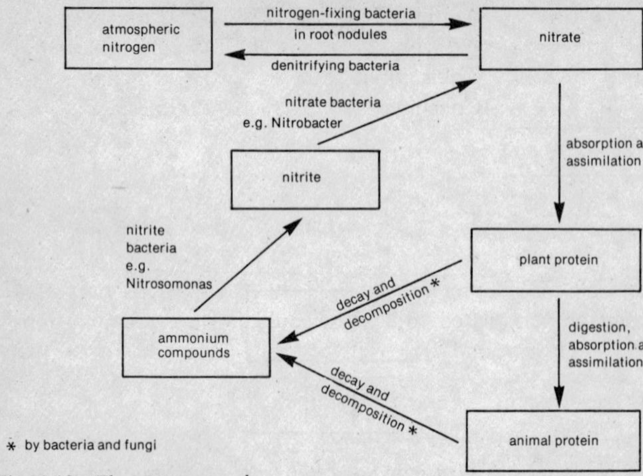

Fig. 4.12. *The nitrogen cycle*

are already within the root of the plant and are therefore readily available to it.

Animals obtain nitrogen by eating plants or other animals.

When organisms die their protein is converted to **ammonium compounds** during decay. These may then be acted on by **nitrifying bacteria** of which there are two sorts. **Nitrite bacteria** convert ammonium compounds to **nitrite** and **nitrate bacteria** convert this nitrite to **nitrate**. These nitrates are then available to plants. In uncultivated areas this recycling of nitrogen by decay maintains a fertile soil. In cultivated areas where crops are harvested and taken away for sale the nitrogen is taken away with them as it is stored in the plants. This means that over a number of years the nitrate content of agricultural land decreases and the land becomes less fertile. This problem is overcome by adding fertilisers that contain nitrates.

The nitrate content of the soil is also affected by the action of **denitrifying bacteria** which convert nitrates into nitrogen gas.

Key Words

Invertebrate	Vertebrate	Mammal
Primate	Evolution	Natural selection
Hominid	Virus	Bacteria

Fungus
Nematode
Respiration
Food web
Decomposer
Antibiotic
Arthropod
Chlorophyll
Consumer
Protozoa
Photosynthesis
Food chain
Producer

Questions

The contents of this chapter are most likely to appear as part of a question from another, related, topic. You could, however, get questions like those given below and they will certainly help you revise this chapter.

1. (a) List the characteristics of mammals.
(b) Describe the ways in which humans differ from other mammals.
2. Look closely at the skulls in Fig. 4.13.
Describe the ways in which the skulls differ and from this information say what changes you think have occurred in the evolution of Homo sapiens.

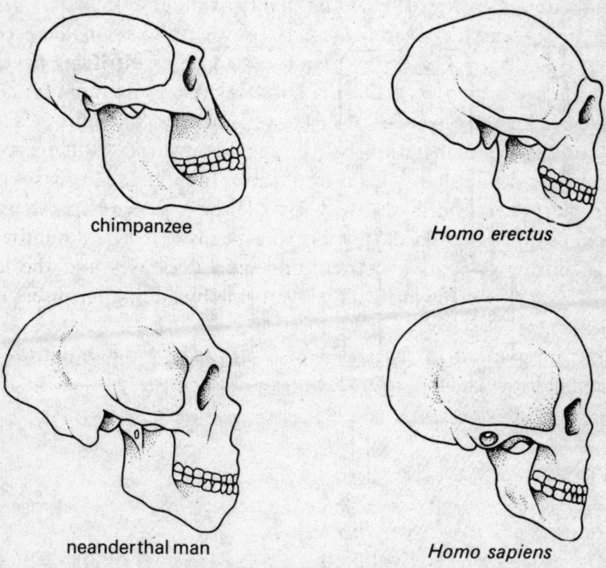

Fig. 4.13. *The skulls of some primates*

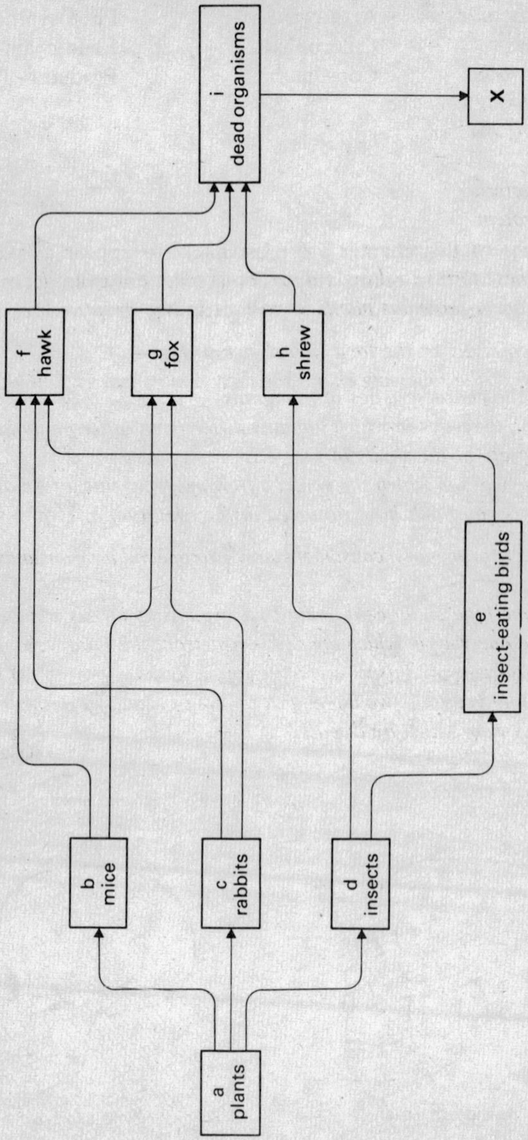

Fig. 4.14. *A food web*

3. The terms listed below are components of the nitrogen cycle.
atmospheric nitrogen
plant protein
nitrite bacteria
nitrogen-fixing bacteria
denitrifying bacteria
nitrite
nitrate bacteria
animal protein
ammonium compounds
(*a*) *Use these terms to draw a diagram of the nitrogen cycle.*
(*b*) *Why are leguminous plants important in crop rotation?*

4. Look carefully at the food web shown in Fig. 4.14.
(*a*) *Which of the following shows the direction of energy flow through the food web?*

A *a, d, e, f*
B *a, c, h, i*
C *h, e, d, a*
D *i, g, b, a*

(*b*) *Name two primary consumers and two secondary consumers in this food web.*
(*c*) *List one food chain containing four organisms in this web.*
(*d*) *Name one way in which energy is lost from the food web.*
(*e*) *What sort of organisms are represented by* X?
(*f*) *What do you think would happen to other organisms in the food web if the rabbits were killed by disease?*

5. *The Human Body – Overview*

In Chapter 3 we looked at the components of the human body – molecules, cells, tissues and organs (see Fig. 3.3). In this chapter we will survey the different tissues and organ systems which work together to form the living, functioning unit we call the body.

The three main cavities (spaces) in the body are shown in Fig. 5.1. The **cranial cavity** contains the brain. The **thoracic** (chest) **cavity** is enclosed by the ribs and diaphragm and contains the lungs and heart (see also Fig. 8.2). The **abdominal cavity** is found in the lower half of the trunk separated from the thoracic cavity by the **diaphragm**. It contains the urinary system (page 158), the reproductive system (page 235) and most of the digestive system (page 90).

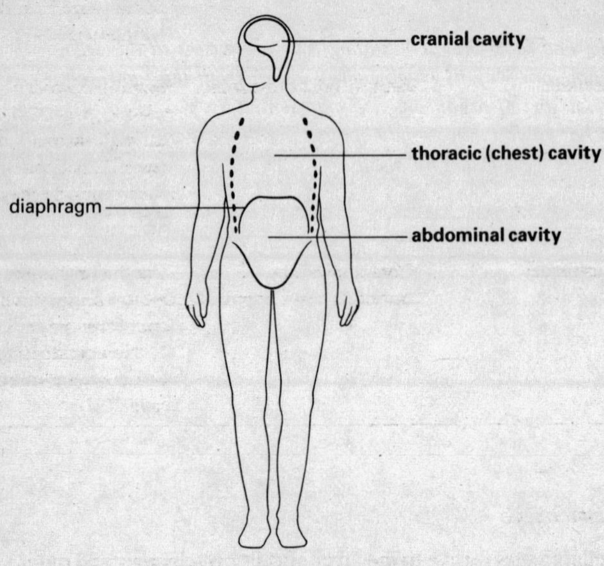

Fig. 5.1. *The main cavities of the body*

5.1. *Types of Tissues*

Four types of tissues are widespread in the body.

Table 5.1. *Human tissues*

Tissue	*Functions*	*Examples*
Epithelial tissue	Lines and protects tubes and cavities within the body. Also protects body surface	Simple epithelium (page 66). Compound (stratified) epithelium (page 66).
Connective tissue: has a matrix (non-living part)	Connects, binds, supports and protects (blood and lymph are exceptions)	Fibrous connective tissues: tendons (page 227), ligaments (page 221) and areolar connective tissue (page 66). Skeletal connective tissues: cartilage (page 220) and bone (page 219). Fluid tissues: blood (page 132) and lymph (page 149)
Muscle tissue	Brings about movement	Smooth (visceral) muscle (page 224). Striped (skeletal) muscle (page 225). Cardiac (heart) muscle (page 225)
Nervous tissue	Communication – transmits nerve impulses	Conducting tissue: motor, sensory and connector (pages 176–7). Non-conducting tissue, myelin sheath (page 177)

Epithelial tissue

Epithelial tissues form a living layer of cells on the inner and outer surfaces of the body. In such tissues the cells are packed tightly together with no spaces between adjacent cells. When the sheet of cells is one cell thick it is called a **simple epithelium** (Fig. 5.2a); where the sheet is several layers thick it is called a **compound (stratified) epithelium** (Fig. 5.2b).

The cells which make up a particular epithelium vary in shape from place to place in the body according to their precise function. For example, a simple epithelium of flattened cells (Fig. 5.2c) is found at surfaces where rapid diffusion of substances takes place e.g. the lining of alveoli in the lungs (page 124) and the lining of blood capillaries (page 146). A simple epithelium of column-shaped cells with numerous projections called **cilia** (Fig. 5.2d) is found lining the respiratory passages (page 118) and lining the oviduct in women (page 237). The beating action of cilia sweeps fluid or particles along. Another type of simple epithelium consists of elongated cells without cilia (Fig. 5.2e) e.g. those lining the stomach and small intestine (page 94), and lining the kidney tubules (page 159). Yet another, glandular tissue, contains epithelial cells which secrete substances e.g. the mucus-secreting cells which line the small intestine (Fig. 5.2e).

Compound (stratified) epithelium is found wherever the lining surface is subject to considerable wear (friction) and has to be replaced, e.g. the skin (page 163) and the linings of the mouth and oesophagus (page 91).

Connective tissue

As their name suggests, connective tissues connect and bind together parts of the body. However, the name is also rather misleading. Two types of connective tissue – blood and lymph – are fluids and do not have a binding function. What *all* connective tissues have in common is a non-living part called the **matrix** which surrounds the living part of the tissue. The three main types of connective tissue are distinguished by different types of matrix – fibrous, solid or liquid:

1. **Fibrous connective tissue** is characterized by the presence of protein fibres running through the matrix. Common examples of this tissue are tendons (page 227), and ligaments (page 221) and areolar or loose connective tissue. **Tendons** connect muscle to bone and in these tissues the protein fibres are white and are made of **collagen** which is tough and inelastic. **Ligaments** connect bone to bone and contain fibres which are mostly yellow and elastic. **Areolar connective tissue** is the packing tissue between organs, and beneath the skin, and its matrix contains a mixture of white and yellow fibres.

2. **Skeletal connective tissue** supports the body and provides it with a rigid framework. It consists of cells embedded in a rigid, hard matrix.

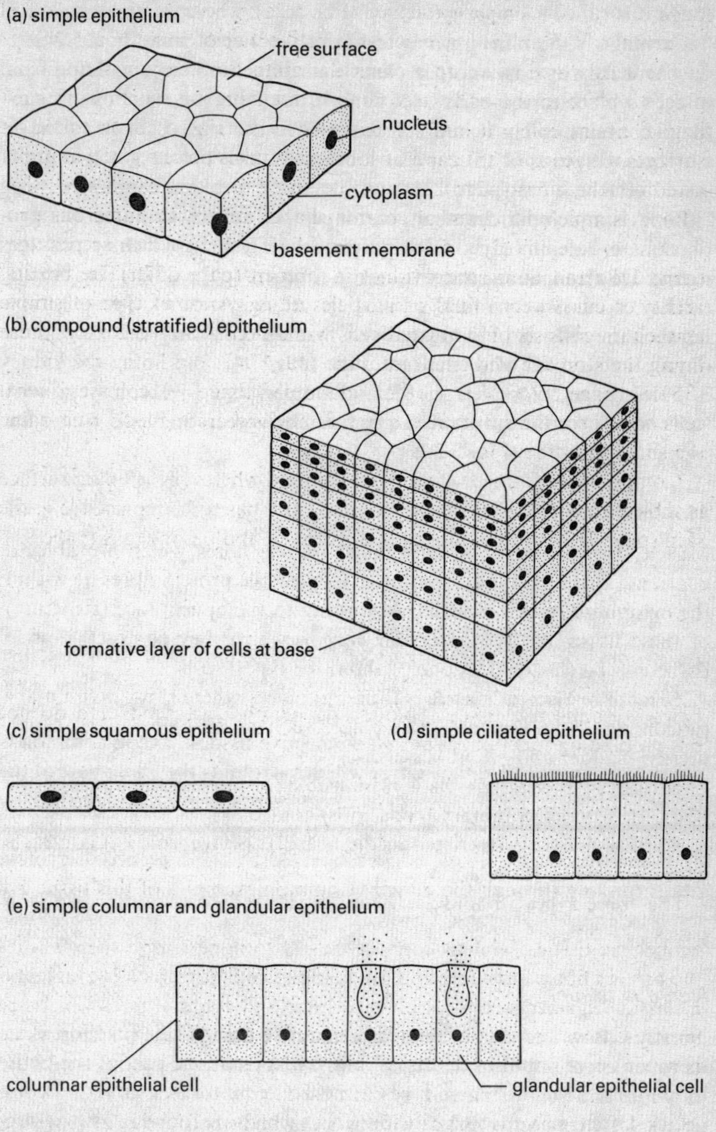

Fig. 5.2. *Different types of epithelium*

There are two kinds of skeletal tissue: cartilage (page 220) and bone (page 219).

Cartilage is the bluish gristle found at the end of some bones where one bone rubs against another. Simple cartilage contains small numbers of cells which secrete a hard yet flexible pale blue matrix. Fibrous cartilage contains collagen and elastic fibres in the matrix. Such cartilage supports the pinna of the ear (ear lobe) and forms the discs between the spinal vertebrae (page 216).

Bone is much harder than cartilage. Its matrix contains calcium phosphate, calcium carbonate and protein. The cells which secrete the matrix are arranged in concentric rings (one inside the other). Despite its rigidity, bone is very much a living tissue. A system of channels runs between the cells and blood vessels so that the cells can receive food and oxygen and get rid of wastes (see page 149).

3. **Fluid tissues**, blood (page 132) and lymph (page 149), consist of cells suspended in a fluid matrix. Lymph is derived from blood (see page 148).

Muscle tissue

Muscle tissue consists of cells called muscle fibres which are able to contract (shorten) and exert a force. Contractile protein fibres lie within the cytoplasm of muscle cells. According to the appearance (structure) of these fibres and the particular way in which they contract, muscle tissue can be classified as one of the three types:

1. **Smooth** or **visceral muscle** is found in places where slow, involuntary (unconscious) movements take place, such as the alimentary canal, uterus, bladder and blood vessels.
2. **Striped** or **skeletal muscle** is responsible for moving the bones of the body. It is under voluntary (conscious) control.
3. **Cardiac muscle** is restricted to the heart. It is **myogenic** – it contracts without nervous stimulation.

The three types of muscle tissue are looked at in more detail on pages 224–5.

Nervous tissue

Nervous tissue consists of neurones or nerve cells. Their function is to transmit nerve impulses (electrical messages) from one part of the body to another. There are three types of neurone: motor, sensory, and connector. Often, nervous tissue includes cells which are found in association with neurones but do not conduct nerve impulses. The commonest are

Schwann cells which form the myelin sheath which surrounds and insulates sensory and motor nerve fibres (page 177).

5.2. *Organs and Organ Systems*

In section 3.7 we saw how cells combine to form tissues and how tissues combine to form organs. Organs tend to work together in organ systems. The body's systems, their organs and functions, are given in Table 5.2.

Table 5.2. *Systems in the body*

System	*Functions*	*Organs or structures*
Digestive system (Chapter 7)	Digestion and absorption of food	Alimentary canal (gut), salivary glands, liver, pancreas
Respiratory (breathing) system (Chapter 8)	Breathing and gas exchange	Lungs and air passages
Circulatory (transport) system (Chapter 9)	Transport	Heart, blood vessels, blood, lymph vessels, lymph
Urinary (excretory) system (Chapter 10)	Excretion	Kidneys, ureters, bladder, urethra
Nervous system (Chapter 11)	Response to stimuli; coordination, intelligence and emotions	Brain and spinal cord, nerves, sense organs
Endocrine (hormonal) system (Chapter 11)	Coordination e.g. of growth and development	Ductless (endocrine) glands
Skeletal system (Chapter 12)	Support, movement and protection	Bones
Muscular system (Chapter 12)	Movement	Muscles
Reproductive system (Chapter 13)	Reproduction	Sex organs (different in the male and female)

The final level of organization in the body is the coordination of all the systems to form the organism (Fig. 3.3). In Chapters 7–13 we shall be discussing how each of the organ systems works, and how they all interact in the course of the body's daily activity. Each system is of vital importance to the body. The failure of any one will cause damage to all the other systems and so to the body as a whole.

Key Words

Cranial cavity
Thoracic (chest) cavity
Abdominal cavity
Diaphragm
Epithelial tissue
Simple epithelium
Compound (stratified) epithelium
Cilia
Connective tissue
Matrix
Fibrous connective tissues
Collagen
Skeletal connective tissues
Fluid tissues
Muscle tissues
Smooth (visceral) muscle
Striped (skeletal) muscle
Cardiac (heart) muscle
Nervous tissue
Conducting tissue
Non-conducting tissue
Digestive system
Respiratory (breathing) system
Circulatory (transport) system
Urinary (excretory) system
Nervous system
Endocrine (hormonal) system
Skeletal system
Muscular system
Reproductive system

Exam Question

Explain how animal cells may be modified in different ways to form three *named tissues.*

[10]
[OXF]

6. *Movement of Substances Into and Out of Cells*

Substances move into and out of cells by one of three processes: diffusion, osmosis or active transport.

As we saw in Chapter 3, the body is largely made up of water. In fact, all cells in the body are surrounded by water and any substance that passes into or out of a cell must be dissolved in water.

6.1. ***Diffusion***

The molecules in a liquid or gas are constantly moving. Unless prevented from doing so by a barrier, they tend to move from a region where they are at a high concentration to a region where they are at a lower concentration. This movement continues until the molecules are evenly distributed. For example, if you drop a small amount of liquid dye into a container of water, the dye molecules will eventually spread throughout the container colouring the whole water. The dye molecules have spread from a region of high concentration to a region of low (initially zero) concentration. This movement of molecules is a physical process termed diffusion.

Definition: Diffusion *is the free movement of molecules of a substance from regions of high concentration to regions of lower concentration.*

In the body, many substances are in solution and diffusion is the usual way they move into, out of or between cells. An example is the diffusion of oxygen and carbon dioxide (gas exchange) across the lining of alveoli in the lungs (see page 124).

Any substance that can pass through a cell membrane will diffuse into or out of a cell if its concentration inside the cell is different to that outside.

As an illustration of this, let us look at a smooth muscle cell in the body. As the muscle cell respires it uses up oxygen and the oxygen concentration in the cell decreases. The concentration of oxygen outside the cell is higher so that oxygen will diffuse into the cell.

Glucose, another substance used up in cell respiration, will diffuse into the cell to replace glucose that has been broken down.

We can summarize the diffusion of substances into and out of the cell in a diagram (Fig. 6.1):

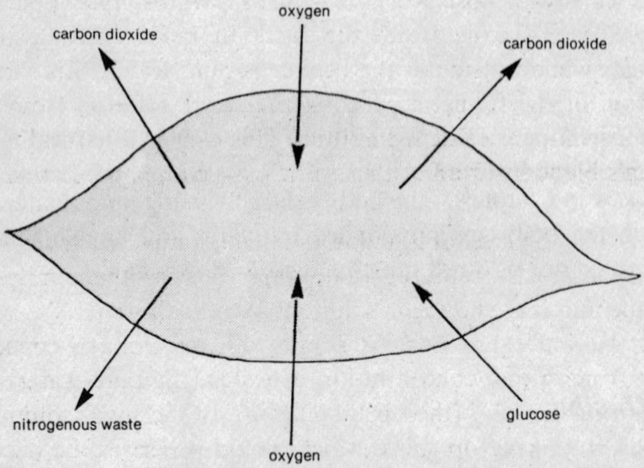

Fig. 6.1. *Diffusion of a smooth muscle cell*

Remember, substances can only diffuse into or out of a cell if they are small enough to pass through the cell membrane. In practice, molecules such as oxygen, carbon dioxide, glucose, amino acids and mineral salts are small enough, whereas larger molecules such as proteins are not.

Finally, in dealing with diffusion, the term **concentration gradient** or **diffusion gradient** is often used. A concentration gradient is determined by the difference in concentration between one region and another. Substances diffuse along a concentration gradient from a high to a low concentration. The greater (steeper) the concentration gradient the faster the rate of diffusion. If diffusion is to be rapid, a steep diffusion gradient must be maintained. The gas exchange surface in the lung maintains a steep diffusion gradient so that diffusion occurs rapidly (see page 124). Similarly, a steep diffusion gradient is maintained between the inside of the ileum and the surrounding blood capillaries (page 95).

6.2. *Osmosis*

Osmosis is a special type of diffusion. It is the diffusion of water across a semi-permeable (also known as selectively permeable) membrane. Cell membranes are semi-permeable and it is by osmosis that water moves into, out of and between cells. A semi-(selectively) permeable membrane is one that allows small molecules e.g. gases and water, to pass across it, but not larger molecules e.g. proteins and disaccharides.

Let us see how osmosis works. Fig. 6.2 shows a simple apparatus used to demonstrate osmosis. Inside the thistle funnel is a strong solution of table sugar while outside in the beaker is pure water. Stretched across the bottom of the funnel separating the sugar solution from the pure water is a semi-permeable membrane. This can be a natural membrane e.g. a pig's bladder, or an artificial one e.g. cellophane. Let us see what happens.

After a time the level of liquid in the thistle funnel will rise. Water has flowed by osmosis from the pure water, across the semi-permeable membrane and into the sugar solution. Why is this so?

What the water has done is simply diffuse along a concentration gradient from a high concentration of water (the pure water) to a low concentration of water (the sugar solution). In the sugar solution, sugar molecules are taking up space which would otherwise be occupied by water, therefore the concentration of water is lower.

This can be put another way. The water is diffusing from a weak solution (of the sugar) to a strong solution.

Definition: Osmosis *is the diffusion of water molecules through a semi-permeable membrane from a weak solution to a strong solution.*

You must be absolutely clear about this definition. Osmosis involves **water** diffusing through a **semi-permeable** membrane.

Let us return to the apparatus in Fig. 6.2. We could apply an external pressure to the sugar solution in the thistle funnel; a pressure that would be just sufficient to stop the flow of water into the sugar solution. The stronger (more concentrated) the solution, the higher its osmotic pressure. Thus, water will diffuse from a solution of low osmotic pressure to one of higher osmotic pressure.

Strictly, the osmotic pressure of a solution is always measured relative to pure water and across a semi-permeable membrane.

Definition: The osmotic pressure *of a solution is the pressure required to prevent the movement of pure water into the solution across a semi-permeable membrane.*

Really, we can only talk of a solution as having an osmotic pressure when it is separated from pure water by a semi-permeable membrane. A solution in a glass bottle or a cell in the body is obviously not in this situation. However, such solutions are potentially capable of exerting an osmotic pressure if separated from pure water by a semi-permeable

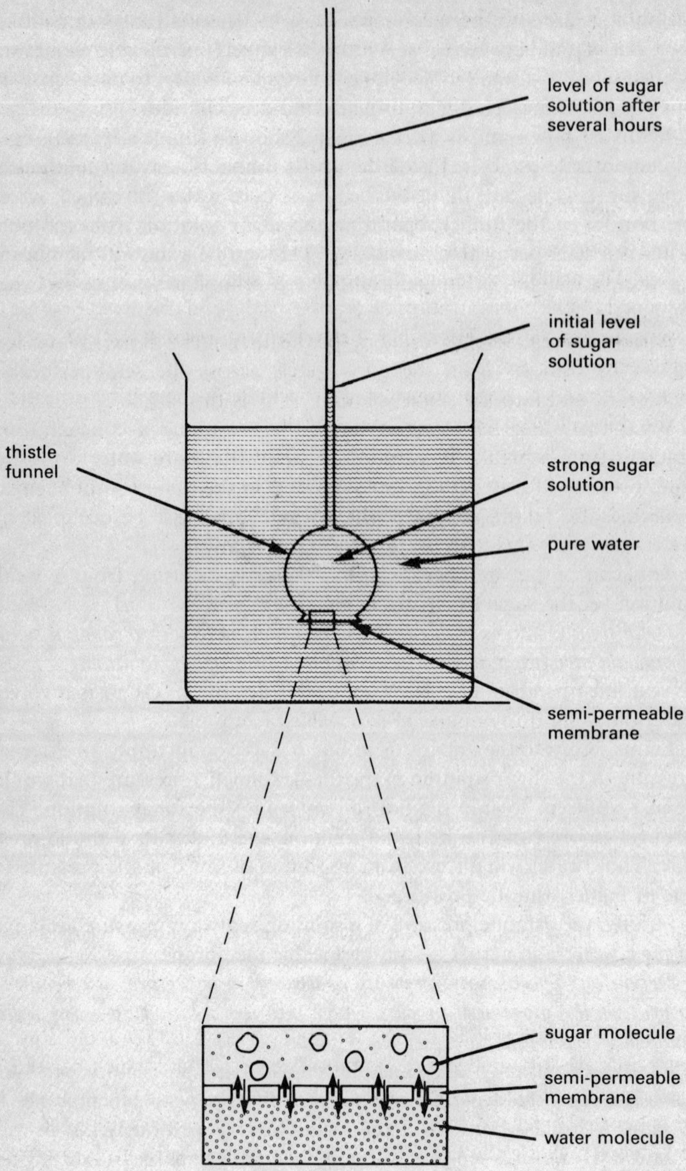

Fig. 6.2. *Demonstration of osmosis*

membrane. For such solutions we say they have an **osmotic potential**, the potential to exert an osmotic pressure. Strictly, we should always use the term osmotic potential when dealing with body fluids or cell contents inside our organism. Throughout this book we will use the term osmotic potential (O.P.).

Osmosis and human cells

The red blood cell is a convenient human cell in which to investigate osmosis. The osmotic potential of a red blood cell, as with other cells, is determined by the concentration of dissolved salts and dissolved organic substances it contains. The higher the concentration of dissolved salts, the greater its O.P.

If a red blood cell is put in water, water will enter the cell by osmosis and the cell will swell up and may eventually burst.

If a red blood cell is put in a solution of greater concentration than its own cell contents e.g. a strong salt solution, then the cell will lose water by osmosis and will shrink and wrinkle (Fig. 6.3).

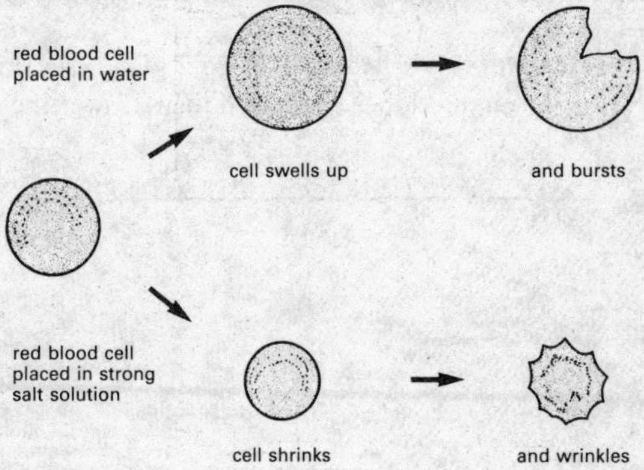

Fig. 6.3. *The effect on a red blood cell of changing the composition of the surrounding fluid*

Swelling up or shrinking can be damaging to a cell. To avoid this, human cells are surrounded by a liquid called tissue fluid which has the same osmotic potential (O.P.) as the cell contents. The O.P. of tissue fluid is kept relatively constant by the action of the kidneys (page 162). The kidneys regulate the O.P. of the blood which in turn gives rise to tissue fluid (see page 148).

6.3. *Active Transport*

Active transport is a chemical process which results in a movement of particles across a membrane in an opposite direction to that expected by diffusion. It occurs when molecules are taken across a membrane from a region of low concentration to a region of higher concentration i.e. against a concentration gradient. Protein 'carrier' molecules within the cell membrane are thought to carry the substances across.

Active transport, as its name implies, is an active process and requires energy. This energy is obtained from respiration. Any factors which influence the rate of respiration also influence the rate of active transport. Thus, low temperature, lack of oxygen and respiratory inhibitors such as cyanide all reduce or stop active transport.

Three examples of active transport are:

1. The selective reabsorption of substances by the kidney tubules (see page 160).
2. The absorption of digested food from the mammalian ileum is aided by active transport (see page 95). Active transport in this case, is used to aid diffusion, by speeding up the rate at which substances are absorbed.
3. The intake of iodine by cells in the thyroid gland (see page 205).

Read back over the chapter once again and then answer the question on page 77.

Definitions

Diffusion
Osmosis
Osmotic pressure

Key Words

Concentration (diffusion) gradient
Semi-(selectively) permeable membrane
Osmotic potential
Active transport

Exam Question

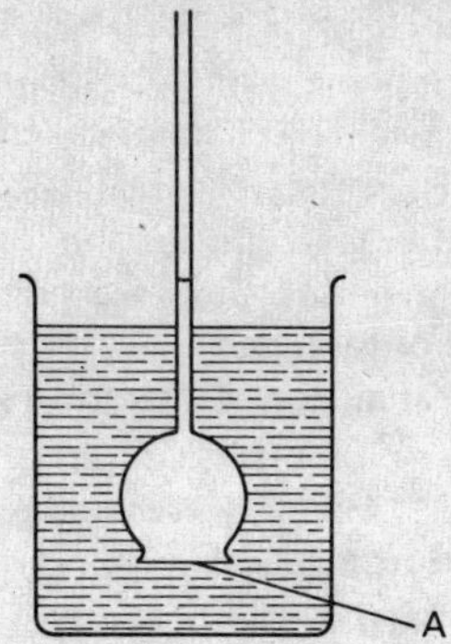

1. The diagram above shows an apparatus used to demonstrate the physical phenomenon of osmosis.

(a) Describe the physical qualities of A. [2]

(b) By an arrow and the letter B indicate on the diagram where a strong sugar solution has been placed. [1]

(c) By an arrow and the letter C indicate the probable fluid level in the tube after 1 hour. [1]

(d) Name one *structure in the living cell which possesses physical properties similar to A.* [1]

[LON]

7. *Feeding (Nutrition)*

Nutrition is the study of food and how it is processed and used by the body. Food is the material from which the body obtains:
1. the energy
2. the raw materials

to build, maintain and repair itself.

7.1. *Types of Nutrition*

There are two main types of nutrition. Green plants (page 41) have **autotrophic** (holophytic) nutrition, while animals and non-green plants have **heterotrophic** nutrition.

Autotrophic organisms make their own organic food from simple inorganic substances, using the energy from sunlight – a process called **photosynthesis** (page 49).

Heterotrophic organisms get their organic food 'ready-made' by feeding on animals or plants. Their supply of organic food is originally made by plants (see page 56).

1. **Holozoic nutrition:** this is typical of most animals, including humans. It involves five stages:

(a) Complex organic food is taken into a cavity within the body (**ingestion**).

(b) Within the cavity, organic food is broken down into simple soluble substances (**digestion**).

(c) The soluble products of digestion are taken up into the organism (**absorption**).

(d) These soluble substances are incorporated into the protoplasm of cells (**assimilation**).

(e) Indigestible waste is removed from the body (**egestion**).

2. **Saprophytic nutrition:** this type of nutrition is shown by many non-green plants, including certain fungi and bacteria (see pages 46–7). The organism (**saprophyte**) secretes digestive enzymes on to dead or decaying organic matter. The organic food is digested and the soluble products of

digestion are absorbed. Saprophytic nutrition differs from holozoic nutrition in that digestion occurs *outside* the organism and the organic food is always obtained from dead or decaying material.

Saprophytes play a very important role in the cycling of materials in nature (see page 58).

3. **Parasitic nutrition:** a parasitic organism (**parasite**) lives in or on another organism (its **host**) from which it obtains its organic food. Examples of parasites which feed on humans and cause disease are given on page 292.

7.2. *Human Nutrition*

Humans have **holozoic nutrition** and are **omnivores** (they feed on plants and animals).

Before food can properly enter the body it must pass across a cell membrane. Complex organic food can enter body cells only if first broken down into small, soluble molecules. The five stages involved in this process are as follows:

1. **Ingestion:** the intake of foods into the mouth.
2. **Digestion:** the breakdown of complex organic foods into small, soluble molecules.
3. **Absorption:** the uptake of soluble food substances into the body across a cell membrane.
4. **Assimilation:** the uptake and use of soluble food substances by cells in the body.
5. **Egestion:** the removal of undigested food from the body. Do not confuse egestion with excretion (page 156) or secretion (below).

Secretion: the production of useful chemical substances by a cell or gland.

To test your understanding of the above terms try answering *Q1* on page 107.

In humans, the alimentary canal (gut) is responsible for the ingestion, digestion, absorption and egestion of food.

The breakdown of foods in the gut involves both mechanical and chemical action. The teeth and tongue physically break down food by chewing (mastication). Digestive enzymes chemically break down foods by hydrolysis (see page 28). These enzymes are found in juices secreted by salivary glands, the pancreas and glands in the gut wall.

Questions on digestive enzymes, together with the conditions under which they operate, are popular (see page 40).

7.3. *The Human Diet*

A balanced diet

Humans require a **balanced diet**. This is one that supplies the different types of food in a digestible form, in adequate amounts and in the right proportions. It also provides the body with sufficient energy for its needs. A balanced diet maintains healthy active life and, where necessary, growth.

The *seven* components of a balanced diet are:
carbohydrates
fats
proteins
vitamins
minerals
water
roughage

The detailed dietary requirements for humans are shown in Tables 7.1, 7.2 and 7.3.

Carbohydrates and fats are primarily responsible for supplying the body with a sufficient supply of energy.

Protein is the main body-building food. Proteins in the body are built up from 20 different amino acids. Eight of these amino acids are needed in the diet – they are called **essential amino acids**. The other 12 amino acids can be made from these essential eight. Proteins in the diet which are rich in essential amino acids are called **first class proteins**.

Vitamins are organic substances required in minute quantities for essential chemical processes in the body. Vitamins cannot be manufactured by the body (except vitamin D); all must be present in adequate quantities in the diet. If the diet is lacking in a particular vitamin, a **deficiency disease** develops with its own characteristic signs and symptoms. If the missing vitamin is later supplied, the signs and symptoms rapidly clear up.

Minerals, like vitamins, are required in the diet in small quantities; in their absence ill health results. Most of the minerals listed in Table 7.3 are rarely absent from the diet. Those most likely to be in short supply are calcium (Ca), iodine (I) and iron (Fe).

Trace metals such as cobalt (Co), manganese (Mn), zinc (Zn) and copper (Cu) are required in tiny quantities. In a varied diet they are normally present in sufficient amounts.

Water makes up about 60 per cent of the body weight and all chemical reactions in the body take place in it. Hydrolysis reactions use water.

Table 7.1. *The different parts of the human diet*

Type of food	*Good sources*	*Main uses in the body*
Carbohydrates		
Starch	Potatoes, flour products	As an energy source. Stored as glycogen
Disaccharides	Table sugar, milk	
Monosaccharides	Honey, fruit	
Proteins		
First class proteins (rich in essential amino acids)	Meat, eggs, milk, cheese Soya beans, nuts	Structural material in cells. Enzymes. General growth and repair of tissues
Second class proteins	Peas, beans	
Fats (lipids)	Unskimmed dairy products e.g. butter, cheese. Vegetable oils	As an energy source. As structural material in cell membranes. Stored as fat in adipose tissue
Vitamins		
At least 20 vitamins are required in minute quantities. Some of the better known ones are listed in Table 7.2.		
Minerals		
About 15 different minerals are required in very small quantities. The major ones are listed in Table 7.3.		
Water	Liquids and most foods	Body 60 per cent water. All chemical reactions take place in it. Intake of water replaces that lost in evaporation from lungs (page 125), sweat (page 165) and urine (page 161)
Roughage	Cereals, vegetables, fruits, wholemeal bread	Indigestible. No food value. Stimulates muscular movements (peristalsis) of gut wall. Lack of roughage can lead to constipation

Table 7.2. *Vitamins in the human diet*

Vitamin	*Good sources*	*Main uses in the body/deficiency effects*
A (fat soluble)	Butter, milk, cod liver oil, certain vegetables e.g. carrots	Maintaining health of mucous membranes. Lack of vitamin (deficiency) increases likelihood of disease infection. Forms part of visual pigment in rod cells of the eye (page 194). Lack of vitamin leads to **night blindness**
B (water soluble) There are over ten B vitamins,*three of which are thiamin (B_1), niacin (nicotinic acid) and cyanocobalamin (B_{12})	B_1 – whole grain of cereal e.g. in wholemeal bread, brown rice, brown flour Other B vitamins – milk, meat, eggs and green vegetables, yeast	Vitamin B_1 and niacin play a role in energy release (respiration). Lack of thiamin leads to paralysis (**beri-beri**), a condition once common in Africa. Lack of niacin leads to gut disorders and the skin disease **pellagra.** Vitamin B_{12} is involved in nucleic acid synthesis and hence formation of new cells. Lack of cyanocobal amin is one cause of **pernicious anaemia**
C ascorbic acid (water soluble) Destroyed by boiling or prolonged exposure to sunlight	Fresh citrus fruits Certain fresh vegetables e.g. potatoes Milk	Repair of tissue damage. Maintaining health of skin and blood vessels. Lack of vitamin leads to **scurvy** (bleeding gums, poor wound healing, and bleeding under skin)
D (fat soluble)	Liver, cod liver oil, dairy products. Also manufactured by the skin when exposed to u.v. light	Used in bone formation. Lack of vitamin leads to skeletal deformity such as **rickets** (bow legs) in children

* Only four of the B complex vitamins are still numbered: B_1, B_2, B_6 and B_{12}.

Table 7.3. *Minerals in the human diet*

Mineral	*Good sources*	*Main uses in the body/deficiency effects*
Calcium (Ca)	Dairy products, bread, fruit, vegetables and tap water in hard water areas	In bone and teeth formation. Lack of mineral leads to brittle bones and teeth. Also needed for blood clotting and proper functioning of nerves and muscles
Iodine (I)	Table salt Sea food	In thyroid gland hormone, thyroxin. Lack of mineral leads to thyroid gland swelling (goitre)
Iron (Fe)	Liver, egg yolk	Formation of haemoglobin (page 134). Shortage may lead to anaemia (shortage of red blood cells)
Phosphorus (P)	Dairy products, meat, eggs, fish	In bone and teeth formation. Lack of mineral leads to brittle bones and teeth. Also needed to make ATP (page 115) and nucleic acids (page 32)
Potassium (K) Sodium (Na)	Plant material Table salt	Important constituents of cells and body fluids. A correct balance of these is required for proper functioning of nerves and muscles
Chlorine (Cl)	Table salt	Important constituent of body fluids. Required for proper functioning of nerves and muscles. Also needed for hydrochloric acid formation in the stomach

Water is also needed to form urine (page 161) and to form sweat (page 165).

Roughage (dietary fibre) is the name given to those parts of the diet which pass through the body undigested. These consist mainly of the cellulose cell walls found in plant material. Fibre adds bulk to the faeces (solid waste) and so stimulates peristalsis (page 90) in the colon. Lack of fibre can lead to constipation.

In practice, a balanced diet for an adult needs to yield about 10,000–15,000 kJ energy per day (see below).

In a balanced diet, the digestible organic portion contains in the region of 20 per cent protein, 20 per cent fat and 60 per cent carbohydrate. A suitable British diet will contain, in addition, some fresh fruit, vegetables, cereal or wholemeal bread, to supply vitamins, minerals and roughage.

An example of a balanced diet for one day is shown in Table 7.4.

The body's energy requirements

The human body requires energy to fuel chemical reactions, to allow muscles to contract, and to maintain a high body temperature. It is obtained from chemical energy stored within bonds between the atoms of organic foods. When the bonds are broken, energy is released.

The energy in organic food is released by the process of respiration (page 112). The amount of energy contained in a sample of food is measured in kilojoules per gram of food (kJ/g). A joule is a unit of energy, and 1,000 joules (J) = 1 kilojoule (kJ).

In the past (and still in slimming books and magazines) the calorie has been used as the unit of energy.

A **calorie** is the amount of heat energy required to raise the temperature of 1 gram of water through 1°C (1 calorie = 4.2 joules).

The amount of energy released from food depends upon its chemical nature. Fats yield about twice as much energy per gram (39 kJ/g) as carbohydrates or proteins (17 kJ/g).

A person's daily energy requirement depends on body size, age, gender and physical activity.

	Energy requirement (average)
Adult male office worker	11,500 kJ/day
Adult female office worker	9,500 kJ/day
Adult male manual worker	12,500–17,500 kJ/day
Male 15 years old	11,000 kJ/day
Male 10 years old	9,000 kJ/day
Male 5 years old	7,000 kJ/day

Table 7.4. *A balanced diet. The food eaten in one day by an 18-year-old female student*

			ORGANIC FOODS			MINERALS*		VITAMINS*				
Food item	*Mass* (g)	*Energy Value* (kJ)	*Protein* (g)	*Fat* (g)	*Carbo-hydrate* (g)	*Calcium*	*Iron*	*A*	*B1*	*B6*	*C*	*D*
Roast Pork	100	1710	12	40	–	√	√	–	√√	√√	–	–
Roast Potatoes	150	1490	6	14	56	√	√√	–	√	√√	–	–
Garlic Sausage	50	770	5	16	7	√	√	–	√	√√	–	–
Plain biscuits	50	900	4	7	38	√	√	–	√	√	–	–
Fruit buns	100	1380	8	9	59	√√	√√	√	√	√√	–	√
Cornflakes	40	580	3	–	35	–	√	–	√√	√	–	√√
Banana	50	160	1	–	10	√	–	√	–	√	√	–
Custard	15	210	–	–	13	√	–	–	–	–	–	–
Milk	560	1520	19	93	27	√√	√	√√	√	√√	√	√
Grapefruit juice	140	120	1	–	7	√	√	–	√	√	√√	–
Sugar	10	165	–	–	10	–	–	–	–	–	–	–
Total	1265	9005	59	179	262							

* √√ = a lot; √ = some; – = little or none

The rate at which the body uses up energy is called the **metabolic rate**. The **basal metabolic rate** is the rate at which energy is used up simply to maintain life processes (breathing, heartbeat, tissue repair, constant body temperature, etc.) while the person is at rest. A person's metabolic rate is the basal rate plus the extra kilojoules required for daily physical activity.

How the daily energy requirement varies with age is shown in Fig. 7.1.

Obesity, dieting and exercise

If the daily intake of food regularly exceeds the amount needed to meet the body's energy demands then the excess energy intake will be stored largely as fat. An excess of body fat is known as **obesity**. Obesity is classified as a medical disease because it reduces a person's life expectancy. Obese people are more likely to suffer from:

1. heart disease (page 145)
2. kidney disorders
3. diabetes (page 162)
4. diseases of the joints, particularly arthritis (page 223).

What causes obesity? The simple answer is: eating more food than the body needs to meet its energy requirements. Unfortunately, some people put on weight while eating only a modest diet, while others seem to get away with eating as much as they like. This difference between individuals is probably partly due to hormonal balance (page 202). Nevertheless, no matter how easily a person puts on weight, obesity occurs *only* when you consume more energy than your body requires.

There are a number of reasons why people eat more than they should. Here are a few:

1. As people get older their rate of metabolism drops, partly because they become less active. They therefore require less food. However, many individuals fail to reduce their food intake as they get older and so develop 'middle-aged spread'.
2. Some people overeat as a result of a psychological disturbance or psychiatric disorder, and as a result get fat. Overeating and weight gain may themselves bring on psychological depression. The person eats more to overcome the depression, they get fatter, and so it goes on.
3. Stress and the pressures of modern Western life tend to work against the regular taking of meals, which may be replaced by lots of high-energy snacks.
4. Social drinking of beer or spirits can lead to obesity, as alcohol is a high-energy food.

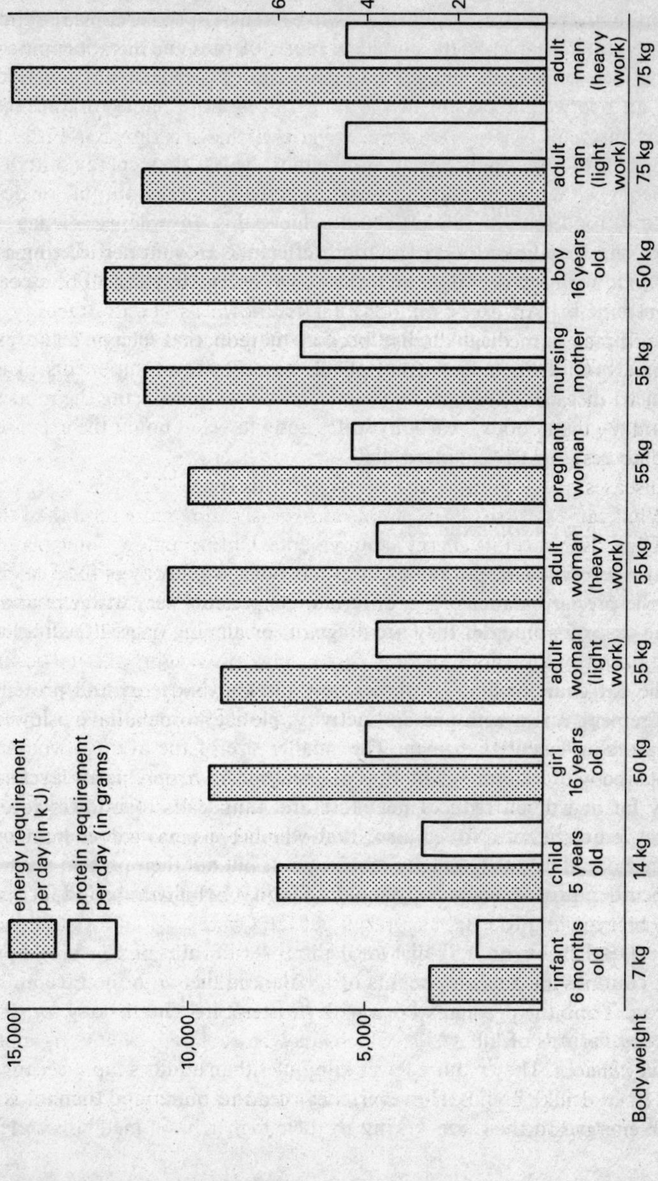

Fig. 7.1. *Variations in the body's energy and protein requirements with age, gender and activity*

Present-day fashion in most dominant Western cultures dictates that obesity is unattractive. However, some people are 'happy being overweight' and are distressed when, bowing to social pressure, they try to lose weight. Perhaps society should be more tolerant and allow people to decide their own 'body image' for themselves. Nevertheless, it must be said, an overweight person in the long run is more liable to contract certain diseases.

In order to lose weight energy intake must be less than energy output. In theory, either an increase in physical activity (energy output) or decrease in food (energy intake) could achieve this. In practice, **dieting** – decreasing food intake – is the more effective. However, if dieting is combined with a programme of increased exercise, the weight reduction programme is likely to be even more successful.

An appropriate weight reduction diet requires that energy intake is reduced but adequate quantities of all the necessary components of a balanced diet are still eaten. In practice, this means reducing the intake of energy-giving foods – carbohydrates and fats – but not at the expense of other parts of the balanced diet.

Special dietary requirements

A balanced diet is needed throughout life, but the quantity of food eaten and the precise balance of the different components vary with age and, in the case of women, if they are pregnant or nursing (breast-feeding) a child.

The bar chart in Fig. 7.1 shows how the body's energy and protein requirement varies with age and activity. Notice, women have a lower energy requirement than men. The smaller size of the average woman compared with the average man, is one reason. Also, the thicker layer of body fat in women reduces heat loss and thus leads to a lower total energy requirement. Notice also, that whether a person does light or heavy work affects their energy requirements but not their protein needs. Remember, protein is the body-building food. Carbohydrate and fat are the energy-giving foods.

Infants. Babies have a milk diet until about 4–6 months of age. Mother's milk contains all the components of a balanced diet with the exception of iron. The baby is usually born with sufficient iron in its body for the first few months of life.

Young children. They require fewer kilojoules than adults simply because they have smaller bodies. However, they consume more food than adults in proportion to their size, owing to their higher basal metabolic rate, and their steady growth. They also need more protein in proportion to the rest of their diet in order to sustain growth.

Teenagers require more food than adults following similar activities. Extra kilojoules and more protein are required to sustain the rapid growth which follows adolescence (see page 252).

Pregnant women and breast-feeding mothers. In their diet they require increased kilojoules, protein, calcium, iron and vitamins. During pregnancy calcium is required for the formation and growth of the baby's skeleton, iron is required for the developing blood system, while extra kilojoules, protein and vitamins are needed to sustain the baby's growth.

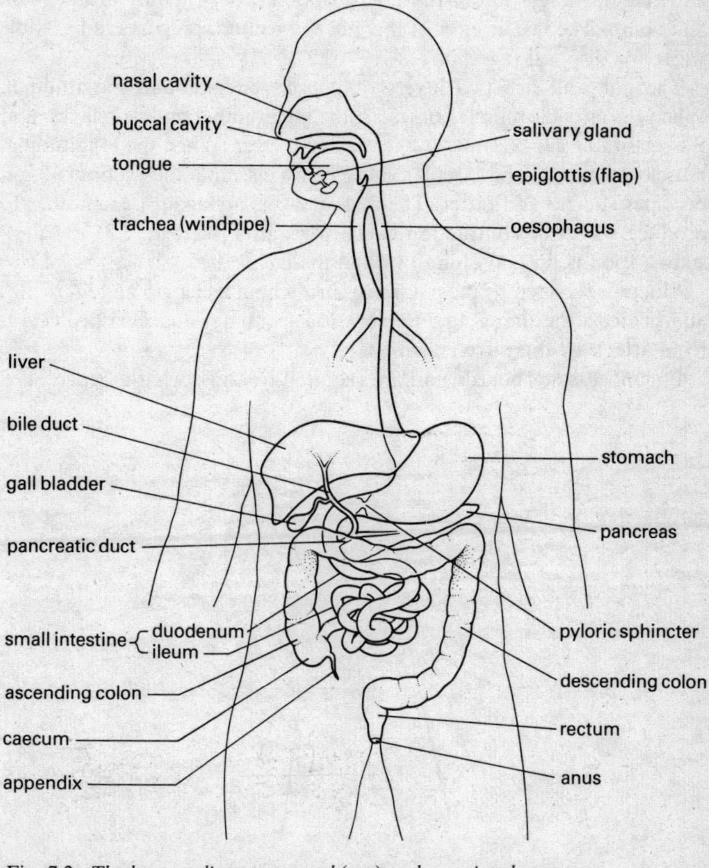

Fig. 7.2. *The human alimentary canal (gut) and associated structures*

The pregnant woman also needs extra energy for the work done in carrying the baby's weight around. The breast-feeding mother requires extra energy for the metabolic activities which lead to milk production.

7.4. *The Human Alimentary Canal* (*Gut*)

The alimentary canal (gut) is the muscular tube which runs from mouth to anus (see Fig. 7.2). Its overall function is to process food and different regions of the gut undertake different parts of this process. From mouth to duodenum, the gut is mainly concerned with the physical breakdown and chemical digestion of food. Absorption occurs mainly in the ileum and colon. The last section of the gut, the rectum, prepares indigestible waste for disposal (egestion).

The gut wall has two layers of muscle, circular and longitudinal. When the circular muscle contracts, the longitudinal muscle relaxes, and the section of gut becomes longer and narrower. When the longitudinal muscle contracts, the circular muscle relaxes, and the section of gut becomes shorter and fatter. The muscle layers act against each other to produce waves of contraction called **peristalsis** (see Fig. 7.3). By peristalsis, food is pushed along through the gut.

Mucus is secreted by the gut lining throughout its length and lubricates and protects the lining against abrasion (rubbing) and also protects it from attack by digestive enzymes.

For most exam boards you are required to know what a generalized

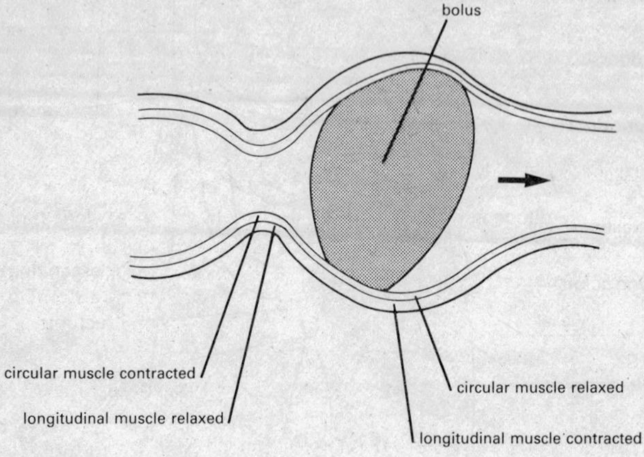

Fig. 7.3. *Peristalsis in the oesophagus*

section of the gut looks like (Fig. 7.4). The structure of the epithelium and mucosa varies according to the function of particular parts of the gut:

1. In the oesophagus, which must be protected from abrasion by rough food items and the high temperature of hot foods, the epithelium is many cells thick, and many mucus-secreting glands are found in the mucosa.
2. In the stomach, the mucosa is folded to form gastric pits, which are lined by a simple epithelium (page 65). The epithelium contains cells which secrete mucus, hydrochloric acid and digestive enzymes.
3. In the ileum, the mucosa is folded to form **villi**, for the absorption of digested foods, and **intestinal glands**, for the secretion of digestive enzymes (Fig. 7.5). A simple epithelium covers the surface of the villi and contains mucus-secreting cells.

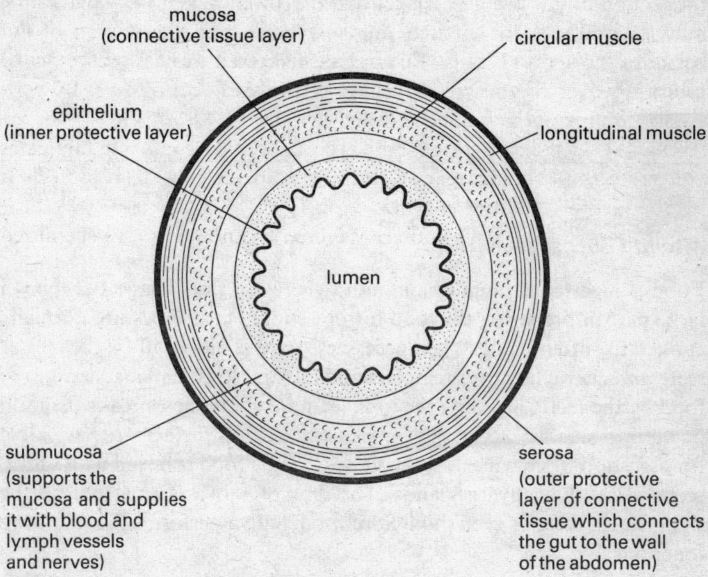

Fig. 7.4. *A generalized transverse section of the gut*

The functions of the different parts of the gut can be summarized as follows:

Table 7.5. *The functions of the different regions of the alimentary canal* (*gut*)

Region	*Functions*
Mouth (buccal cavity)	Ingestion, mastication (chewing), bolus (food ball) formation, some starch digestion.
Oesophagus	Delivery of food from mouth to stomach.
Stomach	Storage of food and delivery to small intestine. Formation of chyme (liquefied food). Some protein digestion. Acid kills bacteria. Alcohol absorption.
Duodenum	Digestion of starch, protein and fat.
Associated organs: Liver	Production of bile which emulsifies (breaks up) fat.
Pancreas	Production of pancreatic juice which contains enzymes for digesting starch, protein and fat.
Ileum	Completes digestion of carbohydrates, proteins and fats. Absorption of end-products of digestion.
Caecum	No particular function in humans.
Appendix	No particular function in humans.
Colon	Water absorption.
Rectum	Formation and storage of faeces (solid waste).
Anus	Egestion.

Mouth (Buccal cavity)

Food is **ingested** through the mouth, where the teeth (page 102) play a large part in preparing the food for digestion. Hard foods are normally cooked to soften them. When necessary, food is bitten off by the incisor teeth and chewed by the premolars and molars. **Mastication** (chewing) of food by the teeth, aided by the tongue and jaw muscles, breaks the food down into smaller pieces. This increases the food surface area available for digestion by enzymes. At the same time the food is mixed with **saliva**, secreted by the salivary glands. The flow of saliva is triggered by the sight, smell, taste or even thought of food. Saliva performs the following functions:

1. it lubricates the food for swallowing
2. it contains the enzyme **salivary amylase (ptyalin)** which digests starch to maltose
3. it dissolves soluble food enabling it to be tasted.

The teeth and tongue mould the food into a ball (**bolus**) which is pushed backwards against the roof of the mouth (the **hard palate**). This sets off the swallowing reflex whereby the bolus is pushed into the oesophagus by the contraction of throat (pharynx) muscles. At the same time the **soft palate** closes over the nasal passages and the epiglottis closes over the entrance of the windpipe (trachea) thus stopping food 'going down the wrong way'.

Oesophagus

Inside the oesophagus, the bolus is squeezed down to the stomach by peristalsis (see Fig. 7.3).

Stomach

The stomach is a muscular bag. Its main functions are:
1. To store food temporarily and deliver it, a little at a time, to the duodenum. This prevents the digestive system becoming overloaded with too much food at once.
2. The stomach secretes **gastric juice**. Muscular contractions of the stomach wall mix together solid food and juice and churn it into a liquid called **chyme**.
3. The digestion of proteins begins in the stomach. The lining of the stomach contains gastric glands which secrete the gastric juice. This secretion contains a number of substances:
(i) **Hydrochloric acid**, which provides the correct pH for pepsin action (see 2), stops activity of the enzyme salivary amylase, and kills bacteria.
(ii) The enzyme **pepsin** which digests proteins to polypeptides and peptides. (NOTE: pepsin, in common with other protein-digesting enzymes, is secreted first in an inactive form. This is to prevent the enzyme-secreting cells, which themselves are largely protein, from being digested.)
(iii) **Rennin**, which is valuable to infants living on milk. It clots milk, so keeping it in the stomach where pepsin can break it down.
4. Some absorption occurs in the stomach. Alcohol and some glucose, minerals, water and water-soluble vitamins are absorbed into the bloodstream across the lining of the stomach.

At the lower end of the stomach is a ring of muscle, the pyloric sphincter. At intervals, this sphincter relaxes and allows small quantities of chyme through to the duodenum.

Duodenum

The duodenum is the first 30 cm (12 inches) of the small intestine. As food passes through the duodenum, secretions from the gall bladder and pancreas are poured into it.

Bile is the thick green fluid produced by the liver and stored in the gall bladder. It empties into the duodenum along the bile duct (see Fig. 7.6). Bile contains sodium bicarbonate, which neutralizes stomach acid, and bile salts, which **emulsify** fats (break fat droplets up into smaller droplets). Bile does *not* contain any enzymes.

Pancreatic juice, produced by the pancreas, enters the duodenum along the pancreatic duct. It contains sodium bicarbonate to neutralize stomach acidity, as well as three digestive enzymes which act on the three main types of organic food – carbohydrates, proteins and fats:

$$\text{Starch} \xrightarrow{\text{pancreatic amylase}} \text{maltose}$$

$$\text{Polypeptides} \xrightarrow{\text{trypsin*}} \text{peptides} + \text{amino acids}$$

$$\text{Fats} \xrightarrow{\text{lipase}} \text{fatty acids} + \text{glycerol}$$

Ileum

The second part of the small intestine, the ileum, is where digestion is completed and where the end-products of digestion are absorbed. In the ileum, pancreatic enzymes are still active. In addition, glands in the ileum lining secrete **intestinal juice** containing enzymes which digest the three main types of organic food down to their soluble constituents:

$$\text{Sucrose} \xrightarrow{\text{sucrase}} \text{glucose} + \text{fructose}$$

$$\text{Maltose} \xrightarrow{\text{maltase}} \text{glucose}$$

$$\text{Lactose} \xrightarrow{\text{lactase}} \text{glucose} + \text{galactose}$$

(all disaccharides) (all monosaccharides)

$$\text{Peptides} \xrightarrow[\text{of enzymes)}]{\text{erepsin (a mixture}} \text{amino acids}$$

$$\text{Fats} \xrightarrow{\text{lipase}} \text{fatty acids} + \text{glycerol}$$

The organic molecules which were originally large and complex are now small and soluble and can be absorbed.

* Trypsin is secreted in the inactive form, trypsinogen, which is activated by the presence of another enzyme, enterokinase, secreted by the lining of the duodenum.

The lining of the ileum is adapted for absorption. Its great length and the presence of thousands of finger-like projections called **villi** (singular: villus) greatly increase the surface area for absorption. In addition, the epithelium of the villi is very thin so allowing rapid passage of dissolved substances through it. Each villus contains a dense network of **blood capillaries** for rapidly transporting away the soluble end products of digestion.

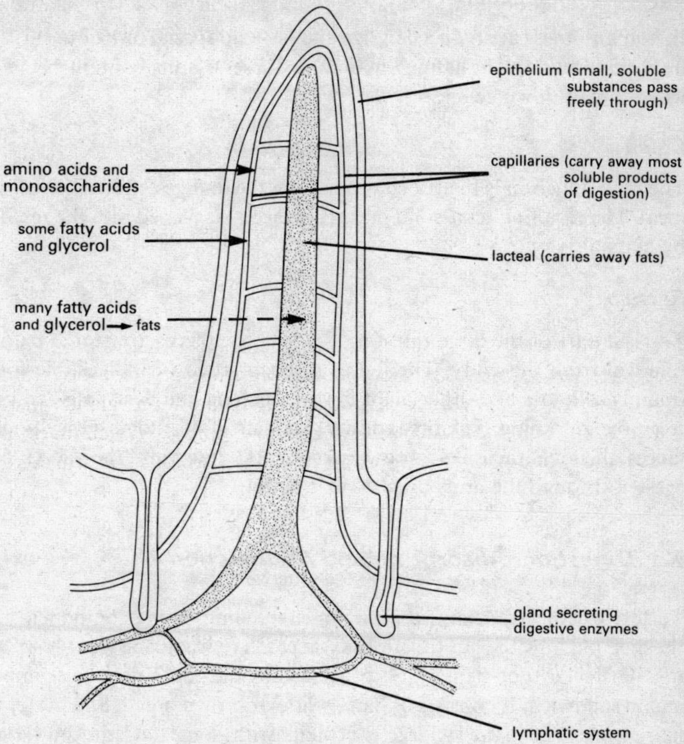

Fig. 7.5. *A villus from the ileum lining*

Absorption across the ileum lining is by a combination of passive diffusion and active uptake (see page 76). Some fatty acids and glycerol recombine in the intestinal epithelium and pass as fats into the lacteals in the centre of villi (see Fig. 7.5). They then travel through the lymphatic system (page 149) before entering the bloodstream. All other products of digestion travel in the bloodstream to the liver (page 108) where their rate of supply to body tissues is regulated. The products of digestion are distributed round the body in the bloodstream and are then delivered to cells via the tissue fluid (page 148). All cells in the body require a supply of organic foods which are finally **assimilated** when they enter the cell. Minerals, vitamins and some water are also absorbed in the ileum.

Caecum and appendix

In humans, these are reduced in size and have no special function. (NOTE: in herbivorous (plant-eating) mammals these regions contain bacteria which break down cellulose).

Colon

The main function is to absorb water from the undigested remains of the meal. The resulting semi-solid mass (the **faeces**) is passed into the rectum by peristalsis.

Rectum

The last part of the large intestine is where the faeces are stored before removal from the body. The faeces are composed of indigestible food (mainly cellulose and other plant fibres), bacteria and dead cells scraped from the gut lining. The breakdown products of haemoglobin help give faeces their characteristic brown colour. At intervals, the faeces are **egested** through the anus by muscular action.

7.5. ***Digestion, Absorption and Assimilation***

To test whether you have a clear understanding of the components of the diet and how the gut functions, you can try visualizing what happens to a particular food item as it is processed by the gut. Take, for example, a ham sandwich. It consists of ham, white or brown bread, and butter or margarine. The ham is largely protein with some fat, the butter or margarine is largely fat, and the bread contains starch, some protein, and, if it is wholemeal bread, roughage. The sandwich also contains a mixture of vitamins, minerals and some water. Now, consider what happens to the sandwich and the different food components it contains, as it travels through the gut. Consider how the sandwich is physically broken down and chemically digested and where different food components are absorbed.

In some exam questions you may be required to follow the chain of events, from ingestion through to assimilation, for an organic food (see, for example, *Q6* on page 109). The following sections provide an overview of digestion, absorption and assimilation for each type of organic food.

Carbohydrates

Carbohydrates are ingested as monosaccharides, disaccharides or polysaccharides. the last two need to be digested to monosaccharides before absorption.

Digestion

In the mouth (buccal cavity):

$$\text{starch} \xrightarrow{\text{salivary amylase}} \text{maltose}$$

In the stomach: no carbohydrate digestion
In the duodenum:

$$\text{starch} \xrightarrow{\text{pancreatic amylase}} \text{maltose}$$

In the ileum:

$$\text{maltose} \xrightarrow{\text{maltase}} \text{glucose}$$

$$\text{sucrose} \xrightarrow{\text{sucrase}} \text{glucose + fructose}$$

$$\text{lactose} \xrightarrow[\text{secreted by ileum lining)}]{\text{lactase (enzymes}} \text{glucose + galactose}$$

(all disaccharides) (all monosaccharides)

All digestible carbohydrates are now monosaccharides and can be absorbed across the lining of the ileum.

Absorption

In the ileum, monosaccharides (mainly glucose) pass through the epithclium of villi, through capillary walls and into the blood plasma. Absorption is by a combination of passive diffusion and active transport (page 76). The glucose then travels in the hepatic portal vein to the liver.

Assimilation

What happens to glucose on reaching the liver depends on the blood glucose level.

1. Glucose is the body's main source of energy. All cells need a supply of glucose for respiration (see page 112).
2. Excess glucose is converted to glycogen in the liver and skeletal muscles. When the blood glucose level drops, the liver converts its glycogen back into glucose and releases it into the bloodstream. In this way, the glucose level in the blood is kept relatively constant.
3. Glucose in large excess is converted to fat and stored in fat (adipose) tissue. Hence, a large amount of carbohydrate in the diet can lead to obesity. However, the fat can be respired later (see page 100).

Proteins are ingested in the form of polypeptide chains of varying length. These have to be broken down to amino acids before absorption.

Digestion

In the mouth: no protein digestion
In the stomach:

$$\text{proteins} \xrightarrow{\text{pepsin (secreted as pepsinogen)}} \text{polypeptides}$$

$$\text{milk protein} \xrightarrow{\text{rennin*}} \text{clotted protein}$$

In the duodenum:

$$\text{proteins} + \text{polypeptides} \xrightarrow[\text{in pancreatic juice}]{\text{trypsin (secreted as trypsinogen)}} \text{peptides} + \text{amino acids}$$

In the ileum (trypsin still active):

$$\text{peptides} \xrightarrow[\text{lining of the ileum)}]{\text{erepsin (several enzymes secreted by the}} \text{amino acids}$$

All proteins have now been digested to amino acids which can be absorbed across the lining of the ileum.

Absorption

As with monosaccharides, amino acids pass into capillaries in villi by passive diffusion and active transport. The amino acids then travel in the hepatic portal vein to the liver.

* Important in children. Milk is clotted so that it remains in the stomach where it can be digested by pepsin.

Assimilation

What happens to amino acids on reaching the liver depends on the body's requirement for protein.

1. All cells in the body need a supply of amino acids to build up their own proteins.
2. Excess amino acids are *not* stored, but in the liver are **deaminated** (their amine group removed). The amine group (NH_2) is altered to the very poisonous ammonia (NH_3) which is then converted to the less harmful substance **urea**. Urea is released into the bloodstream, transported in the blood to the kidneys, and then excreted in the urine (see page 161). The remainder of the amino acid molecule is broken down in the liver to release energy in respiration.

Fats

Fats, unlike carbohydrates or proteins, do not readily mix with water but tend to stay clumped together as large droplets (globules). Before fats can be effectively digested they must be physically broken down into smaller droplets (the process of emulsification). This increases their surface area exposed to digestive enzymes.

Digestion

In the mouth: no fat digestion
In the stomach: no fat digestion
In the duodenum:

$$\text{fat globules} \xrightarrow{\text{bile salts}} \text{fat droplets}$$

$$\text{fat} \xrightarrow[\text{pancreatic juice}]{\text{lipase in}} \text{fatty acids + glycerol}$$

In the ileum (pancreatic lipase still active):

$$\text{fats} \xrightarrow[\text{lining of ileum}]{\text{lipase secreted by}} \text{fatty acids + glycerol}$$

Absorption

In the ileum, only some of the fatty acids and glycerol molecules diffuse into the capillaries of the villi. A large proportion join together again in the intestinal epithelium and pass as fats into the **lacteals**. The fluid in the lacteals enters the lymphatic system which eventually empties its contents into the bloodstream (page 149). Thus, most of the products of fat digestion bypass the liver.

Assimilation

1. Fatty acids and glycerol in the bloodstream are used by all cells for construction and repair of membranes or are broken down in respiration (except in brain cells). The liver converts some excess fatty acids and glycerol to glycogen for storage; the rest is respired.
2. Fats travelling through the lymphatic system enter the bloodstream and can then be stored in adipose tissue under the skin and around certain internal organs e.g. the kidneys. When required for energy, the stored fats are sent to the liver where they are converted to a form which can be readily respired.

7.6. *The Liver*

The liver is the largest organ in the body. It is estimated to have over 500 functions. It is reddish-brown and lies at the top of the abdominal cavity just below the diaphragm (see Fig. 7.6). The liver has the following connections with other parts of the body:

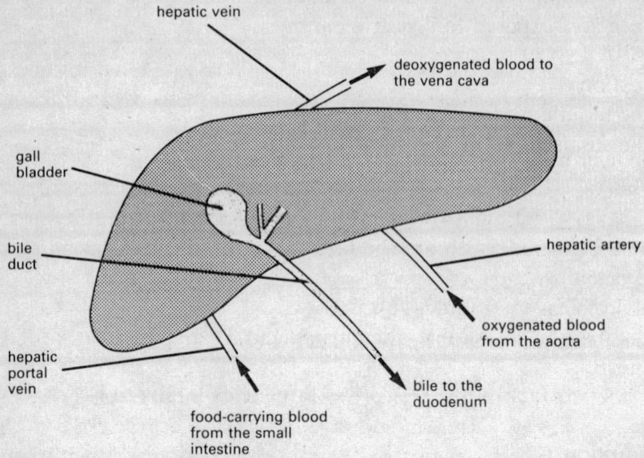

Fig. 7.6. *Connections to and from the liver*

The **hepatic artery** brings oxygenated blood from the aorta while the **hepatic portal vein** brings absorbed food from the alimentary canal.

All blood leaving the liver travels along the **hepatic vein** to the vena cava. Bile stored in the gall bladder empties into the duodenum along the **bile duct**.

The liver is a major homeostatic organ i.e. it helps keep conditions constant within the body. Dissolved food substances absorbed through the gut wall are delivered in the blood straight to the liver. The liver then controls the 'through-flow' of these substances according to the body's needs.

Functions of the liver

The ten main functions of the liver are more easily remembered if grouped into categories.

Three functions concern the major types of organic food – carbohydrates, proteins and fats:

1. The liver controls the blood glucose level by storing excess glucose (as glycogen) and then releasing the glucose when it is required (see page 98). Uptake of glucose by liver cells is stimulated by the hormone insulin (see page 205).
2. In the liver, excess amino acids are deaminated (their amine group removed) and the rest of the molecule is broken down in respiration (see page 99).
3. The liver controls the body's use of fats. When required for energy, body fats are sent to the liver where they are converted to a form which can be broken down in respiration.

The liver has two manufacturing (synthetic) functions:

4. It makes plasma proteins such as fibrinogen (see page 135).
5. It makes bile (page 94) which contains bile salts for emulsifying fats and bile pigments which are the breakdown products of haemoglobin (see 8 below).

The liver has two storage functions:

6. It stores the fat-soluble vitamins A and D and the water-soluble vitamin B_{12}.
7. It stores iron from the breakdown of haemoglobin (see 8 below).

The liver has two 'breaking-down' functions:

8. Old red blood cells are removed from the circulation and their haemoglobin broken down by the liver.
9. Detoxification. The liver breaks down poisonous substances e.g. alcohol and drugs, and converts them to a harmless form.

The liver has one heat-related function:

10. Being such a large active organ, respiration in the liver is the main source of body heat.

7.7. *Teeth*

The teeth play a large part in preparing food for digestion. The chewing action of the teeth, aided by the tongue and jaw muscles, breaks food into small pieces. This increases the food surface area exposed to the action of digestive enzymes. At the same time, saliva is mixed with the food. The saliva lubricates the food for swallowing, dissolves soluble food and begins the digestion process.

Teeth are outgrowths from the skin covering the jaws and are set into sockets in the jawbone. They are supplied with food and oxygen by the pulp cavity (see Fig. 7.7) and they are shaped according to function. Humans, like other mammals (page 41) have four types of teeth: **incisors**, **canines**, **premolars** and **molars**. They are grouped according to position, shape and function (Table 7.6).

Table 7.6. *Types of teeth*

Type	*Position in the jaw*	*Appearance (structure)*	*Function*
Incisor	At the front	Chisel-shaped with single root	Biting or gnawing
Canine	Behind the incisors	Pointed, with single root	Stabbing or tearing
Premolar	Behind the canines	Flattened with 2 cusps and 1 or 2 roots	Grinding and crushing
Molar	Behind the premolars	Flattened with 4 cusps and 2 or 3 roots	Grinding and crushing

Tooth structure

Though teeth vary in shape, all teeth have a similar general structure (see Fig. 7.7). The **crown** of the tooth is the exposed part above the gum; the **root** of the tooth lies below, embedded in the jawbone. Where crown and root meet is called the **neck** of the tooth.

In section, the crown of the tooth consists of three layers: the outer **enamel**, the **dentine**, and the inner **pulp**. In the root, the enamel layer is replaced by **cement**, which holds the tooth into the **fibrous membrane** of the socket.

The number and arrangement of teeth in the jaws is called the **dentition**.

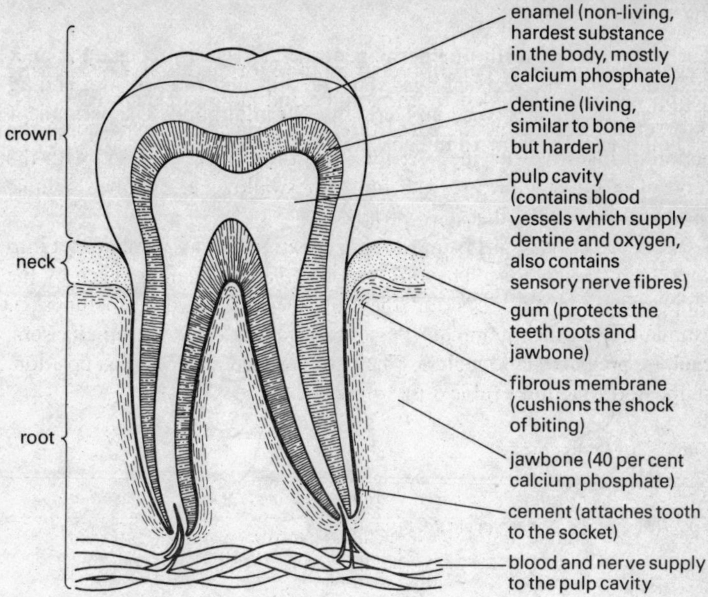

Fig. 7.7. *V. S. of molar tooth*

Milk teeth

Humans possess two natural sets of teeth in their lifetime. The first set, called the **milk** or **deciduous teeth**, erupt through the gums when a child is about 6–30 months old, usually beginning with incisors and ending with molars. The milk set contains 20 teeth, 10 in each jaw (Fig. 7.8).

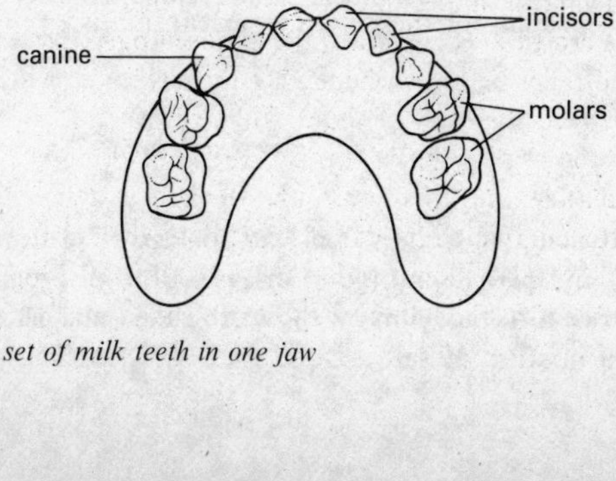

Fig. 7.8. *The set of milk teeth in one jaw*

Permanent teeth

The second set of teeth, the permanent teeth, begin to replace the milk teeth at about six years of age, starting with first molars, and ending with the back molars (wisdom teeth) in early adulthood. The permanent set comprises 32 teeth, 16 in each jaw (Fig. 7.9).

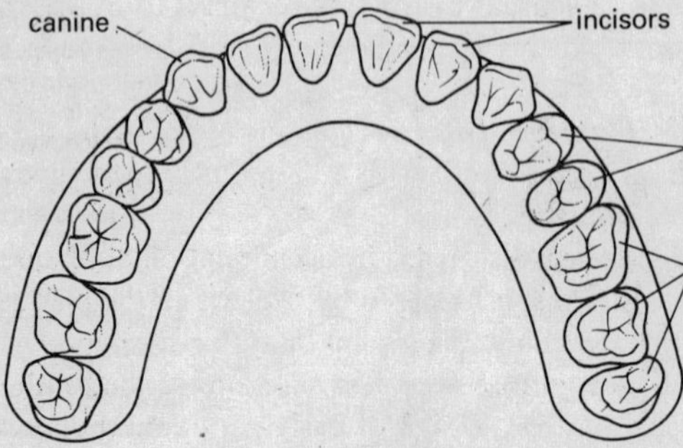

Fig. 7.9. *The set of permanent teeth in one jaw*

Dental formula

The dental formula is a shorthand way of writing down the number of teeth on one side of each jaw starting from the front. For example, the dental formula for human milk teeth is:

$$I\tfrac{2}{2} \quad C\tfrac{1}{1} \quad M\tfrac{2}{2}$$

I refers to incisors, C refers to canines and so on. The figure on top refers to the upper jaw and the figure below, to the lower jaw. The formula indicates that on one side of both upper and lower jaw there are 2 incisors, 1 canine and 2 molars.

The dental formula for the permanent dentition is:

$$I\tfrac{2}{2} \quad C\tfrac{1}{1} \quad P\tfrac{2}{2} \quad M\tfrac{3}{3}$$

Dental disorders

Two types of dental disorders can lead to loss of teeth: **dental caries (tooth decay)** and **periodontal (gum) disease**. Both disorders involve an accumulation of a surface film on the teeth called **plaque**.

Plaque is a mixture of saliva, food and bacteria. The bacteria feed on the food in plaque and release acids which can attack the teeth and gums.

Dental caries (tooth decay) is caused by the action of bacteria which break down sugar in the plaque to form acid. The acid dissolves the mineral salts first in the tooth enamel and then in the dentine, forming a hole (**cavity**). If left untreated, the pulp may become infected and pain (toothache) results. Eventually an abscess may form in the bone underlying the tooth. At this stage, the tooth must be removed and the abscess treated.

Repair of a tooth damaged by caries consists of removing the decayed area using a drill and replacing it with a filling usually of silver and tin mixed with copper and zinc.

Periodontal (gum) **disease** is caused by accumulation of plaque around the neck of the tooth. Poisons released by bacteria in the plaque irritate the gums and cause swelling. The gums may bleed slightly when the teeth are brushed. The gum retreats leaving more of the tooth exposed (getting 'long in the tooth' is a sign of early periodontal disease rather than simply increasing age). Eventually poisons released by the bacteria destroy the fibrous membrane holding the tooth in the socket and the tooth falls out. In Britain, many more teeth are lost in this way, through gum disease, than through tooth decay.

Care of teeth

Tooth decay and gum disease can be effectively prevented by a combination of the following measures:

1. **Restricting the amount of sugar in the diet.** The presence of sugar in the mouth provides food for the acid-producing bacteria. Chewing gum and sweets between meals are best avoided. Other sugar-rich foods such as cake and biscuits are best taken only at meal times.
2. **Removal of plaque by regular cleaning.** Ideally, the teeth should be cleaned thoroughly with a toothbrush and toothpaste after each meal. Failing this, you should brush your teeth last thing at night and first thing in the morning or just after breakfast. The brushing action should be up and down, rather than side to side, to get at food between the teeth. Brush from the gum downwards for the top teeth and upwards for the bottom teeth. This helps prevent food being pushed back to the neck of the tooth. Effective brushing takes at least a full two minutes. The close gap between teeth can be cleaned using dental floss.
3. **The use of fluoride.** Fluoride is a natural component of tooth enamel. It strengthens the enamel and makes it more acid-resistant. The addition

of 1 part per million (1ppm) of fluoride to drinking water has been shown to reduce the incidence of tooth decay and hence fillings in children. Some water authorities add fluoride to the water, others do not. The use of fluoride toothpaste can be beneficial.

4. **Regular visits to the dentist.** Visit the dentist every six months for a check-up from an early age. The dentist can help improve badly-shaped teeth which would otherwise trap plaque in places which are difficult to brush. The dentist will also fill cavities and remove deposits of hardened plaque known as **calculus (tartar)**.

Key Words

Autotrophic (holophytic) nutrition
Photosynthesis
Heterotrophic nutrition
Holozoic nutrition
Ingestion
Digestion
Absorption
Assimilation
Egestion
Saprophytic nutrition
Saprophyte
Parasitic nutrition
Parasite
Host
Omnivore
Secretion
Balanced diet
Carbohydrates
Fats
Proteins
Vitamins
Vitamin A
Night blindness
Vitamin B_1 (thiamin)
Beri-beri
Phosphorus
Potassium
Sodium
Chlorine
Water
Roughage (dietary fibre)
Essential amino acids
First-class proteins
Deficiency disease
Joule
Kilojoule
Calorie
Metabolic rate
Basal metabolic rate
Obesity
Alimentary canal (gut)
Peristalsis
Mouth (buccal cavity)
Mastication (chewing)
Saliva
Salivary amylase (ptyalin)
Bolus
Hard palate
Lipase
Ileum
Intestinal juice
Sucrase
Maltase
Lactase
Erepsin
Villi
Caecum
Appendix
Colon (large intestine)
Faeces
Rectum
Deamination
Urea
Globules
Lacteals
Hepatic artery
Hepatic portal vein
Hepatic vein
Bile duct
Incisors
Canines
Premolars
Molars
Enamel
Dentine

Niacin (nicotinic acid)
Pellagra
Vitamin B_{12} (cyanocobalamin)
Pernicious anaemia
Vitamin C (ascorbic acid)
Scurvy
Vitamin D
Rickets
Minerals
Calcium
Iodine
Goitre
Iron

Soft palate
Oesophagus
Stomach
Chyme
Hydrochloric acid
Pepsin
Rennin
Duodenum
Gall bladder
Pancreas
Bile
Emulsify
Pancreatic juice
Pancreatic amylase
Trypsin

Pulp
Cement
Fibrous membrane
Dentition
Milk (deciduous) teeth
Permanent teeth
Dental formula
Dental caries (tooth decay)
Periodontal (gum) disease
Plaque
Cavity
Calculus (tartar)

Exam Questions

1. The following is a list of biological processes associated with nutrition:
A. mastication;
B. absorption;
C. digestion;
D. ingestion;
E. assimilation;
F. secretion.

For each of the following statements choose the most suitable answer from the above list and write in the appropriate letter. Some letters may be used more than once.
The first one is completed for you.

(*i*) *using the teeth to break up the food;* A
(*ii*) *the breakdown of complex insoluble molecules to simpler molecules;* ____
(*iii*) *the conversion of starch to maltose by amylase;* ____
(*iv*) *the passage of glucose through the villi walls into the blood;* ____
(*v*) *taking food into the body;* ____
(*vi*) *production of saliva during chewing;* ____
(*vii*) *the removal of water from the remains of undigested food in the colon;* ____
(*viii*) *the synthesis of protein from amino acids in a muscle;* ____

[7]
[OXF]

To check your answers see page 79.

2. The diagram shows that part of the alimentary tract which lies beneath the diaphragm.

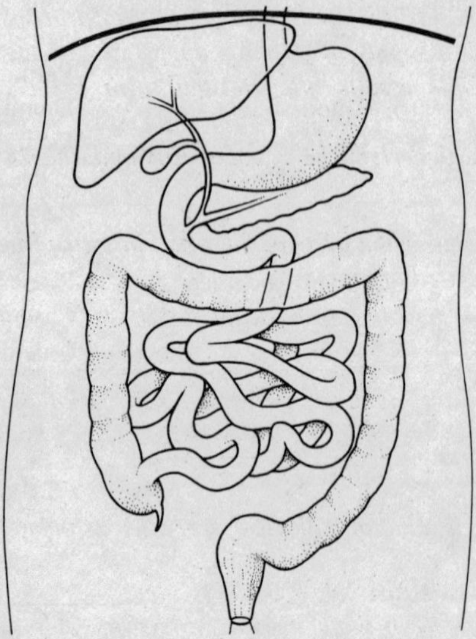

(*a*) *On this diagram, label the parts listed below with the letter shown.*

Where protein digestion begins	*A*
Where starch digestion begins	*B*
A region of high acidity	*C*
Where bile is stored	*D*
Where glucose is absorbed	*E*
Where faeces are stored	*F*

(*b*) *On this diagram, label the following structures:*
oesophagus;
liver;
large intestine;
pancreas. [5]

[WJEC]

3. (*a*) *List the* six *basic substances or groups of substances which should be present in a balanced diet.* [3]

(*b*) *For each of the items named, give* one *function which it serves in the body.* [6]

(*c*) *Name* one *substance which should be present in high concentration in the diet of an expectant mother.*
Explain the reason for its inclusion in the diet. [1]
[WJEC]

4. (*a*) *Describe carefully how you would test for proteins, fats, and reducing sugar. Given a supply of peanuts, apples and cheese make a table to show the probable results after testing them for each of these substances.* [9,9]
(*b*) *What are the underlying causes of obesity and what is recommended for its control?* [7]

5. *Give an account of the parts of the small intestine, their position in the body, and associated organs.* [6]
Explain what happens to food as it passes along the small intestine. [9]

6. *Give a detailed account of:*
(*a*) *the digestion of fats and carbohydrates in the small intestine.* [12]
(*b*) *the absorption, assimilation and storage of* carbohydrate. [8]
[LON]

7. *Complete the following sentences by inserting* one *word in each space provided.*
The liver is situated just below the muscular ________ *and overlaps the* ________ *on the left of the abdomen. Among its many functions are* (*i*) *the conversion of glucose to* ________ *for storage – a process controlled by the hormone* ________, *and* (*ii*) *the storage of the* ________*-soluble vitamins* ________ *and* ________. [6]
To check your answers see page 100. [AEB]

8. (*a*) *What is digestion and why is it necessary?* [5]
(*b*) *Describe the role of the liver in controlling the utilization of the products of digestion.* [15]
A full answer is required for part (*b*) – see pages 97–101. [JMB]

9. (*a*) *What are the kinds and numbers of teeth found in the upper jaw of a normal healthy:*
(*i*) *four-year-old?*
(*ii*) *adult?* [6]
(*b*) *Make a large labelled diagram to show the structure of one of the teeth in the jaw of an adult.* [11]
(*c*) *What are the possible causes of dental caries?*
In what ways may dental caries be prevented? [8]
[OXF]

8. *Respiration, Gas Exchange and Breathing*

As we saw in Chapter 3, respiration is one of the seven characteristic features of living organisms. In Chapter 7, we noted that one of the uses of food was to supply the body with energy. Respiration is the process by which the body extracts energy from food.

Definition: Respiration *is the breakdown of organic foods, within cells, to release energy.*

Respiration occurs in *all* living cells since every cell needs a supply of energy to remain alive. Be careful not to confuse the term respiration with gas exchange or breathing (also called ventilation).

Definition: Gas exchange *is the exchange of oxygen for carbon dioxide between the body and its surroundings.*

In most organisms, when respiration occurs so does gas exchange. This is because most organisms require oxygen for respiration, and produce carbon dioxide as a waste product. To prevent a shortage of oxygen and a build up of carbon dioxide, these gases are exchanged with the surroundings at some point on the body surface. The site where this gas exchange occurs is called the **respiratory** or **gas exchange surface**. In the human body, this surface is the lining of air spaces **(alveoli)** in the lungs.

Breathing or ventilation refers to the movements which cause a renewal of air at the respiratory surface.

Definition: Breathing (ventilation) *is the maintenance of a flow of air over the respiratory surface.*

In humans, breathing is the act of forcing air in and out of the lungs by the use of the diaphragm and intercostal muscles.

The term respiration is sometimes referred to as **internal, cell** or **tissue respiration**; gas exchange and breathing are sometimes grouped under the term **external respiration**. This use of terms can lead to confusion. The more modern naming system used in this book is simpler and clearer.

In its simplest form respiration is represented by the chemical equation:

glucose + oxygen → carbon dioxide + water + energy

$$C_6H_{12}O_6 + 6O_2 \rightarrow 6CO_2 + 6H_2O + \text{energy}$$

As with photosynthesis (page 49), this represents a simplification of a complex series of reactions.

The key feature of respiration is that it releases energy. The body needs a continual supply of energy to carry out essential processes. These processes include:

1. Building up large molecules from small molecules (anabolic metabolism, page 20).
2. In growth, cell division and the formation of new cells (page 265).
3. Muscle contraction to do mechanical work (page 224).
4. The transmission of nerve impulses (page 177).
5. Active transport of substances into and out of cells (page 76).
6. In addition, heat energy is needed to maintain a high body temperature (page 166).

Energy is the capacity to do work. It exists in a variety of forms such as heat, light, electrical, chemical and mechanical energy. Energy cannot be created or destroyed, but it can be changed from one form into another.

In respiration, chemical energy is converted into heat energy and usable chemical energy. The chemical energy comes from the bonds which link atoms inside an organic food molecule. We normally say this molecule is glucose, but it could be some other sugar, a fatty acid or glycerol, or, less often, an amino acid. Energy is released when the bonds inside the food molecule are broken. Some of the energy (about 35 per cent) is given off as heat and some is trapped and stored as usable chemical energy within a substance called **adenosine triphosphate** (ATP). The ATP then delivers the energy to those parts of the cell which require it.

The chemical energy within the glucose molecule originally came from the sun as light energy. Plants are able to trap this and convert it into chemical energy during **photosynthesis**:

$$\text{carbon dioxide} + \text{water} \xrightarrow[\text{chlorophyll}]{\text{light energy (sunlight)}} \text{glucose} + \text{oxygen}$$

$$6CO_2 + 6H_2O \longrightarrow C_6H_{12}O_6 + 6O_2$$

(store of chemical energy)

When the chemical bonds within glucose are broken, energy is released:

$$C_6H_{12}O_6 + 6O_2 \longrightarrow 6CO_2 + 6H_2O + \text{energy}$$

Essentially, respiration is the reverse of photosynthesis. Photosynthesis stores energy while respiration releases it:

$$\text{carbon dioxide} + \text{water} \underset{\text{RESPIRATION}}{\overset{\text{PHOTOSYNTHESIS}}{\rightleftharpoons}} \text{glucose} + \text{oxygen}$$

light energy → PHOTOSYNTHESIS; RESPIRATION → heat and chemical energy

8.1. *Aerobic and Anaerobic Respiration*

Two forms of respiration occur in the human body: **aerobic** and **anaerobic**. Aerobic respiration requires oxygen, anaerobic respiration does not.

Table 8.1. *Summary of differences in aerobic and anaerobic respiration in the human body*

Aerobic respiration	*Anaerobic respiration*
1. Occurs in all cells	1. Occurs in skeletal muscle during vigorous physical exercise
2. Equation: $C_6H_{12}O_6 + 6O_2 \longrightarrow$ glucose oxygen $6CO_2 + 6H_2O + 2{,}880kJ$ carbon water energy dioxide	2. Equation: $C_6H_{12}O_6 \longrightarrow$ glucose $2CH_3CH(OH)COOH + 150kJ$ lactic acid energy (3-carbon compound)
3. Uses oxygen	3. Does not use oxygen
4. Within the cell, the reactions take place in mitochondria (see page 24)	4. Within the cell, the reactions take place 'free' in the cytoplasm
5. All or most of the available energy within the glucose molecule is released (equivalent to 36 molecules of ATP)	5. Only part of the energy within the glucose molecule is released (equivalent to 2 molecules of ATP)
6. Water is a product of the reaction	6. Water is not a product of the reaction.

Aerobic respiration is the main type and occurs in *all* living cells of the body. Anaerobic respiration occurs in muscle cells undergoing vigorous exercise, when oxygen is in short supply.

Aerobic respiration is much more efficient than anaerobic respiration and releases much more energy from each glucose molecule. In aerobic respiration the glucose is broken down into very simple substances. In anaerobic respiration, however, the end-products are still complex and contain much unreleased energy.

The key features of aerobic and anaerobic respiration in humans are summarized in Table 8.1. Do not worry if you cannot remember the chemical formulae; the names and energy output are more important.

Aerobic and anaerobic respiration are not two completely different processes; rather, they represent two different stages in a single process:

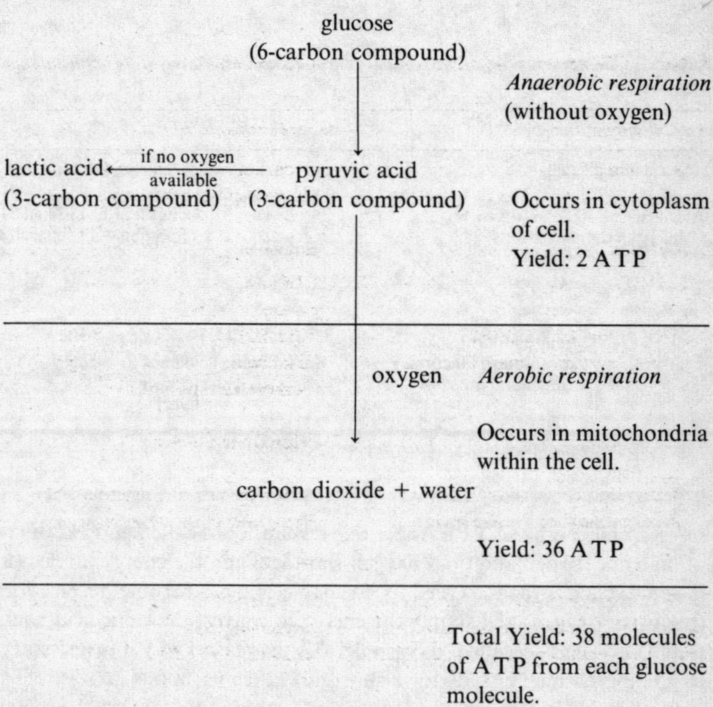

In the presence of oxygen, all cells in the body oxidize glucose to the simple molecules carbon dioxide and water and the maximum amount of energy is extracted.

During vigorous physical exercise e.g. running or swimming, not enough oxygen may reach contracting skeletal muscle (page 224) to supply the energy needs of all the tissues. Although the bloodstream carries oxygen to the muscle cells as fast as possible, oxygen may not be arriving at the cells in large enough quantities. Under these circumstances, aerobic respiration is supplemented by anaerobic respiration.

When oxygen is lacking, anaerobic respiration breaks down glucose as far as pyruvic acid, which is then converted to **lactic acid**. When lactic acid accumulates in muscle cells, it interferes with their normal working, and may cause pain and cramp. Thus, as lactic acid accumulates, it is removed and carried away in the bloodstream. On reaching the liver, the lactic acid is converted back to glucose. To do this, however, requires

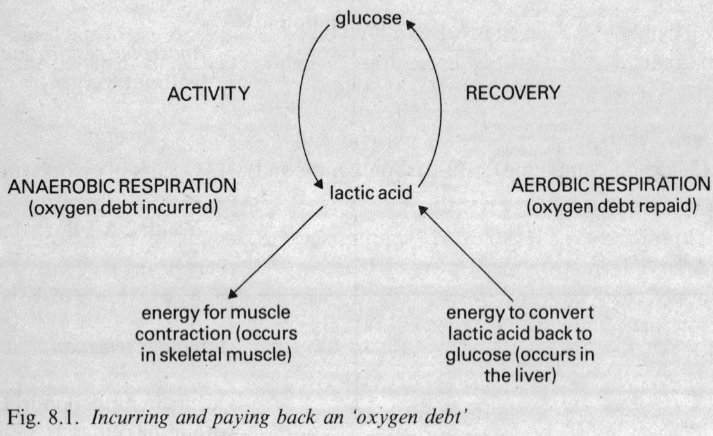

Fig. 8.1. *Incurring and paying back an 'oxygen debt'*

oxygen and energy (ATP). Anaerobic respiration is called upon at times of high energy demand (and oxygen shortage) and the energy it releases is 'paid back' when oxygen is available. Later, aerobic respiration (requiring oxygen) will supply the energy to convert the lactic acid back to glucose. This so-called **'oxygen debt'** is the reason why it is necessary to go on breathing heavily for a short time after strenuous exercise. The 'oxygen debt' is being paid off; oxygen is needed to convert the lactic acid back to glucose. The glucose is then returned to the muscle and stored as glycogen.

8.2. *ATP*

Of the energy released in respiration reactions, about 40 per cent is usable chemical energy. Inside the cell, this energy is trapped as a temporary energy store inside the substance adenosine triphosphate, ATP. This chemical then delivers the stored energy to any reaction or process in the cell which requires it. ATP carries energy from the respiration reactions that release it to those reactions in the cell that require it.

The ATP molecule contains three phosphate groups, and it stores energy in the chemical bond between the middle and outer phosphate groups. This bond is formed, using energy from respiration, by adding a phosphate group to a molecule of the substance, **adenosine diphosphate, ADP**:

$$\underset{\text{ADP}}{\text{A–P–P}} + \underset{\text{phosphate}}{\text{P}} + \underset{\text{from respiration}}{\text{energy}} \longrightarrow \underset{\text{ATP}}{\text{A–P–P}\sim\text{P}}$$

The bond so formed is called a high-energy bond because of the large amount of stored energy it contains. When broken by hydrolysis, the energy is released, and ADP is reformed:

$$\underset{\text{ATP}}{\text{A–P–P}\sim\text{P}} \longrightarrow \underset{\text{ADP}}{\text{A–P–P}} + \underset{\text{phosphate}}{\text{P}} + \underset{\text{to do work in the cell}}{\text{energy}}$$

In this way ATP is recycled within the cell. It is built up using energy released from the breakdown of glucose, and then broken down to supply energy to any process in the cell that requires it. Each ATP molecule represents a 'packet' of available energy.

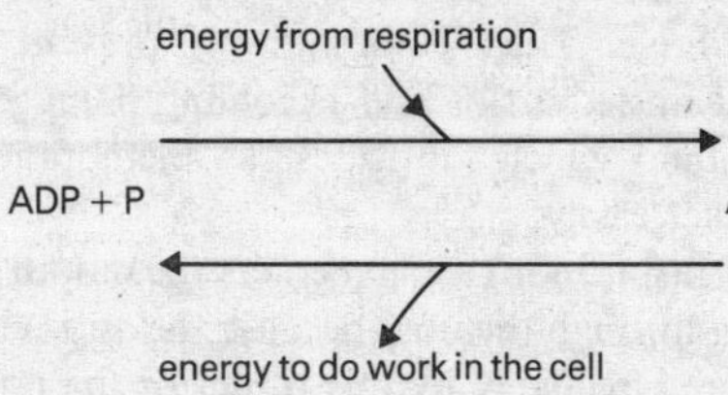

8.3. *The Human Respiratory System*

Most organisms require oxygen for respiration and produce carbon dioxide as a waste product. At some point on the body surface these gases must be exchanged between the organism and its surroundings. Oxygen diffuses into the organism and carbon dioxide diffuses out, along a concentration (diffusion) gradient (see page 72).

In small organisms such as Protozoa (page 48) all parts of the body are only a short distance from the external environment and gas exchange occurs over the entire body surface. However, in larger organisms made up of millions of cells, the inner parts of the body are too far away from the outside to obtain their oxygen and get rid of waste carbon dioxide by diffusion alone. One part of the body surface becomes specialized for its job as a respiratory surface, and a transport system is used to deliver gases to and from all cells in the body. In humans, the lining of air sacs (alveoli) in the lungs provides the respiratory surface, and the blood system (page 132) transports gases around the body.

The air within the air sacs is renewed by breathing (ventilation). Air is forced in and out of the lungs by means of repeated contraction and relaxation of the diaphragm and intercostal muscles (see Fig. 8.4).

The organs responsible for gas exchange and breathing – the lungs and air passages (Fig. 8.2) – make up the respiratory (breathing) system.

The lungs occupy most of the **thoracic cavity**. This airtight cavity is protected by the sternum and ribs (page 217) at the front and sides, and by the vertebral column (page 216) at the back. The **diaphragm** is a sheet of fibrous tissue with muscles attached. It separates the thoracic cavity (thorax) from the abdominal cavity.

The lungs are separated from the ribs by an airtight space, the **pleural cavity**. This is bordered on the inside and outside by the **pleural membranes**. These membranes line the outer surface of the lungs and the inside of the thoracic cavity. Most importantly, these membranes make the pleural cavity airtight, so that pressure changes in the thorax are transmitted to the lungs. The membranes also prevent the lungs from rubbing directly against the ribs and becoming damaged. The pleural cavity contains a fluid which lubricates the membranes so that they move past each other easily.

On breathing in (inspiration) air first enters the mouth or nostrils. It is better to breathe in through the nose because the air is cleaned, warmed and moistened more effectively by this route. In the nose, a system of narrow nasal passages supported by cartilage increases the surface area of epithelium in contact with the air. **Olfactory cells** (page 189) are found on the upper surface of the nasal cavity. These cells are stimulated by the presence of particular chemicals in air and provide us with the sense of smell.

The air breathed in (called inspired or inhaled air) passes through the

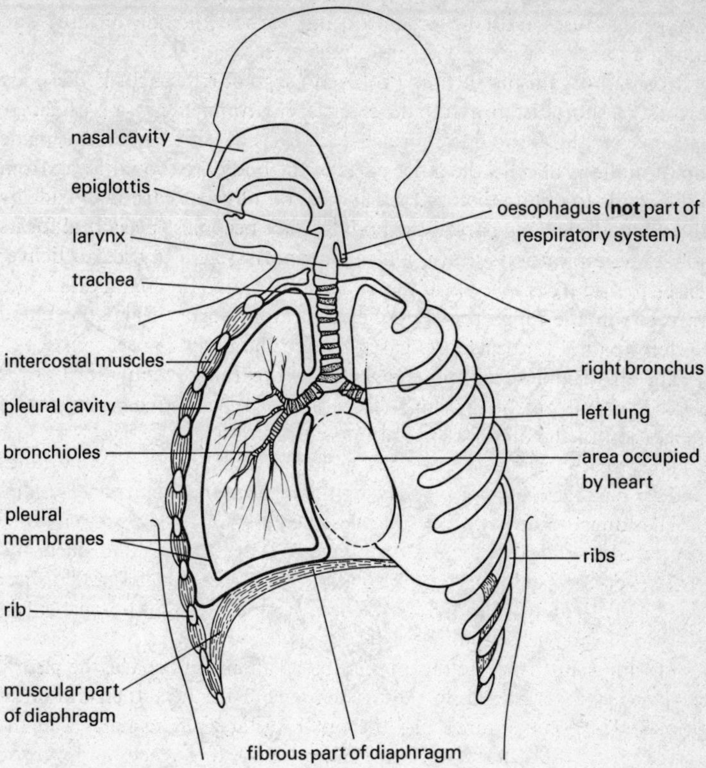

Fig. 8.2. *The human respiratory system*

pharynx, down the **trachea** (windpipe), and then through the two **bronchi** (singular bronchus) and into thousands of **bronchioles** in the lungs. The bronchioles end in groups of **alveoli** (singular alveolus) looking rather like microscopic bunches of grapes (see Fig. 8.3). Each alveolus is covered by a network of capillaries. Gas exchange takes place between the alveoli and the overlying capillaries.

As air from the atmosphere enters the respiratory system, dust particles and bacteria are trapped by sticky mucus. This mucus is secreted by the epithelium lining the nasal passages, trachea and bronchi. The epithelium lining these passages is **ciliated** (see page 66). The beating action of the tiny cilia sweeps mucus and trapped particles to the throat (pharynx)

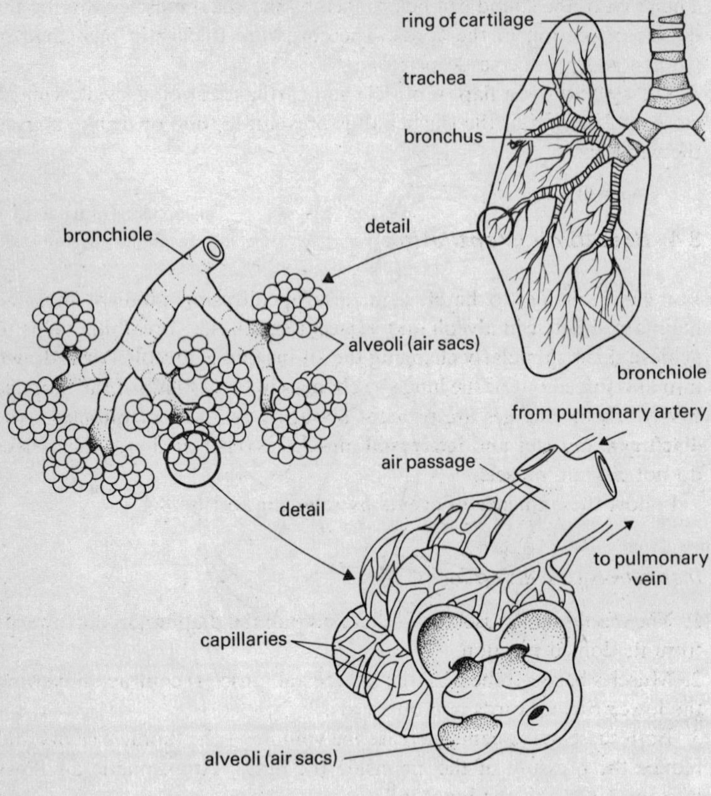

Fig. 8.3. *Detail of human lung showing smaller air passages and alveoli*

where the mucus is swallowed. The lining of the air passages can become inflamed by the presence of chemicals e.g. when a person smokes, or by large numbers of micro-organisms e.g. when a person has a cold. At such times large amounts of mucus build up in the pharynx and this triggers the coughing reflex.

The trachea (windpipe) and bronchi contain horseshoe-shaped **rings of cartilage**. These rings serve to support the air passages so that they do not close when the air pressure inside them drops.

Near the top of the trachea is the **larynx** or voice box. It contains two folds of tissue, the **vocal cords**. These cords can be pulled taut by vocal muscles. As air passes over the cords, they vibrate and sound is produced.

The pitch of the sound can be changed by the vocal muscles altering the degree of tension in the cords. The cords are thicker in men than in women and produce a deeper tone.

The **epiglottis** is a flap of muscle and cartilage. During swallowing, it closes off the top of the trachea thus preventing food or drink entering the windpipe.

8.4. *Breathing* (*Ventilation*)

For gas exchange to be efficient, a steep diffusion gradient must be maintained between alveoli and adjacent capillaries. Breathing helps to achieve this by regularly changing the air inside the alveoli. Air is drawn into and forced out of the lungs by changes in the volume of the thoracic cavity. These changes are brought about by two sets of muscles – the **diaphragm** muscles and **intercostal** muscles. NOTE: the lungs themselves do not contain muscle.

Follow the sequence of events by referring to Fig. 8.4.

Inspiration (*breathing in*)

1. The diaphragm muscles contract and pull the diaphragm downwards from its domed position.
2. Muscles between the ribs (the intercostal muscles) contract and swing the lower ribs upwards and outwards.
3. Both these movements increase the volume of the thoracic cavity and reduce the pressure of the air inside the lungs. Atmospheric air flows into the lungs and the lungs inflate.

Expiration (*breathing out*)

1. The diaphragm muscles relax, and gentle pressure from the organs in the abdominal cavity pushes the diaphragm back to its original domed position.
2. The intercostal muscles relax and under gravity the lower ribs swing downwards and inwards to their original position.
3. Both these movements decrease the volume of the thoracic cavity and increase the air pressure inside the lungs. The lungs, helped by their elasticity, expel some of the air and deflate to their original size.

During forced breathing, for example during strenuous physical exercise, muscles of the abdominal wall come into play. During expiration,

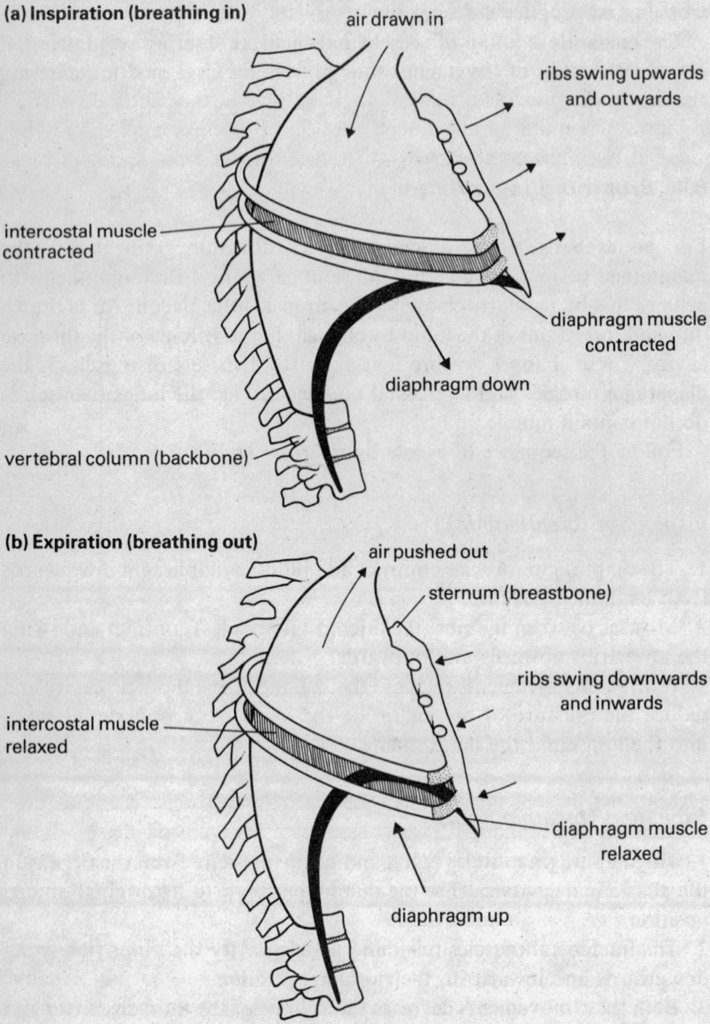

Fig. 8.4. *Breathing movements* (*only two ribs are shown*)

these abdominal muscles contract, squeeze on the abdominal organs, and forcibly push the diaphragm upwards forcing air out of the lungs.

During normal breathing (what you are doing now) an adult man breathes in and out about 0.5 litre of air in each breath. This is **tidal air**. During very deep breathing a maximum of 4 litres of air can be breathed in and out. This is called the **vital capacity**. One litre of air, the **residual air**, always remains in the lungs trapped by friction and cannot be breathed out. The **total capacity** of the lungs, the vital capacity plus residual air, is 5 litres (see Fig. 8.5).

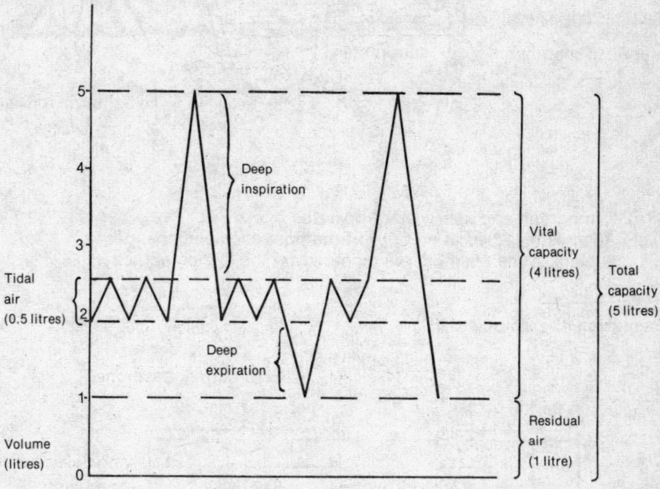

Fig. 8.5. *Volumes of air in the lungs*

About 0.2 litre of air occupies the trachea and bronchi and is unavailable for gas exchange. This volume of air is the **dead space**.

You need to understand what the above terms refer to, and what volumes they represent. The volumes given above are approximate average values for an adult man.

A **spirometer** is the apparatus normally used to measure lung volumes. Changes in volume during inspiration and expiration are usually recorded as a trace on a revolving drum. This can be calibrated to give the number of breaths per minute. Examination questions may ask you to interpret results obtained in this way (see *Qs. 3* and *4* on page 131).

As you will notice from Fig. 8.6, both the volume of each breath and the rate of breathing (number of breaths/minute) is higher during exer-

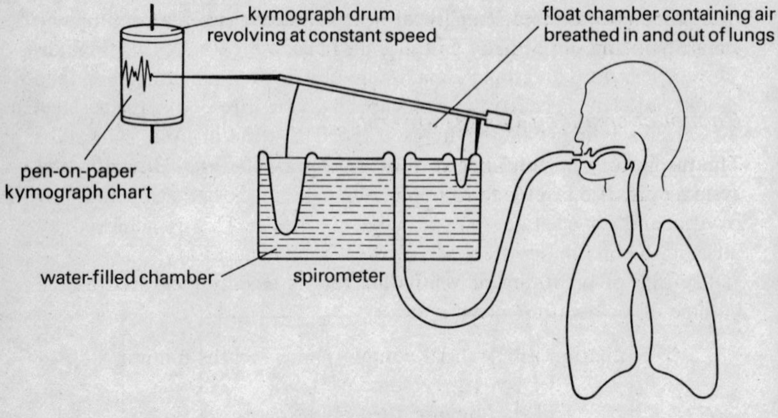

(a) Kymograph and spirometer apparatus in use.
As air is breathed in and out of the float chamber, changes in volume of the chamber are recorded on the kymograph chart.

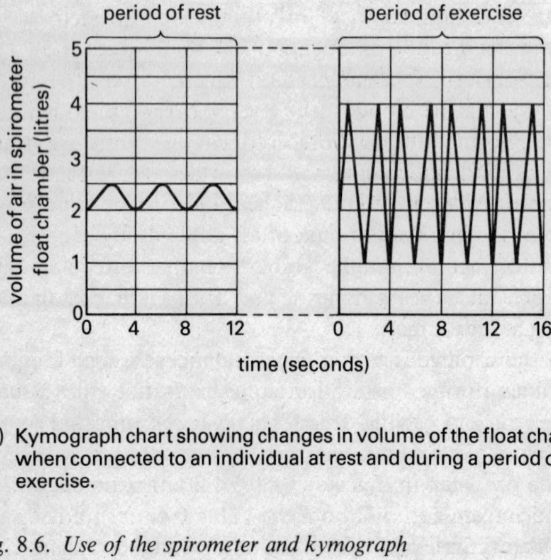

(b) Kymograph chart showing changes in volume of the float chamber when connected to an individual at rest and during a period of exercise.

Fig. 8.6. *Use of the spirometer and kymograph*

cise. This is necessary to increase the rate of delivery of oxygen to, and the removal of carbon dioxide from, the muscles being exercised. At the same time the rate and strength of heartbeat increases to speed up the transport of the respiratory gases (page 124).

Control of breathing (ventilation) rate

The respiratory system aims to maximize gas exchange. However, the system must also be able to respond to changes in the body's demand for oxygen and its need to remove carbon dioxide. This is achieved by altering the breathing rate and heartbeat rate as necessary.

The rate of breathing or **ventilation rate** is usually measured as the volume of air breathed per minute:

Ventilation rate = tidal volume × no. breaths/minute
(the volume of air breathed in and out with each breath)

The normal breathing rate is about 15–20 breaths/minute. This rate may double or triple during and just after periods of strenuous physical exercise. At such times the tidal volume may increase from its normal value of 0.5 litre and reach 3 litres.

Ventilation rate (rate and depth of breathing) is controlled by the **respiratory centre** in the medulla oblongata of the brain (page 185). This centre contains sensory cells **(chemoreceptors)** which are sensitive to the level of carbon dioxide in the blood. If the level of carbon dioxide in the blood is higher than normal, the chemoreceptors in this centre are stimulated. At the same time, chemoreceptors in the aorta and carotid arteries, sensitive to carbon dioxide, are stimulated and send nerve impulses to the respiratory centre. The respiratory centre responds by sending an *increased* number of nerve impulses/second to the intercostal and diaphragm muscles. This increases the rate and depth of breathing. This in turn speeds up gas exchange.

Heartbeat rate is controlled by the **cardiovascular centre**, also found in the medulla oblongata. When carbon dioxide levels rise, the chemoreceptors in the aorta and carotid arteries send nerve impulses to the cardiovascular centre. This centre responds by sending *fewer* nerve impulses/second to the heart pacemaker (page 143). This results in an increase in the rate and strength of heartbeats. This in turn speeds up the transport of respiratory gases.

During normal breathing a steady rate and depth of breathing is maintained by reflex action (page 180) involving the respiratory centre. This reflex can be overriden by the higher centres of the brain. You can consciously alter your breathing, making it faster or slower, deeper or shallower. However, as soon as your attention wanders, the automatic reflex is re-established.

8.5. *Gas Exchange at Alveoli*

There are over 250 million alveoli in each lung. These air sacs have a number of features which maximize gas exchange across their lining:
1. The lining of the alveoli is thin-walled (to allow gases to diffuse through rapidly).
2. The lining is moist (gases must be in solution before they can pass across a cell membrane).
3. The lining is rounded (to give a large surface area for maximizing diffusion).
4. The alveoli are richly supplied with blood (to transport gases rapidly to and from the alveoli and hence maintain a steep diffusion gradient).
5. The alveoli are well ventilated (to transport gases rapidly to and from the alveoli and to maintain a steep diffusion gradient).

Compare these features with those of villi described on page 95. Both villi and alveoli are adapted for rapid diffusion. Short-answer questions on these adaptations are fairly popular in exams.

The air in the alveolus (alveolar air) has a higher concentration of oxygen than the blood arriving in the overlying capillary. There is thus a concentration (diffusion) gradient between the inside of the alveolus and the blood. Oxygen dissolves in the moisture lining the alveolus and diffuses across two layers of cells (the wall of the alveolus and the epithelium of the capillary) and into the blood. In the blood it diffuses into red blood cells (page 134) and combines loosely with the protein **haemoglobin** to form **oxyhaemoglobin**.

Haemoglobin is a respiratory pigment. Because of its attraction for oxygen it enables the blood to carry large amounts of the gas. Haemoglobin gives blood its red colour. Oxyhaemoglobin is bright red whereas haemoglobin is dark, almost purplish, red; hence, oxygenated blood is brighter than deoxygenated blood.

Carbon dioxide is carried in the blood as the **hydrogen carbonate ion**. Blood arriving at the alveolus is rich in carbon dioxide. The concentration of carbon dioxide in the alveolar air is lower. Thus, the diffusion gradient for carbon dioxide is in the opposite direction to that of oxygen. In the capillaries the hydrogen carbonate ion breaks down to release carbon dioxide, which diffuses from the blood into the alveolus.

The blood leaving the alveolus is rich in oxygen (oxygenated) and low in carbon dioxide. The lung capillaries join to form the pulmonary veins which take blood back to the heart. From there, the blood is pumped round the body to supply all the tissues with oxygen. The path taken by blood is shown on page 141.

The composition of alveolar air remains nearly constant despite the continual loss of oxygen to the blood, and gain of carbon dioxide from the blood. Replacement oxygen diffuses across from inspired air and carbon dioxide is lost to expired air (see Fig. 8.7).

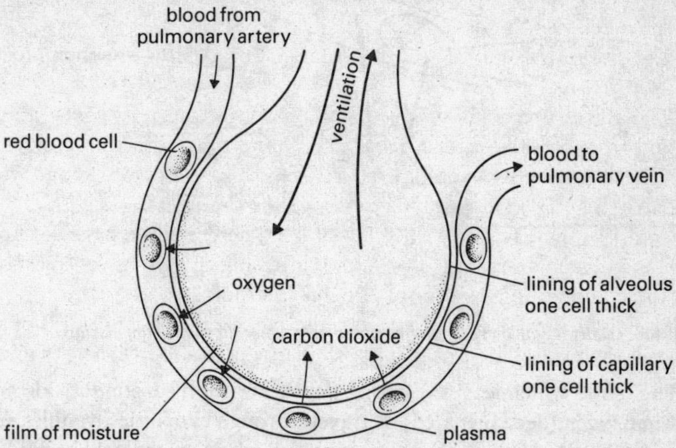

Fig. 8.7. *Gas exchange at an alveolus*

Table 8.2. *Composition of gases in breathed air*

	Inspired air	*Expired air*	*Alveolar air*
Oxygen	20%	16%	14%
Carbon dioxide	0.04%	4%	6%
Nitrogen	79%	79%	80%
Water vapour	Variable	Saturated	Saturated

8.6. *Supplying Tissues with Oxygen and Removing Carbon Dioxide*

When oxygenated blood arrives at respiring tissues, the oxyhaemoglobin releases its oxygen and breaks down to haemoglobin. The oxygen diffuses through the capillary wall, across the tissue fluid, and into respiring cells. (See Fig. 8.8.)

At the same time, carbon dioxide diffuses in the opposite direction – from the respiring cells, across the tissue fluid and into the blood. On reaching the blood, most of the carbon dioxide combines with water to form hydrogen carbonate ions.

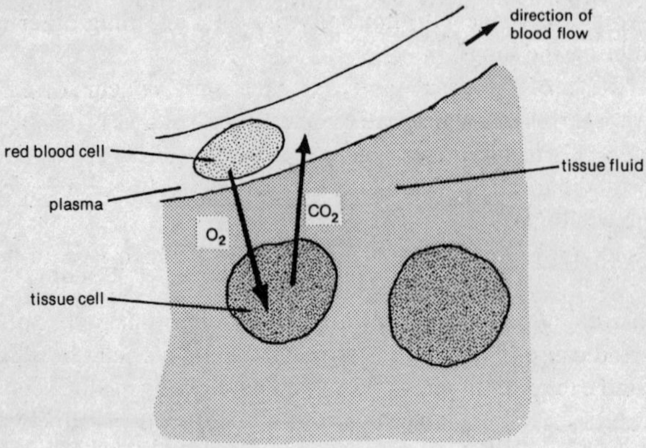

Fig. 8.8. *Delivery of oxygen and removal of carbon dioxide from tissues*

The blood which leaves respiring tissues is rich in carbon dioxide and low in oxygen (deoxygenated). It travels through capillaries, venules and veins back to the heart and from there is pumped to the lungs (see page 142).

To summarize, oxygen is carried in the blood as oxyhaemoglobin within red blood cells. Haemoglobin picks up and releases oxygen under the following conditions:

$$\text{Haemoglobin} + \text{oxygen} \underset{\substack{\text{at body tissues, where the} \\ [O_2] \text{ is low, } [CO_2] \text{ is} \\ \text{high and acidity is high*}}}{\overset{\substack{\text{in the lungs, where the} \\ [O_2] \text{ is high, } [CO_2] \text{ is} \\ \text{low and acidity is low*}}}{\rightleftharpoons}} \text{Oxyhaemoglobin}$$

Carbon dioxide is carried in the blood plasma mostly as hydrogen carbonate ions. Hydrogen carbonate is broken down and formed under the following conditions:

$$\text{Hydrogen carbonate} \underset{\substack{\text{at body tissues, where the} \\ [O_2] \text{ is low, } [CO_2] \text{ is} \\ \text{high and acidity is high*}}}{\overset{\substack{\text{in the lungs, where the} \\ [O_2] \text{ is high, } [CO_2] \text{ is} \\ \text{low and acidity is low*}}}{\rightleftharpoons}} \text{Carbon dioxide + water}$$

The enzyme **carbonic anhydrase**, found in red blood cells, catalyses this reaction.

8.7. *Respiratory Disorders*

Several mechanisms in the body ensure that the respiratory surface in the lungs is kept clean and that the respiratory passages remain unblocked:
1. The epiglottis (page 119) normally prevents anything other than air from entering the lungs.
2. The linings of the nasal cavity, trachea and bronchi secrete mucus which traps airborne particles and bacteria. The mucus is then wafted by cilia (page 117) to the throat where it is swallowed.
3. The coughing reflex generally dislodges any large particles which do enter the windpipe.
4. The sneezing reflex dislodges large particles which irritate the nasal lining.

The breathing in of smoke, dust particles and other pollutants over a long period can overpower the respiratory system's self-cleaning mechanisms and can result in one or more of the following medical conditions:
1. **Bronchitis.** This is inflammation of the bronchi which become narrowed with swelling. Increased mucus production causes them to become partially blocked. Coughing and soreness result and may become extremely serious (chronic) bronchitis. Bronchitis is more common among smokers and those living in smoky industrial towns. The passing of the Clean Air Act in 1964 has reduced the incidence of bronchitis in industrial towns.
2. **Respiratory infections** such as colds (page 292) or, more seriously, pneumonia (page 292) occur more among those who live in smoky areas. Smoke particles slow down the action of cilia and cause mucus to build up in the respiratory passages and lungs. As a result, microbes and dust particles accumulate, increasing the risk of infections and damage to tissues.
3. **Pneumoconiosis** is the name given to a group of diseases caused by

* When carbon dioxide combines with water it first forms **carbonic acid** which then breaks down to form hydrogen carbonate ions. This is why a high level of acidity is found whenever the concentration of carbon dioxide is high.

inhaling various forms of dust. These conditions are often associated with a particular occupation. **Silicosis**, for example, is usually associated with mining or quarrying. Particles of silica cause damage to the lungs, and stimulate increased production of mucus. This may lead to coughs, breathlessness, bronchitis, and an increase in respiratory infections. **Asbestosis**, caused by inhaling asbestos fibres, has similar symptoms, but in addition can lead to lung cancer. Blue asbestos, strongly linked with causing cancer, has now been banned in the United Kingdom.

In industry, regulations have been brought in to reduce the likelihood of contracting these dust-related diseases. The wearing of masks, ventilation of factories, and the damping down of dusty surfaces, are some of the preventative measures used.

4. **Allergic reactions.** Coughing, sneezing and a runny nose (caused by excess mucus production) are the symptoms of hay fever – a condition triggered by the pollen of plants. These symptoms arise because some people are **allergic** to the proteins and waxes that make up the outer coats of pollen grains; their bodies treat these chemicals as 'foreign' and produce antibodies against them (see page 150).

5. **Cigarette smoke**, like all forms of smoke, consists of fine particles suspended in a hot gas. Cigarette smoke is particularly dangerous to health because:

(a) Particles in tobacco smoke slow down the beating action of cilia; in heavy smokers the cilia may gradually become destroyed. The characteristic 'smoker's cough' is an attempt to clear the mucus which accumulates when the cilia do not operate effectively. The reduction in air-cleaning efficiency means that particles and microbes are more likely to enter the lungs and cause physical damage and respiratory infection. In extreme cases this can lead to irreparable damage and loss of alveoli – a condition called **emphysema** – whereby the victim becomes short of breath.

(b) Certain tars and other chemicals in tobacco smoke are **carcinogenic** (cancer promoting) and over time may cause **lung cancer**.

(c) **Nicotine** in tobacco smoke is absorbed into the blood and has a number of effects on the body (see page 290). Nicotine causes an increase in blood pressure both by constricting (narrowing) arteries and increasing the rate of heart beat. Nicotine also raises blood fatty acid concentrations and causes platelets to stick together more readily and to the walls of arteries. The net result is to increase the likelihood of arterial deposition – 'hardening of the arteries' (page 145). This in turn increases the likelihood of coronary thrombosis and other heart problems (see page 145).

(d) **Carbon monoxide** in tobacco smoke diffuses into the blood and combines with haemoglobin to form carboxyhaemoglobin. This prevents some of the haemoglobin from combining with oxygen and thus reduces the blood's oxygen-carrying capacity (see also page 134).

(e) **Tar and other chemicals** deposited in the lungs by smoking line the alveoli and impair gas exchange. This reduces a person's ability to undertake physical exercise.

(f) **Smoking during pregnancy** can result in reduced physical development of the foetus, a lower birthweight and a greater likelihood of stillbirth or infant death. Nicotine in the mother's blood reaches the baby via the placenta and seems to reduce tissue growth directly. Carbon monoxide also reaches the baby's blood, reduces its oxygen-carrying capacity and deprives the foetus of much needed oxygen.

Definitions

Respiration
Gas exchange
Breathing (ventilation)

Key Words

Respiratory (gas exchange) surface
Internal respiration
External respiration
Adenosine triphosphate (ATP)
Aerobic respiration
Anaerobic respiration
Lactic acid
Oxygen debt
Adenosine diphosphate (ADP)
Thoracic cavity
Diaphragm
Pleural cavity
Pleural membranes
Olfactory cells
Pharynx
Trachea (windpipe)
Bronchi (singular: bronchus)
Bronchioles
Alveoli (singular: alveolus)
Ciliated epithelium
Larynx
Vocal cords
Epiglottis
Diaphragm muscles
Intercostal muscles
Inspiration
Expiration
Tidal air
Vital capacity
Residual air
Total capacity
Dead space
Spirometer
Ventilation rate
Respiratory centre
Chemoreceptors
Cardiovascular centre
Haemoglobin
Oxyhaemoglobin
Hydrogen carbonate ion
Carbonic acid
Bronchitis
Pneumoconiosis
Silicosis
Asbestosis
Allergic reactions
Emphysema
Carcinogenic
Nicotine
Carbon monoxide

Exam Questions

1. List three *changes which occur to the air as it passes through the nasal cavity during inspiration.*

(*a*) ....

(*b*) ....

(*c*) ....

[3]

[AEB]

2. The graph represents the lung volume changes based on a number of spirometer readings during various breathing actions.

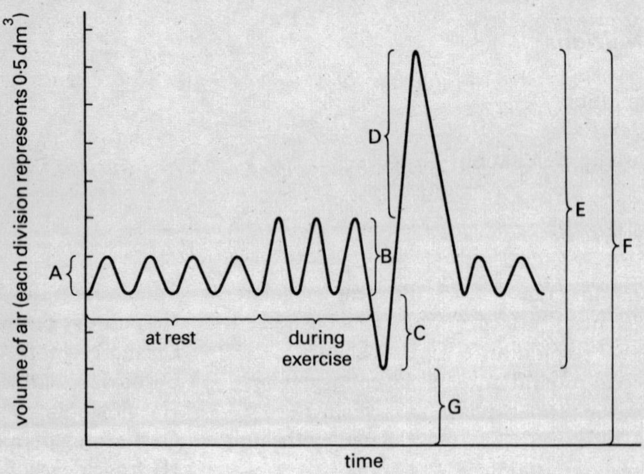

(*a*) (*i*) *What is meant by the term 'tidal volume'?* [2]

(*ii*) *Describe concisely an experiment which may be used to measure the volume of a person's tidal air.* [3]

(*b*) *State the letter labelling*

(*i*) *Residual air volume*

(*ii*) *Vital capacity*

(*iii*) *Inspiratory reserve volume*

(*iv*) *Total lung capacity.* [4]

(*c*) *At rest the subject breathes at a rate of 16 breaths per minute. During exercise the subject breathes at a rate of 21 breaths per minute. What volume of air will the subject breathe during*

(i) 5 minutes at rest?
(ii) 2 minutes of exercise? [2]
(d) Describe clearly the role of the diaphragm, ribs, external intercostal muscles and abdominal muscles in bringing about an inflow of air into the lungs during inspiration. [9]
[Total 20]
[AEB]

3. *(a) The table below shows the results of observations made on the breathing of a 20 year old woman.*

	Volume of single inspiration cm^3 (ml)	*Breaths per minute*
At rest, before exercise	*500*	*19*
During vigorous exercise	*1100*	*36*

(i) From the table calculate the total volume of air inspired in each minute at rest and during vigorous exercise. [2]
(ii) If the volume of oxygen in atmospheric air is 20% and 16% of exhaled air consists of oxygen, calculate the volume of oxygen entering the blood each minute at rest. Show your working. [3]
(iii) Why does the body require oxygen when at rest? [3]
(iv) In the example above, the volume of oxygen entering the blood during exercise is 1584 cm^3 *(ml) per minute. Explain the reasons for this increase compared with your answer to (iii) above.* [5]
(b) Describe the function of each of the following in breathing:
(i) cartilaginous rings in the trachea [1]
(ii) pleural membranes [3]
(iii) diaphragm. [3]
[LON]

4. *(a) Explain how oxygen is obtained by the body from the atmosphere, is transported to muscle in the arm, and is used in chemical processes when the muscle is active.*
(b) Why do muscles fatigue and why is it important to exercise muscles each day? [18, 7]
[OXF]

9. *Transport and the Circulatory System*

All living cells within an organism have to be supplied with the substances they need and must get rid of waste substances produced by chemical reactions in the cell. In small organisms substances outside the body can diffuse quickly across the short distance to the inside. In large organisms the distance between outside and inside is greater and diffusion would be too slow. If the organism lives on land it will probably have an outer covering to prevent water loss, so diffusion would not be possible anyway.

To overcome this problem large organisms have developed special transport systems to move substances around. Substances from the outside are taken into the body through specialized organs (e.g. oxygen at the lungs) and then carried to the rest of the body.

In mammals this transport system is called the circulatory system and is made up of three components:

1. circulatory fluids (blood and lymph)
2. tubes or vessels to carry these fluids (arteries, veins, capillaries, lymph vessels).
3. a pump to move the fluids around (the heart).

9.1. *Blood*

Fig. 9.1 shows the components of blood as seen with a light microscope. The **plasma** is the liquid part of the blood and is about 90 per cent water with a number of substances dissolved in it:

(a) food substances – monosaccharides (e.g. glucose), amino acids, fatty acids, glycerol and vitamins;

(b) mineral salts e.g. sodium chloride ($NaCl$) and sodium bicarbonate ($NaHCO_3$);

(c) plasma proteins.

Table 9.1 shows which substances are carried by the blood, with their origins, destinations and the means by which they are transported.

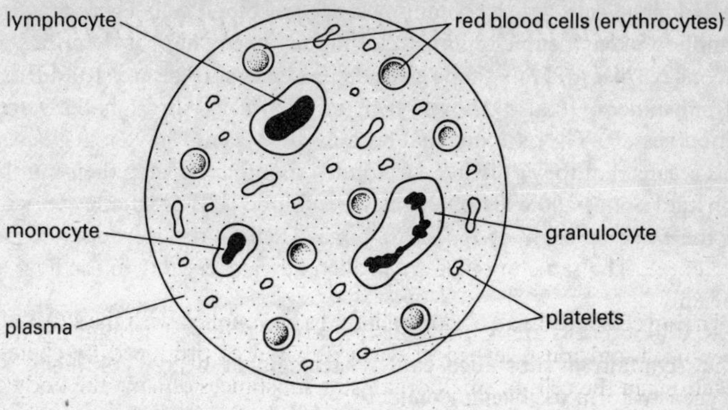

Fig. 9.1. *The components of blood*

Table 9.1. *Substances carried by the blood*

Substance	*From*	*To*	*How carried*
Oxygen	lungs	all tissues	oxyhaemoglobin
Carbon dioxide	all tissues	lungs	sodium bicarbonate in plasma
Glucose Amino acids	} ileum	all tissues	dissolved in plasma
Fatty acids	ileum to lymphatic system to blood	all tissues	in plasma
Urea	liver	kidneys	in plasma
Hormones	endocrine glands	all tissues but only affect certain cells	in plasma
Antibodies	lymph glands and bone marrow	wherever needed to fight disease	in plasma
Heat	liver and muscles	whole body	all of blood

Red blood cells are the commonest type of blood cell. There are about 5 million in each cubic millimetre of blood. Their shape is described as a biconcave disc and this shape gives them a large surface area for diffusion of substances. It also allows them to slip easily through the narrow blood vessels. They are unusual because they do not have a nucleus and this means that they only live for about 4 months. To keep their numbers constant about 200,000,000,000 new red blood cells are made every day, in the bone marrow of the short bones such as the sternum, ribs and vertebrae. The same number are broken down every day in the liver and spleen.

Red blood cells are responsible for carrying oxygen around the body. They contain a substance called **haemoglobin** which combines with oxygen to form **oxyhaemoglobin**.

Haemoglobin can also combine with carbon monoxide (a gas produced by car engines) to form **carboxyhaemoglobin** which cannot then combine with oxygen. This is why it is important to avoid breathing exhaust fumes, particularly when doing some form of exercise, such as jogging.

Red blood cells also carry carbon dioxide which is produced by cells as a waste product. This is done with the aid of an enzyme, **carbonic anhydrase**, which changes the carbon dioxide to bicarbonate. Some of this bicarbonate remains in the red blood cells while the rest is carried in the plasma.

White blood cells come in various shapes and sizes and are involved in the defence of the body against disease (page 150). They are made in the bone marrow, lymphatic system and spleen and there are 5,000–10,000 per cubic millimetre of blood. Their role in the body's defence is discussed later in this chapter.

Platelets are responsible for blood clot formation at the site of an injury, preventing the loss of too much blood. Platelets are much smaller than red and white blood cells and there are about 250,000–500,000 per cubic millimetre of blood. When a blood vessel is damaged the platelets release an enzyme called **thrombokinase** which initiates the sequence of events leading to the formation of a blood clot, as summarized in Fig. 9.2.

The formation of blood clots is a complicated process which helps to prevent accidental formation of clots which can cause very serious problems. If a clot occurs in the brain it can cause a stroke, if it occurs in the heart it can cause a heart attack (coronary thrombosis).

Table 9.2 summarizes the information you need to know about the structures in mammalian blood.

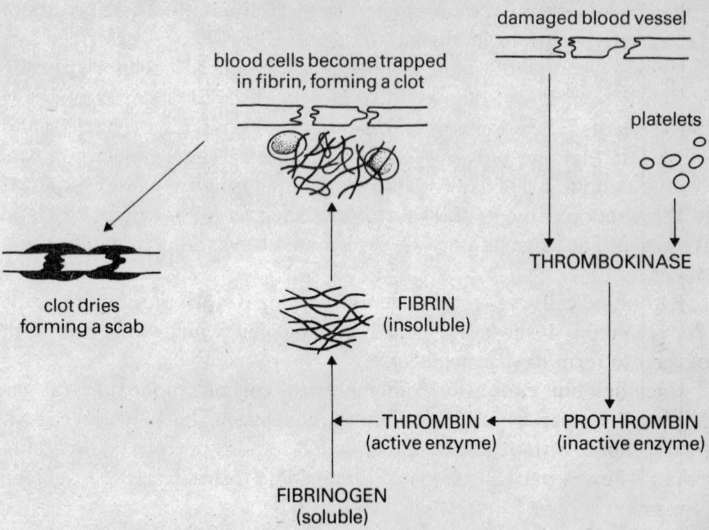

Fig. 9.2. *Blood clot formation*

Functions of blood

One of the main roles of the blood is to transport substances around the body (see Table 9.3). It is also involved in defence against infection (page 150) and control of body temperature (see Chapter 10).

9.2. *The Heart and Circulatory System*

Blood is able to move around the body (circulate) because of the pumping action of the heart. The heart and blood vessels together are called the circulatory system. Mammals have a **double circulatory system** made up of two parts. The **pulmonary circulation** takes blood to and from the lungs, the **systemic circulation** refers to blood flowing around the rest of the body. Fig. 9.3 shows how this double circulation is arranged.

You will be required to know the names of the main blood vessels of the circulatory system. These are shown in Fig. 9.4.

When trying to remember the names of the blood vessels you should find it useful to learn the following points:

1. arteries carry blood away from the heart

Table 9.2. *The structures in mammalian blood*

	Appearance	*Number/mm³*	*Site of formation*	*Function*
Red blood cells 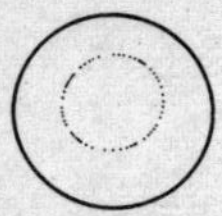	i) biconcave (thin central region) ii) no nucleus iii) red due to presence of haemoglobin	5 million	Red bone marrow	Oxygen transport (see text) Bicarbonate formation (see text)
White blood cells Two types: 1. Granulocytes 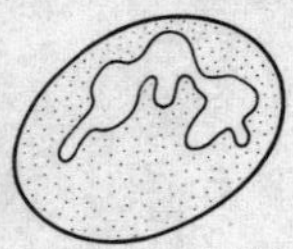	i) granular (grainy) cytoplasm ii) lobed (lumpy) nucleus	7,000	Red bone marrow	Phagocytic – engulf bacteria
2. Agranulocytes Two types: a) lymphocytes 	i) non-granular cytoplasm ii) large nucleus	2,500	Lymph nodes	Secrete antibodies

b) monocytes 	i) non-granular cytoplasm ii) kidney-shaped nucleus	500	Red bone marrow	Phagocytic – engulf bacteria
Platelets 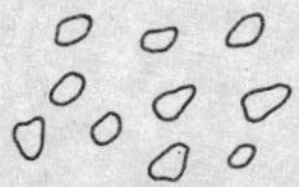	cell fragments	$\frac{1}{4}$ million	Red bone marrow	Blood clotting

NOTE: In a sample of normal human blood the above structures are present in the ratio red blood cell : white blood cell : platelet
500 : 1 : 25

Table 9.3. *Mammalian blood vessels: their structure and function*

	Structure	*Function*
Arteries 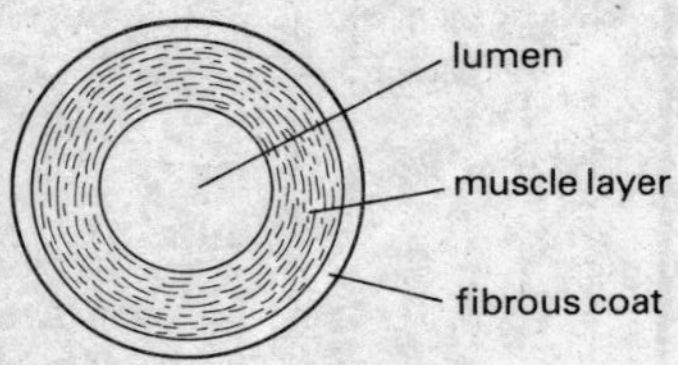 T.S. artery	i) thick-walled small lumen (bore) ii) thick muscle layer with many elastic fibres iii) no valves	i) carry blood *away* from the heart under high pressure ii) carry *oxygenated* blood (except pulmonary artery) iii) elastic recoil helps reinforce pumping action of the heart and maintain steady blood flow iv) dilation (widening) or constriction (narrowing) of arteries diverts blood flow to particular regions of the body
Veins 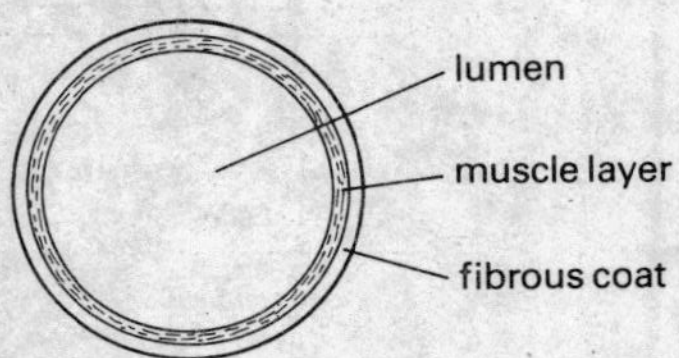 T.S. vein	i) thin-walled with large lumen ii) thin muscle layer with few elastic fibres iii) valves present	i) carry blood *towards* the heart under low pressure ii) carry *deoxygenated blood* (except pulmonary vein)

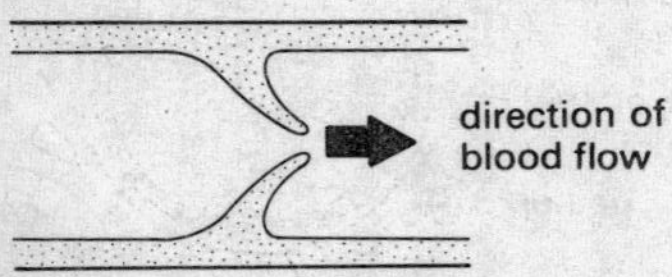

L.S. vein showing valve

Capillaries

	Structure	Function
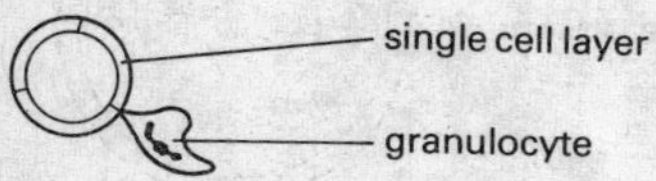	i) wall one cell thick ii) no muscle layer iii) no valves	i) carry blood between arteries and veins ii) plasma forced out of capillaries under high pressure to form tissue fluid (see page 148) iii) granulocytes and monocytes can squeeze out of capillaries and into surrounding tissues

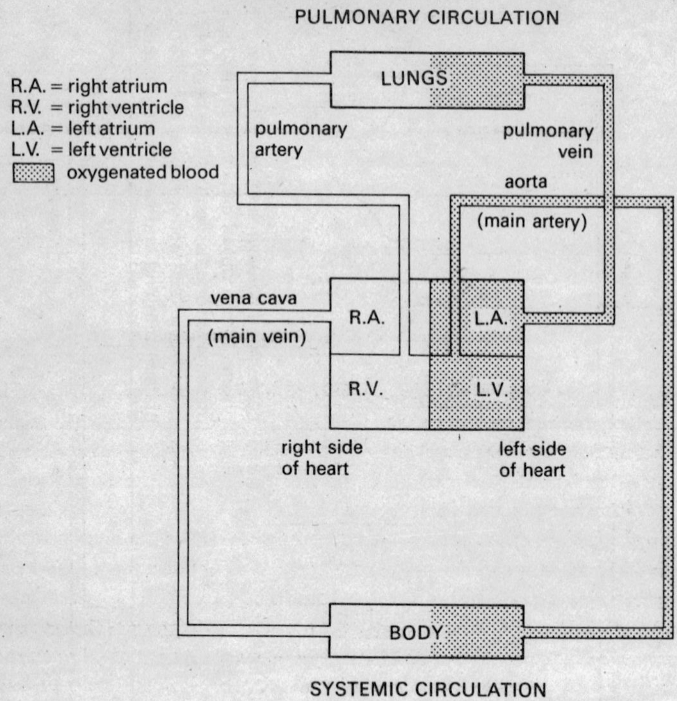

Fig. 9.3. *The double circulation of mammals*

2. veins carry blood towards the heart
3. pulmonary refers to the lungs
4. hepatic refers to the liver
5. renal refers to the kidneys.

If you remember these points it is easier to work out the name of a blood vessel if you can't remember its name. For example, the vessel supplying the liver will be the hepatic 'something' and that 'something' must be 'artery' because it is carrying blood away from the heart.

NOTE: The hepatic portal vein is exceptional. It is a vein because it is carrying blood towards the heart but it does not go directly there: it stops off at the liver first. This is why it is called a 'portal' vein.

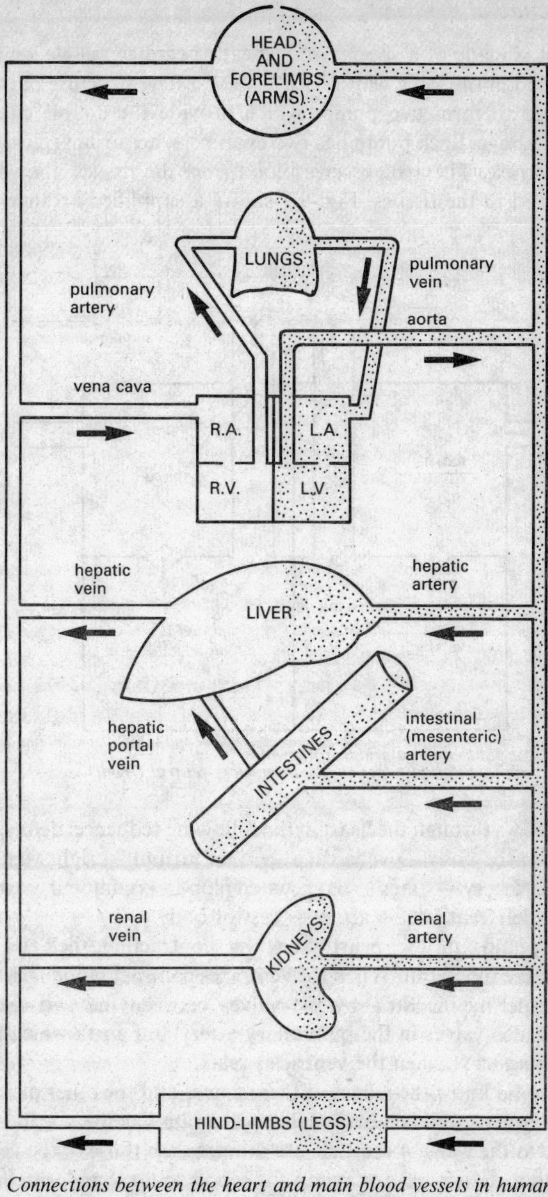

Fig. 9.4. *Connections between the heart and main blood vessels in humans*

The structure of the heart

The heart is made of a special muscle called **cardiac muscle** which does not get tired in the same way as other muscle. The structure of the heart is arranged to form two pumps which provide the double circulation described above. Each pump has two chambers, an atrium (plural: atria) and a ventricle. The atria receive blood *from* the tissues, the ventricles pump blood *to* the tissues. Fig. 9.5 shows a simplified arrangement of the heart.

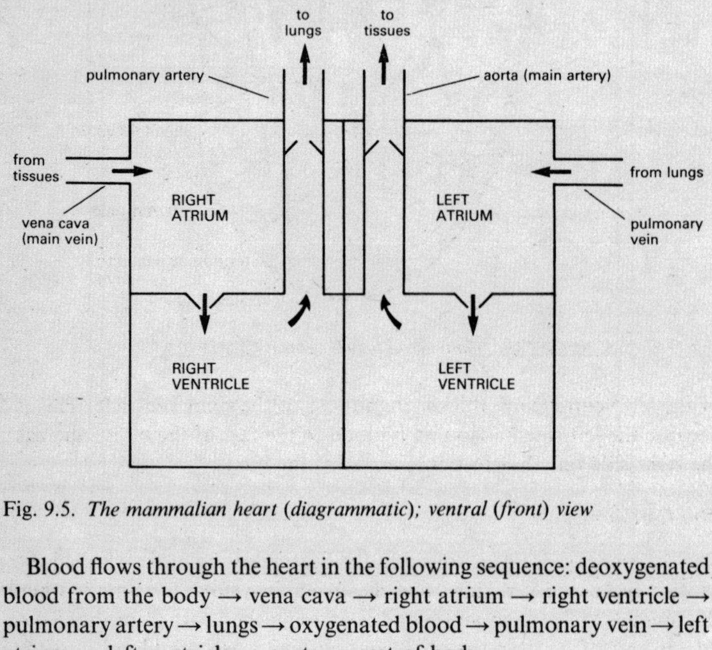

Fig. 9.5. *The mammalian heart (diagrammatic); ventral (front) view*

Blood flows through the heart in the following sequence: deoxygenated blood from the body → vena cava → right atrium → right ventricle → pulmonary artery → lungs → oxygenated blood → pulmonary vein → left atrium → left ventricle → aorta → rest of body.

These pumps in the heart work by contracting their walls and squeezing the blood out. When the ventricles contract blood is prevented from re-entering the atria by the valves between the two chambers. There are also valves in the pulmonary artery and aorta which prevent blood falling back when the ventricles relax.

You should know the names of these valves and the other parts of the heart and you should be able to label a diagram like the one in Fig. 9.6.

Note that the walls of the atria are thinner than those of the ventricles because they do not have to pump the blood so far. Similarly, the walls

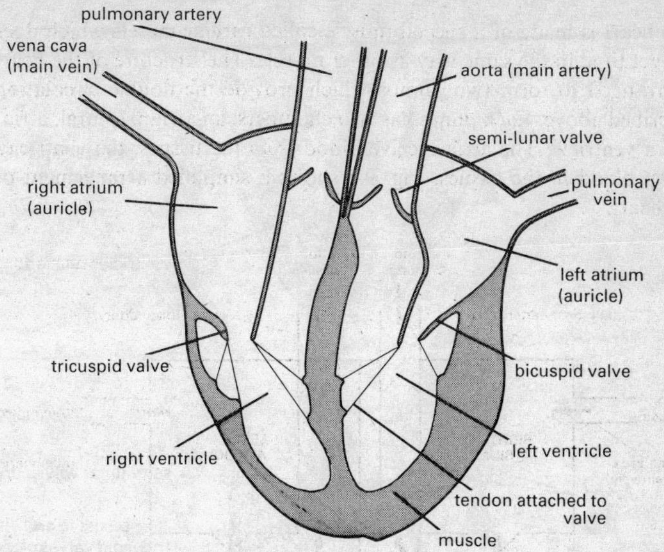

Fig. 9.6. *V.S. through the mammalian heart: ventral (front) view*

of the left ventricle are thicker than those of the right ventricle. This is because the left side has to pump blood to the rest of the body whereas the right side only has to pump as far as the lungs.

The Cardiac Cycle

The sequence of events involved in the beating of the heart is called the **cardiac cycle**, and is divided into **diastole** and **systole**. Diastole is when the muscles are relaxed and blood is entering the heart from the veins. At the end of diastole the atria contract and push the blood into the ventricles. At systole the ventricles contract and force blood into the arteries (see Fig. 9.7).

The sound of a heart beating is often described as 'lub-dub'. The 'lub' is the sound of the bicuspid and tricuspid valves closing. The 'dub' is the sound of the semi-lunar valves closing.

Controlling heartbeat

In a healthy young resting adult the heart beats 70–80 times per minute. This is known as the resting rate and is higher in children. The rate of

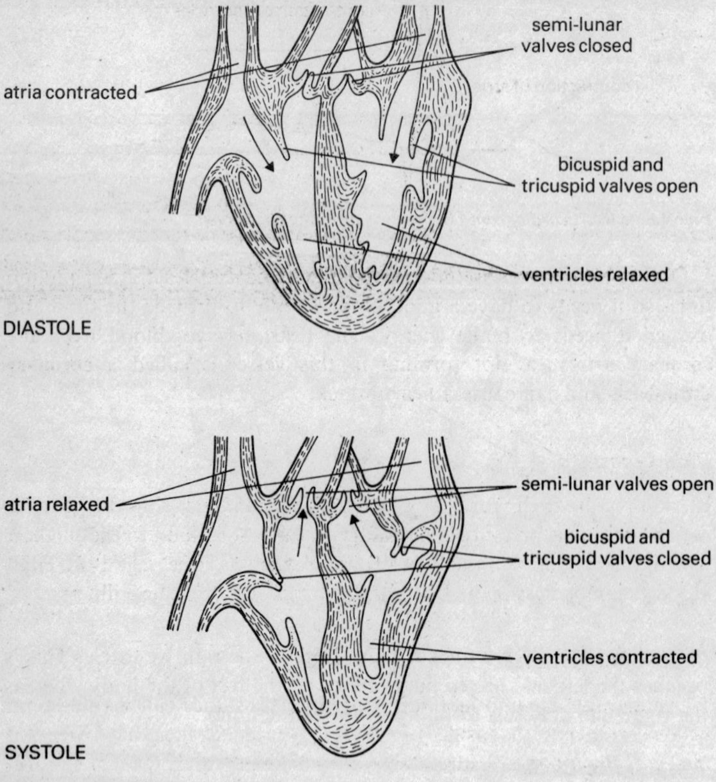

Fig. 9.7. *The cardiac cycle*

heartbeat is controlled by a special area called the **pacemaker**. Electrical impulses from the pacemaker spread along special conducting tissues over the surface of the heart and ensure that contraction of the muscle is synchronized. This electrical activity can be detected by a machine called an **electrocardiograph** which produces a graph called a **electrocardiogram** (E.C.G.) showing how the heart is beating. An E.C.G. of a normal heart is shown in Fig. 9.8.

The rate of heartbeat can be affected by the nervous system and a hormone called adrenaline (see page 205). The heart will beat faster during exercise, excitement, when the body temperature is high and when food is being digested.

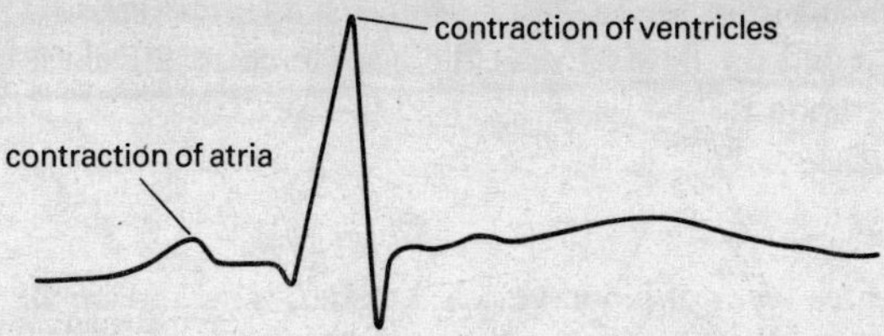

Fig. 9.8. *Electrocardiogram (E.C.G.) of a normal heartbeat*

During an average lifetime the heart will beat at least 2,500 million times so it needs to have a good blood supply to provide the food and oxygen it needs to make energy. The heart receives blood from the **coronary artery**, a clot forming in this vessel is called a **coronary thrombosis** and can cause a heart attack.

Blood pressure

Blood pressure is the force at which blood is pumped from the heart to the arteries. This pressure is necessary to carry the blood to the furthest part of the body and in the formation of tissue fluid (see page 148). High blood pressure strains the heart and arteries and can cause illness.

Causes of heart disease

1. Animal fats contain large amounts of a substance called **cholesterol** which can stick to the insides of arteries. This makes them narrower and increases the blood pressure; it may also flake off causing a clot to form (thrombosis).
2. Smoking may also cause cholesterol to stick to artery walls. Smoking also reduces the amount of oxygen in the blood so the heart does not receive as much oxygen as it needs and does not beat smoothly.
3. Obesity (being overweight) can put a strain on the heart because the body has to work harder to move the extra weight around.
4. Stress can also put a strain on the heart. When a person is tense their heart beats faster. If they are tense for long periods of time the heart does not get a chance to rest and becomes overworked.

Exercise is very important in keeping the heart healthy. Regular exercise can make the heart muscle stronger in the same way that other muscles can be strengthened by training. During exercise the blood is pumped around the body faster than usual and this helps to keep the blood vessels clear.

It is very dangerous for an unfit person to suddenly exercise vigorously. They must build up slowly to get the heart used to the extra demands being made upon it.

Blood vessels

There are three types of blood vessels: **arteries, veins** and **capillaries**. The arteries receive blood from the heart and have thick, muscular walls to withstand the pressure. As the blood travels along the arteries their walls stretch. Where the arteries are close to the surface of the skin this rhythmic stretching of the arteries can be felt as a **pulse**. The arteries divide into smaller vessels called **arterioles** which further divide to form capillaries. The capillaries carry the blood very close to the cells within the tissues. Their walls are only one cell thick which helps in the formation of tissue fluid (see page 148).

The capillaries re-unite to form small veins called **venules** which themselves join to form veins.

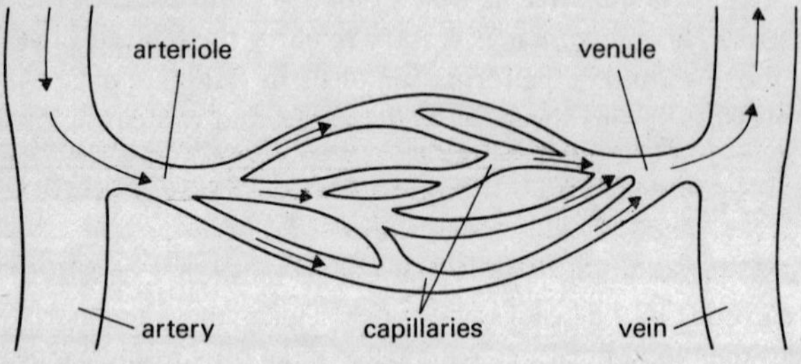

Fig. 9.9. *How blood is carried to and from the cells*

Blood entering the veins is no longer under pressure yet it has to be able to get back to the heart. This is achieved by the action of the muscles that lie alongside the veins. As these muscles contract they squeeze the blood along in the veins. The presence of valves makes sure that the blood only flows in one direction.

Table 9.3 shows the differences between the types of blood vessels.

Changes in blood composition

As blood travels around the body it gains and loses substances depending on which organ or tissue it is passing through. The changes that occur are summarized in Table 9.4.

Table 9.4. *Changes In Blood Composition*

Region of the body	*Blood gains*	*Blood loses*
All tissues	Carbon dioxide Nitrogenous waste	Oxygen Food (monosaccharides, amino acids, etc.)
Lungs	Oxygen	Carbon dioxide Water
Small intestine	Dissolved foods – water, minerals, vitamins, monosaccharides, amino acids, glycerol, fatty acids	
Liver	Controlled amounts of glucose and fats Urea Heat	Glucose (for storage as glycogen) Fatty acids and glycerol Excess amino acids Old red blood cells
Kidneys		Urea Water Salts
Bones	Red blood cells Granulocytes and monocytes (types of white blood cell)	Iron (for Hb in red blood cells) Calcium and phosphate (for bone growth)
Skin	Vitamin D	Heat Salts in urea (in sweat)
At the veins of the neck where the lymphatic system empties into the bloodstream	Lymph containing fats and lymphocytes	

9.3. *Formation of Tissue Fluid*

Although capillaries carry the blood close to the cells, diffusion of chemicals is made even more efficient by bringing these substances closer. At the tissues the blood plasma is forced through the walls of the capillaries by the pressure of the blood. The walls of the capillaries act as a filter so that the blood cells and large protein molecules remain in the capillaries. The fluid that leaves the capillaries contains the following substances:

1. water
2. dissolved oxygen
3. glucose
4. fatty acids
5. glycerol
6. amino acids
7. minerals
8. vitamins
9. hormones

Substances required by the cells diffuse into them while waste products, such as carbon dioxide, diffuse from the cells into the tissue fluid.

Some of this tissue fluid is then re-absorbed into the capillaries, the rest enters the lymphatic system.

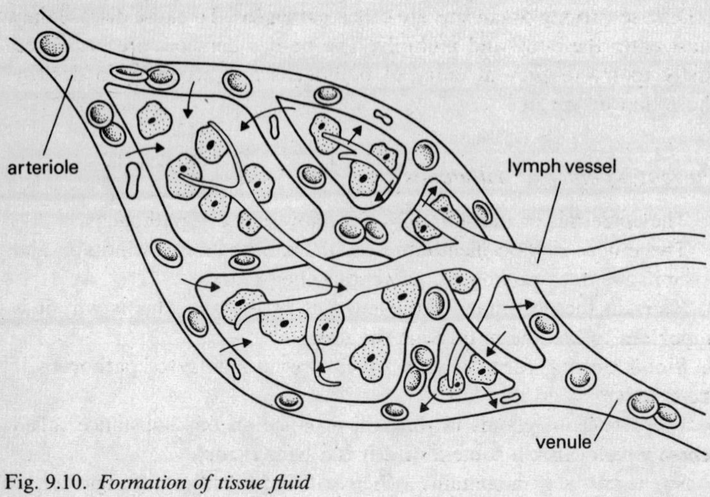

Fig. 9.10. *Formation of tissue fluid*

9.4. *The Lymphatic System*

In tissues there are tiny, blind-ending tubes called lymphatics. The tissue fluid that drains into them is called **lymph**. The **lymphatic system** is a network of these tubes, similar in structure to veins. Eventually lymph is returned to the blood just before it enters the right atrium.

Spaced along the lymph vessels are collections of cells called **lymph nodes**. In some parts of the body the lymph nodes are grouped together to form **lymph glands**. These glands are found in the neck, groin and armpits.

In the villi of the small intestine there are special lymphatics called **lacteals** which receive fatty acids and glycerol from digested food (see Chapter 7).

The lymphatic system also plays a role in defence against disease and this is discussed in the next section.

9.5. *Defence Against Disease*

Diseases are caused by the following micro-organisms:

1. viruses
2. some bacteria
3. some Protozoa
4. some fungi.

Disease-causing organisms are called **pathogens**. To cause disease they must enter the body and multiply. The body's defences are organized firstly to try to prevent entry of pathogens and secondly to destroy those that do get in.

Preventing entry of pathogens

1. The epidermis of the skin does not allow entry of pathogens.
2. The mucus on the membranes in the mouth, nose, windpipe and oesophagus traps pathogens, preventing their entry.
3. Hairs in the nose filter pathogens out of the air. This is why it is important to breathe in through the nose.
4. Blood clotting forms a scab which prevents entry of pathogens if there is damage to the skin.
5. The sebaceous glands in the skin produce an oily substance called **sebum** which can kill bacteria (i.e. it is a bactericide).
6. Sweat on the skin contains a chemical that kills fungi (fungicide).

7. Tears contain a bactericide.
8. Gastric juice (page 93) contains acid which kills bacteria.
9. Pathogens trapped in mucus in the nose and windpipe are moved by cilia to the mouth where they are swallowed.

Dealing with pathogens inside the body

1. **Phagocytes** (granulocytes and monocytes). These are found in the blood and lymph nodes and kill bacteria by engulfing them in a process called phagocytosis, as shown in Fig. 9.11.

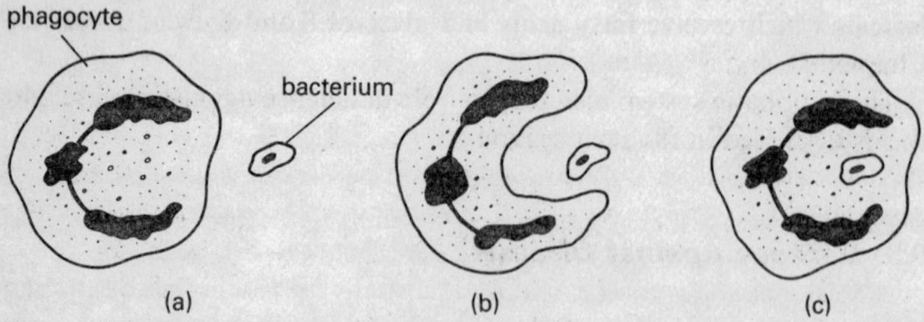

Fig. 9.11. *Phagocytosis*

Monocytes are twice as big as granulocytes. They are able to squeeze through the capillaries into the tissues where they become known as **macrophages**. In the tissues they remove debris from damaged tissues and attack bacteria at the site of infection. Pus from an infected wound consists of dead white blood cells and liquefied tissues.

Phagocytes are also found in the lymph nodes, where they engulf bacteria and foreign matter.

2. **Interferon** is a protein that can prevent the reproduction of viruses. It is produced by many cells in the body.

3. **Antibodies.** Pathogens may secrete or contain chemicals called **antigens** and these are recognized by the body as foreign materials. When antigens are poisonous they are called **toxins**. The body responds by forming antibodies which are produced by the lymphocytes.

Definition: Immunity *is the body's ability to resist infection by producing antibodies.*

Most lymphocytes are found in the lymph nodes. During infection the lymph nodes become swollen and we get 'swollen glands'. Other areas that contain lymphocytes are the spleen, thymus gland, tonsils and appendix.

Antibodies are proteins which can be classified into four main groups:

1. **Opsonins** combine with antigens on the surface of a pathogen and make it easier for the phagocytes to engulf it.
2. **Lysins** kill pathogens by causing them to burst into fragments.
3. **Agglutinins** cause pathogens to stick together in clumps (agglutinate) so they are unable to harm the body.
4. **Anti-toxins** combine with toxins, making them harmless.

Antibodies are specific to a particular antigen, so there is a different antibody for each disease. When we get a disease our bodies produce antibodies to fight that particular disease. These antibodies remain in the body for many years after we have recovered and prevent us suffering from that disease again.

Immunity can be classified as passive or active.

Passive immunity is when immunity is achieved by receiving 'ready-made' antibodies from another organism. These could be acquired naturally; for example a foetus receives antibodies from its mother. They can also be supplied by vaccination (see Chapter 16).

Active immunity can be achieved naturally by catching a disease and developing an immunity to it. It can also be induced by vaccination (Chapter 16).

Transplants. The body's ability to recognize foreign materials and fight against them presents problems when an organ is transplanted. The immune system sees tissue from another person as 'foreign' and attacks it as though it were a pathogen. To prevent rejection of the transplanted organ patients are treated with drugs that repress the immune system. This creates further dangers of infection and such patients have to be isolated to prevent their exposure to pathogens.

9.6. *Blood Groups*

There are four blood groups, called A, B, A B and O. They are different because of the antigens on the red blood cells and the antibodies in the plasma.

Group A: This blood group has A antigens on the red blood cells and anti-B antibodies in the plasma.

Group B: has B antigens on the red blood cells and anti-A antibodies in the plasma.

Group A B: has A and B antigens on the red blood cells and no anti-A or anti-B antibodies in the plasma.

Group O: has no A or B antigens on the red blood cells and both anti-A and anti-B antibodies in the plasma.

Doctors have to be very careful when giving a blood transfusion because it is not possible to mix all of the blood groups. For example, if blood groups A and B were mixed the A antigens in group A blood would be attacked by the anti-A antibodies in the group B blood. Similarly, the B antigens in the group B blood would be attacked by the anti-B antibodies in group A blood.

Table 9.5 shows the ways in which blood groups can be mixed.

Table 9.5. *How blood groups can be mixed*

Blood group	*Donate to*	*Receive from*
A	A,AB	A,O
B	B,AB	B,O
AB	AB	A,B,AB,O
O	A,B,AB,O	O

People with blood group O can donate blood to people of any other blood group so they are called **universal donors**.

The Rhesus factor

Most people (about 85 per cent) have an antigen on their red blood cells called the **rhesus factor**. These people are rhesus positive (Rh+); people without it are rhesus negative (Rh−).

If a person who is Rh− receives blood from a Rh+ person they will develop antibodies to the rhesus factor in the Rh+ blood. This does not happen the first time because there are no antibodies already in the blood. Once the Rh− blood has been exposed to the rhesus factor, however, it becomes **sensitized** to it, so the next time Rh+ blood is introduced the antibodies formed after the first transfusion agglutinate it.

Rh+ people can receive Rh− blood any number of times without any problems.

A Rh+ father and a Rh− mother can have a Rh+ baby. If there is a fault in the placenta, Rh+ blood from the foetus may enter the mother's (Rh−) blood. This will sensitize the mother's blood to the rhesus factor.

If she has a second Rh+ child the mother's sensitized blood may attack the blood cells of the foetus.

There are now substances available to prevent a Rh− mother developing antibodies to the rhesus factor.

Key Words

Blood
Plasma
Haemoglobin
Platelets
Thrombokinase
Heart
Pacemaker
Electrocardiogram (E.C.G.)
Artery
Vein
Capillary
Interferon
Rhesus factor
Red blood cells
White blood cells
Carbonic anhydrase
Cardiac cycle
Diastole
Systole
Double circulatory system
Pulmonary circulation
Systemic circulation
Lymphatic system
Lymph node
Pathogens
Sebum
Phagocyte
Granulocyte
Monocyte
Lymphocyte
Macrophage
Blood groups

Exam Questions

1. *The figure below shows the external structure of the heart.*

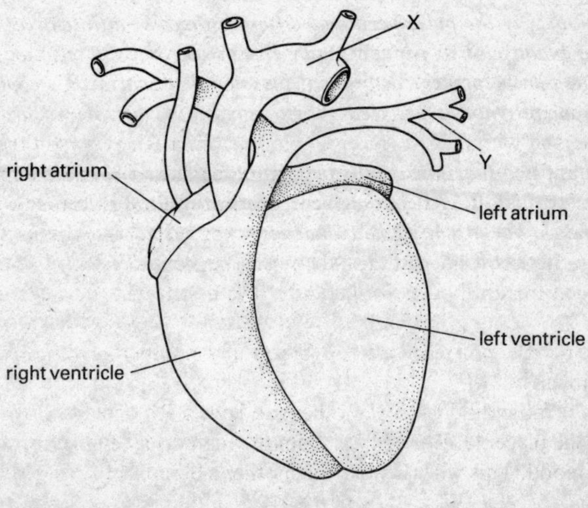

(*a*) *Name the blood vessels that carry deoxygenated blood.*
(*b*) *Name the vessels labelled X and Y.*
(*c*) *Draw large, labelled diagrams of a red blood cell and a white blood cell.*

2. *When you take your pulse you usually feel the radial artery at your wrist. Pulses can be taken at other places in the body. The graph below shows the pulses in three blood vessels.*

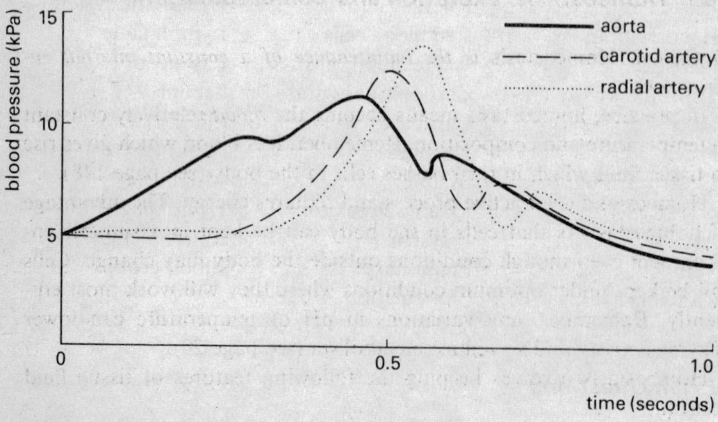

(*a*) *In which of these three vessels does the pulse occur first?*
(*b*) *In which vessel does the pulse occur last?*
(*c*) *Explain why the pulse occurs at different times in different vessels.*

3. *For a blood clot to form, vitamin K must be present. The action of vitamin K can be prevented by a rat poison called warfarin. People who suffer from thrombosis are treated with small amounts of warfarin. Explain.*

4. (*a*) *State two functions of the lymphatic system.*
(*b*) *With the aid of labelled diagrams, explain what a granulocyte would do if it met a bacterium in the blood.*
(*c*) *Where would you expect to find macrophages in the body?*

10. *Keeping Conditions in the Body Constant (Homeostasis)*

10.1. ***Homeostasis, Excretion and Osmoregulation***

Definition: Homeostasis *is the maintenance of a constant internal environment.*

In practice, homeostasis means keeping the *blood* relatively constant in temperature and composition. Remember, it is blood which gives rise to tissue fluid which in turn bathes cells in the body (see page 148).

Homeostasis is an active process and requires energy. The advantage of homeostasis is that cells in the body can be kept in a suitable environment even though conditions outside the body may change. Cells can be kept under optimum conditions where they will work most efficiently. Remember, any variations in pH or temperature can lower enzyme activity and so reduce metabolism (see page 20).

Homeostasis involves keeping the following features of tissue fluid constant:

1. the balance of chemical constituents such as salts, dissolved foods and waste products
2. the salt/water balance (osmotic pressure, see page 73)
3. the levels of oxygen and carbon dioxide
4. temperature
5. pH (acidity/alkalinity).

The four major sets of organs (homeostatic organs) which regulate these features are given in Table 10.1.

Two important aspects of homeostasis are **excretion** and **osmoregulation**.

Definition: Excretion *is the removal from the body of the waste products of metabolism.*

Be careful *not* to confuse excretion with egestion (page 96) or secretion (page 79).

Definition: Osmoregulation *is the process by which the salt/water balance (osmotic pressure) of body fluids is kept constant.*

The removal of waste products of **metabolism** is a vital part of homeostasis. It prevents the accumulation of substances which are poison-

Table 10.1. *The body's organs concerned with homeostasis*

Organs	*Blood factors regulated*	*Blood levels in a healthy adult*
Liver and pancreas	Glucose	100 mg/100 cm^3 or 1 g/litre
Kidneys	Water Salts pH (acidity/alkalinity) Urea	90 per cent 0.7 g/litre pH 7.4 0.3 g/litre
Lungs	Carbon dioxide Oxygen	550 cm^3/litre 190 cm^3/litre
Skin and liver	Temperature	36.8 °C

ous or which would otherwise interfere with the normal functioning of body cells. These excreted waste substances are called **excretory products**.

The term excretion has also come to include the removal of excess or poisonous substances which have been absorbed. For example, it is not possible to tell whether excreted water has come from metabolism (e.g. respiration) or whether it has been absorbed from the diet.

The body's main excretory products and excretory structures are shown in Table 10.2.

Students commonly confuse excretion with egestion. Faeces contain mainly *egested* material, that is, substances which have not been digested and have not been absorbed. Only a small proportion of faeces is truly excreted material e.g. bile salts.

10.2. *The Kidneys*

The kidneys are the major organs concerned with excretion and osmoregulation. The kidneys remove the following substances from blood:

1. urea
2. excess water
3. excess salts
4. excess hydrogen ions (to keep blood pH constant)
5. foreign substances such as drugs, poisons, etc.

Table 10.2. *Excretory products and excretory structures in the human body*

Excretory products	*Source*	*Excretory structures concerned with their removal*
Carbon dioxide	From respiration	The *lungs* excrete carbon dioxide in expired air.
Water	From respiration or absorbed from the diet	The *kidneys* remove water in *urine*, the *lungs* in exhaled air and the *skin* in sweat.
Urea	From the deamination of excess proteins (page 101)	The *kidneys* excrete urea in urine and the *skin* a small amount in sweat.
Mineral salts	Absorbed from the diet	The *kidneys* excrete salts in urine and the *skin* a small amount in sweat.
Bile pigments	From the breakdown of haemoglobin from red blood cells	The *liver* excretes bile pigments as part of bile. Later removed in the faeces.

NOTE: Water, salts and a little urea are also lost in the faeces.

6. hormones.

The removals of these substances are excretory functions: in addition 2 and 3 are osmoregulatory functions.

The above substances are excreted by the kidneys in the **urine**.

Kidney structure

The kidneys are a pair of bean-shaped, reddish-brown organs enclosed in a transparent membrane. They are attached to the back of the abdominal cavity. The kidneys and their associated structures comprise the **renal system** (Fig. 10.1).

The kidneys are connected to other parts of the body by three vessels:

1. the **renal artery**, which delivers blood to the kidney from the aorta.
2. the **renal vein**, which carries blood away from the kidney and to the inferior vena cava.
3. the **ureter**, which carries urine away to the bladder.

In vertical section (Fig. 10.2) the kidney consists of a dark outer

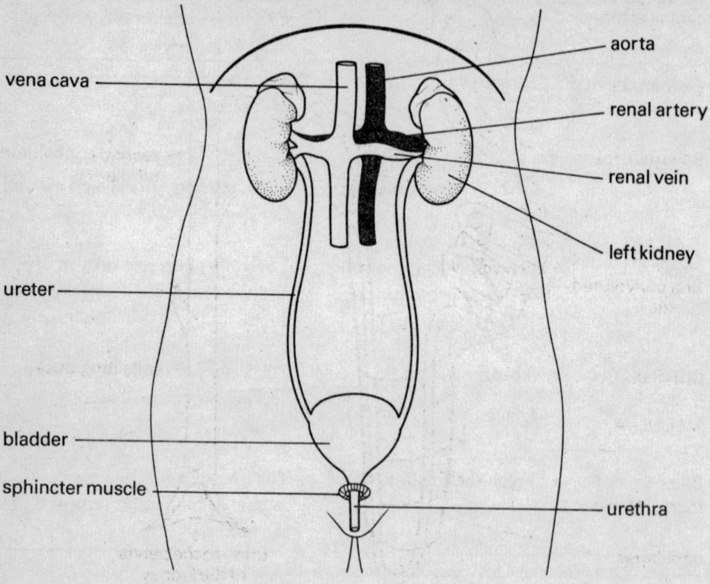

Fig. 10.1 *The human renal system*

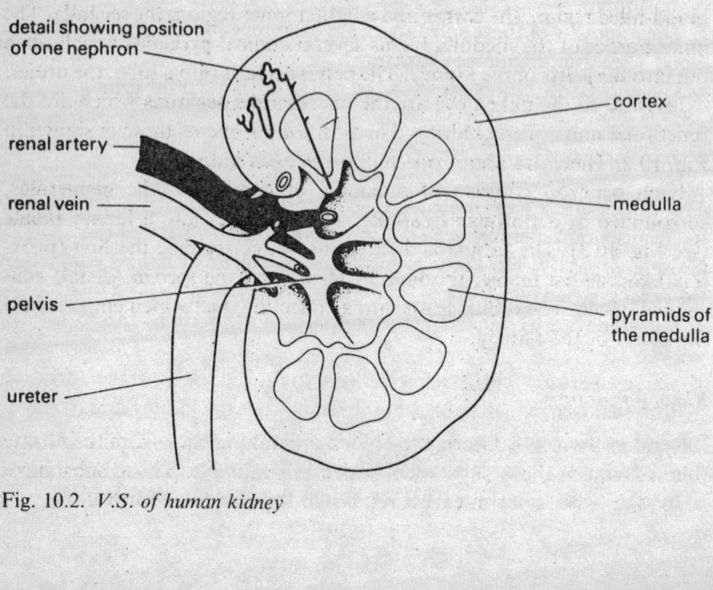

Fig. 10.2. *V.S. of human kidney*

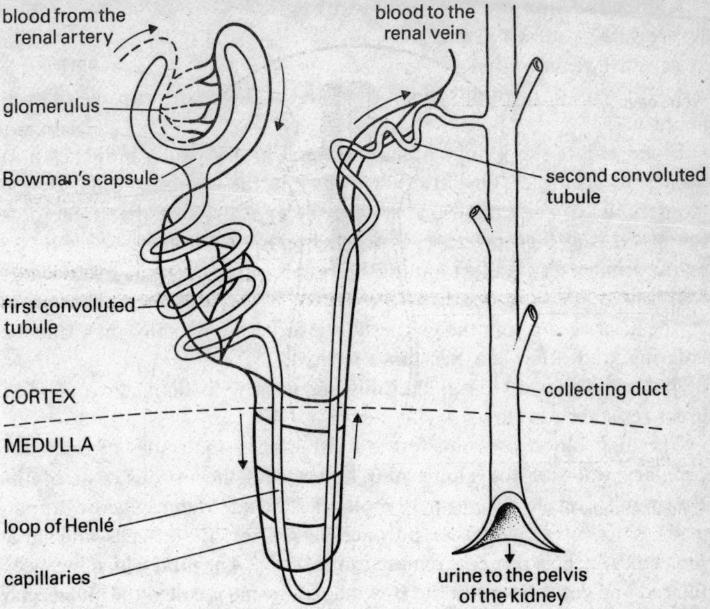

Fig. 10.3. *A nephron from the human kidney*

blood-filled region, the **cortex** and a lighter inner region, the **medulla**. The inner border of the medulla forms several conical **pyramids** which open out into the **pelvis** of the kidney. The pelvis extends into a tube, the ureter.

Invisible to the naked eye are the microscopic **nephrons** which are the functional units of the kidney. The position of one of these is shown in Fig. 10.2. There are about one million in each kidney.

Each nephron consists of a bundle of capillaries, the **glomerulus**, surrounded by a **Bowman's capsule**, which empties into a **kidney tubule** (see Fig. 10.3). The tubule is divided into three regions; the **first** (proximal) **convoluted tubule**, the **loop of Henlé** and the **second** (distal) **convoluted tubule**. The tubule leads into a collecting duct which empties into the pelvis of the kidney.

Kidney function

The kidneys work by filtering the blood and taking back from the filtrate (filtered liquid) those substances which are valuable. Those substances which are harmful or in excess remain in the filtrate to form urine.

Kidney function involves two processes:

1. **pressure** or **ultra-filtration**
2. **selective reabsorption**

1. **Pressure** or **ultra-filtration** occurs in the Bowman's capsule of each nephron.

Blood enters the kidney along the renal artery which branches into numerous arterioles. One arteriole leads into the knot of capillaries, the glomerulus, of each nephron. Within the capillaries of the glomerulus the blood is at high pressure. Pressure builds up because:

1. the renal artery is short and the blood pressure generated by the heart is still high;
2. the arteriole leaving the glomerulus is larger in diameter than the one entering, and offers less resistance to flow;
3. the capillaries of the glomerulus are narrow in diameter and offer great resistance to flow.

The high blood pressure forces most smaller molecules through the capillary walls of the glomerulus and across the porous wall of the Bowman's capsule. These small molecules include water, glucose, amino acids, salts, urea and other nitrogenous wastes. Blood cells and large molecules such as proteins remain in the blood. The fluid which has been filtered and collects within the Bowman's capsule is called the **glomerular filtrate**.

2. **Selective reabsorption** occurs in the kidney tubule and collecting duct of each nephron.

Selective reabsorption involves taking back (reabsorbing) valuable substances from the glomerular filtrate, otherwise these substances would pass out of the body and be lost. These substances are absorbed into a network of capillaries which wrap around the kidney tubule. These capillaries arise from the arteriole which comes out of the glomerulus (see Fig. 10.3).

As Table 10.3 shows, different regions of the kidney tubule reabsorb different substances. Water is taken up by osmosis (page 72) while the other valuable components are taken up by active transport (page 76) against a concentration gradient. Active transport requires energy expenditure and, not surprisingly, the cells lining the kidney tubule are richly supplied with mitochondria (page 24). On their inner surface these cells have a cell membrane folded to form microvilli which increase the surface area for absorption.

The end-product of ultra-filtration and reabsorption is urine. This empties from the collecting ducts into the pelvis of the kidney.

Urine

From the kidney pelvis, urine drips into the ureter. Urine is propelled along this tube by peristalsis and empties into a muscular sac, the **bladder**, where urine is stored. The bladder has a capacity of about 400 cm^3. Periodically, when the bladder is full, urine is squirted out of the bladder and along the **urethra** and out of the body. (Do not confuse the ure*thra* with the ure*ter*.)

The release of urine is termed **micturition** and is controlled by a ring of muscle, a sphincter, at the base of the bladder. When the bladder fills with urine, stretch receptors in its walls are triggered and send nerve impulses to the spinal cord and brain. In babies and young children this results in a reflex action which delivers nerve impulses to the bladder sphincter. The sphincter muscle relaxes and urine is released. In babies this is a simple reflex action (page 180); when the bladder fills, urine is automatically passed out of the body. During 'potty training' children are encouraged to override this reflex and to pass urine only at appropriate times. Thus for most people, from early childhood onwards, micturition comes under voluntary control.

A human produces about 1.5 litres of urine per day. The composition of urine is shown in Table 10.3. In addition to water, urea and salts, urine contains hormones (variously modified) and possibly some poisons or drugs in small amounts. The exact composition of urine varies according to diet, activity and health.

As Table 10.3 shows, urine normally contains neither glucose nor

Table 10.3. *Comparison of blood plasma and urine*

	Concentration in grams per 100 cm^3 (= percentage composition)	
Constituent	*In plasma*	*In urine*
Water	90–91	95–96
Urea	0.03	2.0
Sodium chloride and other salts	0.7	1.5
Glucose	0.1	0.0
Proteins	7–9	0.0

protein. The presence of glucose in urine is an indication of the condition **diabetes mellitus**. This is an inability to control blood glucose level due to lack of the hormone insulin (page 205). Glucose is present in the urine if excess glucose is being carried in the blood plasma. Under these conditions, a large amount of glucose enters the glomerular filtrate and not all the glucose is reabsorbed.

Control of salt/water balance (osmoregulation)

The salt/water balance (osmotic pressure) of the blood must be kept within narrow limits. The body is about 67 per cent water, and death will occur if about 20 per cent of this water is lost and not replaced.

Water is lost from the body in urine, sweat, expired breath and faeces. Water is regained mainly by drinking and eating, but some is produced as a by-product of respiration.

About 100 cm^3 of water is filtered out of the blood and into the kidney tubule every minute. Normally about 99 cm^3 of this is reabsorbed, but this can be varied. In hot weather, the body loses much water by sweating (page 167). To keep water in the body, the kidney tubules reabsorb as much water as possible. As a result, a small volume of concentrated urine is produced. After drinking large volumes of liquid, the O.P. of body fluids may be lowered. In forming urine, the kidneys will reabsorb as little water as possible, and a large volume of dilute urine will be produced.

The amount of water lost in the urine is controlled by **anti-diuretic hormone** (ADH, page 205). ADH has the effect of increasing the permeability of the collecting duct to water, so that more water is reabsorbed and the urine becomes more concentrated.

The O.P. of blood is detected by the hypothalamus which in turn controls the release of ADH by the pituitary gland (see page 205). When the blood O.P. is high, the hypothalamus sends nerve impulses to the pituitary gland to release ADH. ADH causes more water to be reabsorbed by the collecting ducts and kidney tubules so that a small volume of concentrated urine is produced. When the blood O.P. is low, the hypothalamus sends fewer nerve impulses to the pituitary gland. Less ADH is released and as a result less water is reabsorbed by the kidneys. A relatively large volume of dilute urine results.

Read carefully the last paragraph again. What conditions might result in the blood O.P. rising above normal? What conditions might result in the blood O.P. dropping below normal?

Another mechanism helps maintain the salt/water balance of the blood. It does so by controlling the reabsorption of sodium ions by the kidney tubules.

During sweating, sodium ions are lost from the body fluids; salt is excreted onto the skin as part of the sweat. If the blood sodium ion concentration falls, the hormone **aldosterone** is released by the cortex of the adrenal gland (page 205). Aldosterone stimulates reabsorption of sodium ions in the kidney tubules, particularly in the second convoluted tubules.

10.3. *The Skin*

The skin has two main layers:

1. an outer layer, the **epidermis**
2. an inner layer, the **dermis**

A layer of **subcutaneous fat** lies below the dermis.

1. **Epidermis:** this is the protective surface layer of the skin. It is many cells thick. At its base is the **germinative (Malpighian) layer**, an active layer of cells which constantly divides to produce new epidermis. Above the germinative layer is the **granular layer**. This contains newly-produced epidermal cells which are in the process of being converted into cornified cells. As cells move through the granular layer, they become flattened, lose their nuclei and have the protein **keratin** deposited in them. The cells finally die and form part of the **cornified layer**. This protective layer of dead cells is constantly worn away by friction and is replaced by new cells from below. Keratin helps to waterproof the surface of the skin as well as reducing water loss from the tissues below.

Certain cells in the germinative layer contain the dark pigment **melanin**, which absorbs ultra-violet radiation. Downfolds of the epidermis form the sweat glands, sebaceous glands and hair follicles, which lie deep in the dermis.

The epidermis is an example of a compound (stratified) epithelium (page 66). It varies in thickness, being particularly thick in those regions subject to abrasion e.g. soles of feet and palms of hand.

2. **Dermis:** this is largely connective tissue (page 66) containing few cells, but many elastic and collagen fibres. These fibres provide elasticity and tensile strength. Phagocytic white blood cells called **macrophages** move slowly through the dermis where they engulf micro-organisms and other foreign matter. Various structures lie within the dermis: hair follicles, glands, capillaries, muscles, nerves and sense organs.

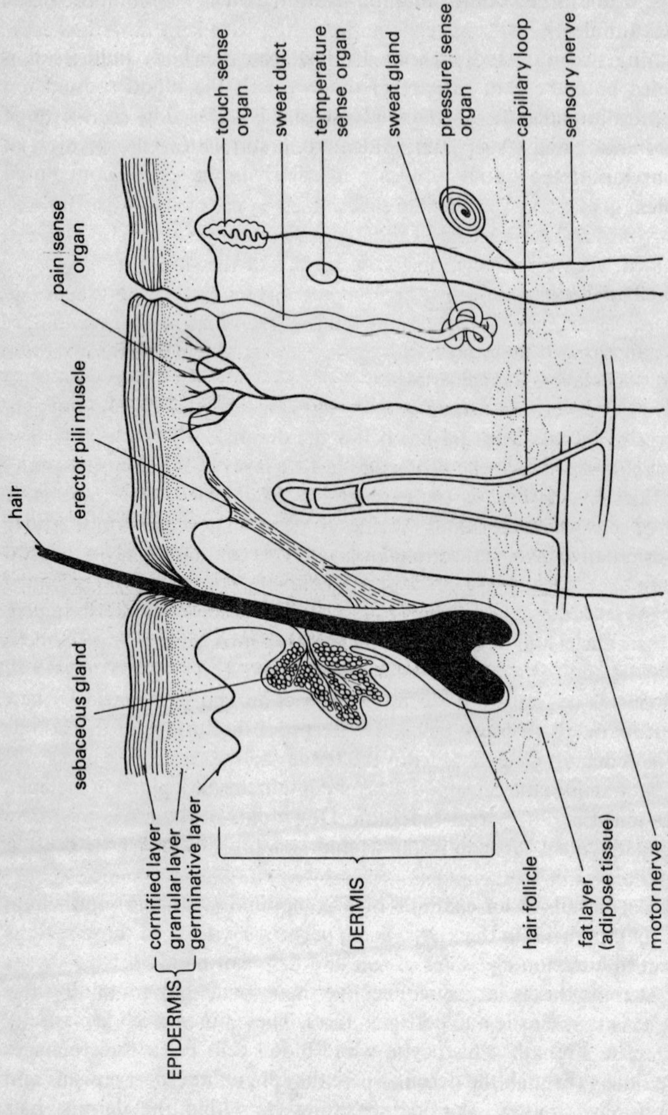

Fig. 10.4. *V.S. of mammalian skin*

The **hair follicle** is a deep downfold of the granular and germinative layers. The follicle secretes the non-living hair which is composed of a cylinder of dead epidermal cells impregnated with keratin. Attached to the hair is an *erector pili* muscle which, when it contracts, pulls the hair upright.

Sebaceous glands open into the hair follicle and secrete an oily fluid, **sebum**, which helps keep the hair and skin surface supple, waterproof and bacteria-free.

Sweat glands consist of coiled tubes, lined by cells which absorb tissue fluid from surrounding tissues and capillaries. The resulting fluid (sweat) is passed, via sweat ducts, on to the surface of the skin.

Capillaries in the dermis bring food and oxygen to the skin tissues and remove waste. Some give rise to the fluid, sweat, and some form capillary loops. Both play an important part in temperature regulation (section 10.4).

Five types of **sensory receptor** in the skin detect heat, cold, touch, pain and pressure. **Motor nerves** (page 176) stimulate muscles and glands, while **sensory nerves** (page 176) run from the skin's sensory receptors to the brain.

The layer of **subcutaneous fat** below the dermis protects underlying organs from mechanical damage and acts as an energy store and insulator.

Skin function

The skin's functions relate to it being the boundary layer of the body. Its functions are:

1. **Protection** – the outer dead layer of the epidermis is impermeable and prevents loss of water.
– the skin protects against mechanical damage and friction
– a dark pigment **melanin** in the Malpighian layer prevents ultra-violet light (from sunlight) penetrating the body and damaging vital organs
– the skin prevents entry of micro-organisms (page 46), the sebum kills bacteria
– the fat layer and hairs reduce heat loss.

2. **Temperature regulation** – sweating, and widening (dilation) and narrowing (constriction) of blood vessels control heat loss through the skin (see page 167).

3. **Vitamin D production** – in the presence of ultra-violet light (in sunlight) certain fats are converted to vitamin D. Vitamin D is otherwise provided by the diet.

4. **Sensitivity** – the skin is sensitive to touch, heat, cold, pain and pressure. These are protective functions, enabling the body to respond to adverse conditions; they also provide considerable information about the outside world.
5. **Excretion** – water, urea and dissolved salts are excreted in the sweat. The loss of these substances is incidental. The main function of sweat is to increase heat loss.

NOTE: Structures such as teeth (page 102), mammary glands (page 251), hairs and nails are modified skin tissues.

10.4. *Control of Body Temperature*

Humans, like all mammals and birds, are **endothermic**, meaning we can control our body temperature *internally* by physiological means. We can maintain a **constant body temperature** largely independent of our surroundings. This has two major advantages:
1. We can maintain an optimum temperature for metabolism.
2. We can be active all the year round and at all times of day, whatever the external temperature.

In humans, the body temperature is kept at about 37°C, which is near the optimum temperature for enzyme action. Death occurs if the body temperature rises much above 42°C or drops much below 30°C.

To maintain our body temperature at 37°C (usually well above the temperature of the surroundings) we must generate our own body heat, largely from respiration. To keep body temperature constant we need to balance the heat we gain against the heat we lose so that:

heat gained by body = heat lost from body

The body gains heat from:
1. **Metabolism**; respiration in the liver and muscles releases a large amount of heat energy.
2. Heat **radiation** from the sun or nearby hot objects.
3. Heat **conduction** from the air or any hot objects in contact with the body (including hot food or drink which is ingested).

The body loses heat by:
1. **Evaporation** of sweat from the skin or water from the lungs. (NOTE: **latent heat** is needed to convert a liquid into a gas.)
2. Heat **radiation** to the surroundings.
3. Heat **conduction** to the surrounding air or any cool objects in contact with the body.

4. Heat loss by **convection** (warm air next to the body rises and is replaced by colder air).
5. Some heat is lost in urine and faeces.

A small structure, the **hypothalamus**, at the base of the fore-brain (page 185) acts as a thermostat, monitoring blood temperature. If this rises above normal, nerve impulses are relayed to the sweat glands, blood vessels and erector muscles in the skin to increase heat loss. If blood temperature drops below normal, the hypothalamus controls an appropriate set of responses to reduce heat loss and increase heat production. The responses to overheating and overcooling are shown below. The control mechanism is summarized on page 209.

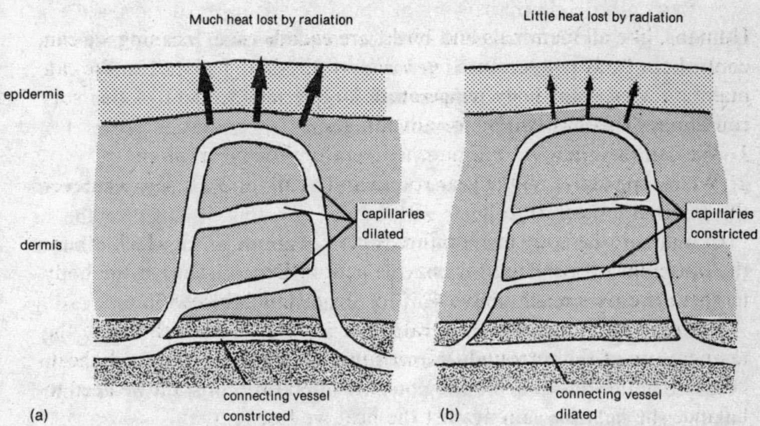

Fig. 10.5. (*a*) *Vasodilation;* (*b*) *vasoconstriction*

1. **Control of overheating** (blood temperature in humans rises above 37°C). Body temperature may rise during vigorous exercise, when the body is fighting infection, or if the air temperature is high. The following responses, controlled by the hypothalamus, lower body temperature:

(*a*) **Increased sweating.** Sweat glands form sweat from the water, salts and urea they receive from blood capillaries. As the water in sweat evaporates from the skin's surface, so the skin is cooled.

(*b*) **Vasodilation** (widening of capillaries in the dermis, see Fig. 10.5). The blood flow to the skin is increased and heat loss by radiation, convection and conduction is increased.

(*c*) **Reduced muscular activity.** (NOTE: respiration supplies muscles with the energy required for contraction but also produces heat as a by-product.)

(*d*) **Hair lies flat against the skin.** Not very important in humans (see below).

(*e*) **Voluntary actions** may be employed such as removing clothes, reducing artificial heating or switching on a fan.

(*f*) **Reduced rate of metabolism.** In the long term the appetite may be reduced and less food broken down in respiration or stored (insulation).

Failure of the above mechanisms to lower body temperature may result in heat stroke, **hyperthermia**, and then heat death.

2. **Control of overcooling** (blood temperature drops below 37°C):

(*a*) **Sweating stops.**

(*b*) **Vasoconstriction** (narrowing of blood vessels in the dermis, see Fig. 10.5). The blood flow to the skin is decreased and heat loss by radiation, convection and conduction is reduced.

(*c*) **Increased voluntary muscular activity** increases heat production.

(*d*) **Increased involuntary muscular activity** (shivering) increases heat production.

(*e*) **Hair stands on end** ('goose flesh'). This is of little importance in humans, but in other animals with a thick covering of hair (fur) the air trapped between erect hairs significantly reduces heat loss by radiation, convection and conduction.

(*f*) **Voluntary actions** such as putting on additional clothes or increasing artificial heating may be employed.

(*g*) **Increased rate of metabolism.** In the long term appetite may be increased and more food broken down by respiration in the liver or stored as fat as insulation.

Failure of the above mechanisms to raise body temperature may result in reduced 'deep body' or 'core' temperature, **hypothermia**, and then cold death.

Mechanism of temperature control

The skin contains sensory receptors informing us of changes in the temperature of our surroundings. However, the hypothalamus is not only the control centre for temperature regulation, it also contains temperature receptors (see page 190).

If the blood reaching the hypothalamus is below 37°C, vasoconstriction, 'goose flesh' and other responses will occur to raise body temperature. This will happen whatever the external temperature. Temperature receptors in the hypothalamus override the stimulus being received by temperature receptors in the skin.

If the blood reaching the hypothalamus is above 37°C, vasodilation, sweating and other responses will occur to lower body temperature. This will happen whatever the external temperature. Again, temperature receptors in the hypothalamus override the stimulus being received by temperature receptors in the skin.

Experiments which illustrate this principle are often included in exam questions. Such experiments show that the body's main 'thermostat' is situated in the hypothalamus and is sensitive to changes in blood temperature rather than changes in external temperature.

Definitions

Homeostasis
Excretion
Osmoregulation

Key Words

Liver
Lungs
Kidneys
Skin
Excretory products
Renal system
Renal artery
Renal vein
Bile pigments
Urea
Cortex
Medulla
Ureter
Nephron
Pyramids
Pelvis
Glomerulus
Bowman's capsule
Glomerular filtrate
Kidney tubule
First convoluted tubule
Loop of Henlé
Second convoluted tubule
Collecting duct
Urine
Pressure (ultra) filtration
Selective reabsorption
Bladder
Urethra
Micturition
Diabetes mellitus
Anti-diuretic hormone (ADH)
Aldosterone
Epidermis
Dermis
Subcutaneous fat
Germinative (Malpighian) layer
Granular layer
Keratin
Cornified layer
Melanin
Macrophages
Hair follicle
Sebaceous glands
Sebum
Sweat glands
Capillaries
Sensory receptors
Motor nerves
Sensory nerves
Endothermic
Radiation
Conduction
Convection
Evaporation
Hypothalamus
Sweating
Latent heat
Vasodilation
Vasoconstriction
Hyperthermia
Hypothermia

Exam Questions

1. (*a*) *One of the main functions of the skin is protection. Explain concisely how the skin protects the body against:*
(*i*) *the entry of bacteria,* (*ii*) *dehydration,* (*iii*) *ultra-violet radiation.* [6]
(*b*) *The diagram represents a 'Heat Balance' for the human body.*

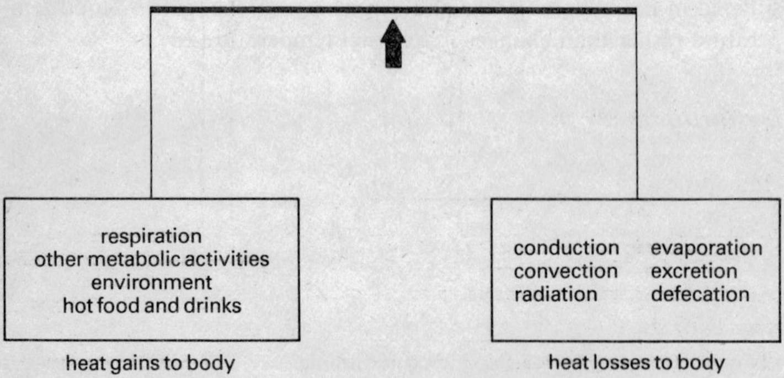

Heat losses and heat gains by the body must be balanced.
(*i*) *Explain why the maintenance of this balance is essential.* [3]
(*ii*) *Explain how the skin can reduce heat loss by radiation.* [3]
(*iii*) *On a very hot summer's day the skin produces a lot of sweat. Explain the value and consequences of this action.* [5]
(*c*) *Explain why the hands should be washed before handling food.* [3]

[Total 20]

[AEB]

2. *The figure below is a diagram of part of a kidney tubule and its associated blood vessels. The arrows indicate the direction of flow of fluids.*
(*a*) *Name the artery which supplies blood to A.*
(*b*) *Name the structure labelled C.*
(*c*) *Name the structure B, which is enclosed by structure C.*
(*d*) *Name the part of the kidney tubule marked E.*
(*e*) *Name the fluid found in C.*
(*f*) *What happens to some of the sodium chloride at the point marked D?*
(*g*) *The concentration of sodium chloride in the tubule is lower than the concentration in plasma. By what process is sodium chloride transferred from the tubule to the plasma in the blood vessel?*

[Total 10]

[CAM]

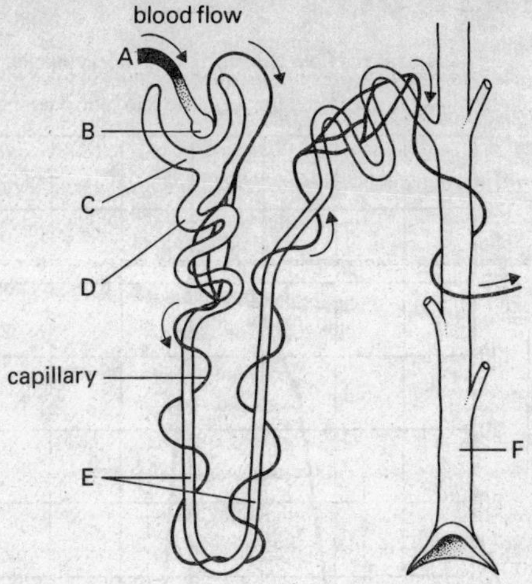

3. (a) Draw a labelled diagram of a nephron. [5]
(b) Describe the rolé of the nephron in
(i) the formation of urine,
(ii) osmoregulation. [15]
[JMB]

4. The graph on page 172 shows the rate of blood flow through muscle tissue and skin in the lower leg of a resting man. After 20 minutes the normal constant room temperature is suddenly raised, kept at this new level for 60 minutes, and then suddenly returned to its former lower constant level (20°C).
(a) From the graph describe the change in blood supply to the lower leg with the sudden rise *in room temperature.* [3]
(b) Explain how the changes described in (a) are brought about. [7]
(c) From the graph describe the change in blood supply to the lower leg with the sudden fall *in room temperature.* [4]
(d) Explain how the changes described in (c) are brought about. [6]
[LON]

5. (a) Why is it important for the temperature inside the body to be kept at about 37°C? [4]
(b) What changes take place in the body when a person moves from a cold room to a warm place at 30°C? How do the changes help the person to keep his body temperature constant? [8]

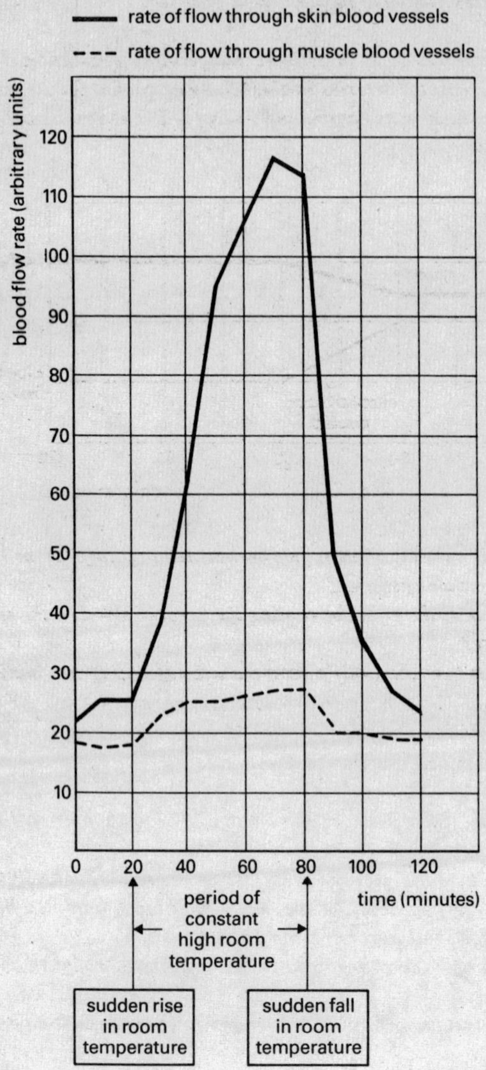
rate of flow through skin blood vessels
rate of flow through muscle blood vessels
blood flow rate (arbitrary units)
120
110
100
90
80
70
60
50
40
30
20
10
0
20
40
60
80
100
120
time (minutes)
period of constant high room temperature
sudden rise in room temperature
sudden fall in room temperature

(*c*) *Make a large, clear drawing of a section through human skin to show the structures you have mentioned in part* (*b*). [8]

[CAM]

6. *In an experiment to investigate temperature regulation, blood passing through the carotid arteries to the head was cooled for 30 minutes, whilst body temperature was continuously recorded. The results are shown in the graph below.*

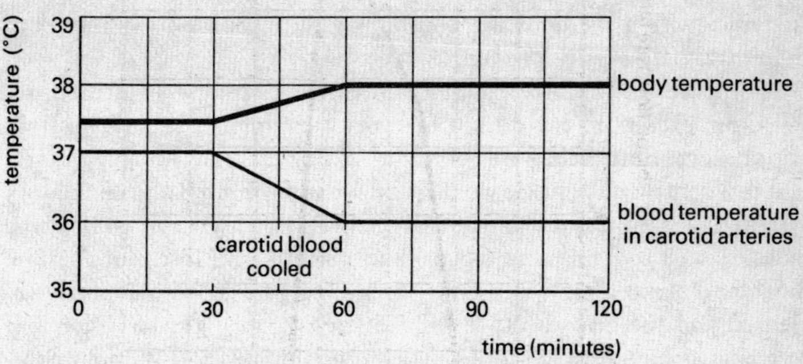

(*a*) *For this subject, what is the normal temperature* (*i*) *in the body and* (*ii*) *in the carotid arteries?* [2]

(*b*) (*i*) *What is the effect of cooling the carotid blood on the subject's body temperature?* [1]

(*ii*) *Explain how the body's temperature-regulating mechanisms produce this effect.* [17]

[LON]

11. Control and Coordination

Activities within the body are coordinated in response to stimuli both *from inside and outside the body.*

The processes we have examined in earlier chapters – nutrition, respiration, excretion, etc. do not take place completely separately from one another. Rather they are coordinated. For example, aerobic respiration in a contracting muscle would soon cease if the lungs and circulatory system failed to deliver enough oxygen. During exercise, contracting muscles need to gain more oxygen and glucose, and lose more carbon dioxide. To meet these demands, breathing rate is automatically increased and the heart beats faster. This results in a greater volume of oxygenated blood being sent to the contracting muscles. Without coordination, bodily activities would soon break down; for example, a runner would collapse after a few metres through lack of an increased oxygen supply to his/her muscles.

The activities of organs and organ systems are not only closely linked to each other but are also linked to changes outside the body. In response to environmental changes the human body makes adjustments which tend to keep its internal conditions constant (see homeostasis, page 155). Thus, patterns of activity in the body react to external as well as internal changes. For example, changes in temperature of the surroundings result in appropriate responses in behaviour e.g. putting on or taking off extra layers of clothes.

Coordination in the human body is brought about by two systems:

1. the **nervous system** which uses electrical **nerve impulses**;
2. the **endocrine system** which uses chemical messengers called **hormones**.

11.1. *The Human Nervous System*

The nervous system is divided into two parts:

1. the **central nervous system** (CNS) – the brain and spinal cord;
2. the **peripheral nervous system** (PNS) – the nerves which run into and out of the CNS.

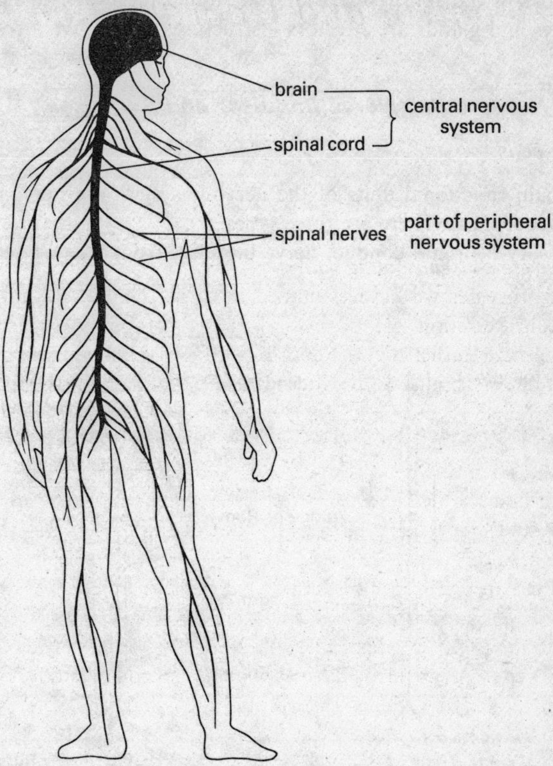

Fig. 11.1. *The human nervous system*

Information is transmitted through the nervous system in the form of nerve impulses (local electric currents set up by the flow of sodium ions – page 178). Stimuli from inside or outside the body trigger **sensory receptors** to generate nerve impulses. These impulses travel along **sensory nerve cells** into the CNS. The CNS 'processes' the information contained in the incoming nerve impulses and can make decisions on the basis of this and other information stored in memory. The CNS generates nerve impulses which then travel along **motor nerve cells** to **effectors**, which give an appropriate response to the original stimulus.

Examples of sensory receptors are sense organs such as the eye (page 190) and the ear (page 198) and various sensory cells such as pressure receptors in the skin (page 165) and stretch receptors in the muscles. Muscles and glands are effectors – structures which give a response.

11.2. *Nerve Cells, Nerve Impulses and Synapses*

Nerve cells

The main functional units of the nervous system are nerve cells (also called neurones). There are three types:

1. **Sensory neurones** conduct nerve impulses from sensory receptors to the CNS.

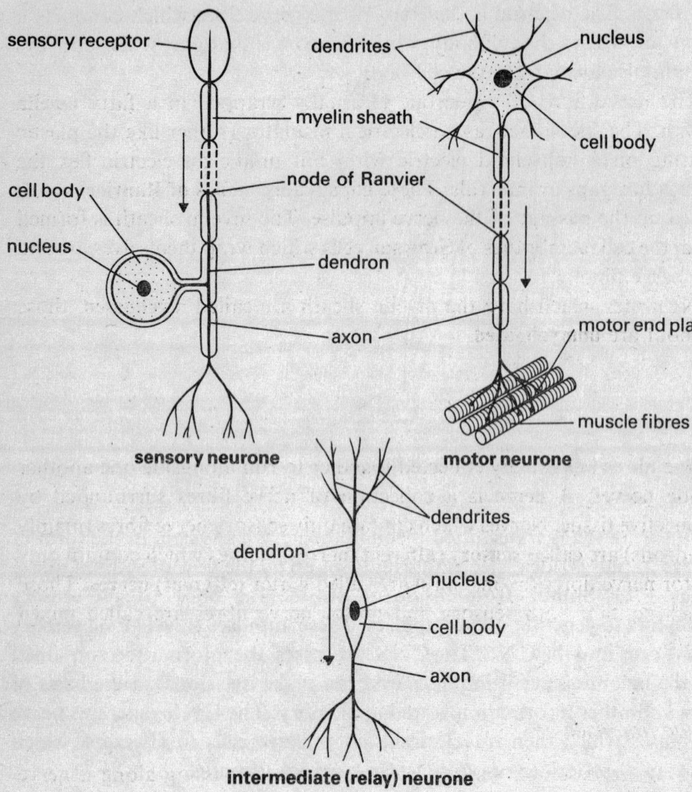

Fig. 11.2. *Three types of nerve cell (neurone)*

2. **Intermediate** (also called **relay** or **connector**) **neurones** transmit nerve impulses within the CNS.
3. **Motor neurones** conduct nerve impulses from the CNS to effectors.

The three types of nerve cells are illustrated in Fig. 11.2. You should learn these diagrams well – questions on sensory or motor neurones in particular regularly come up in exams. A nerve cell functions by sending nerve impulses from one part of the cell to another. In sensory and motor neurones, the cell is elongated so that the nerve impulse can be conveyed a long distance. The elongated part of the nerve cell is called the **nerve fibre**. The swollen part of the cell containing the nucleus is called the **cell body**.

In comparing sensory and motor neurones notice the position of the cell body. The **dendron** is that part of the nerve fibre which conducts a nerve impulse to the cell body, while the **axon** is that part which conveys the impulse away from the cell body.

The nerve fibre of a neurone is usually wrapped in a fatty **myelin sheath**. The sheath acts as an electrical insulator (rather like the plastic coating on a household electric wire) but unlike an electric flex the sheath has gaps at intervals. These gaps (called **nodes of Ranvier**) act to speed up the passage of the nerve impulse. The myelin sheath is formed from the cell membranes of **Schwann cells** which wrap themselves around the nerve fibre.

Neurones which have the myelin sheath are called **myelinated**, those without are **unmyelinated**.

Nerves

Nerve fibres are usually collected together to run alongside one another inside nerves. A **nerve** is a collection of nerve fibres surrounded by connective tissue. Nerves which contain only sensory nerve fibres (mainly dendrons) are called **sensory (afferent) nerves**. Nerves which contain only motor nerve fibres (axons only) are called **motor (efferent) nerves**. Those which contain both sensory and motor nerve fibres are called **mixed nerves**.

Nerve impulses

A nerve impulse is a wave of electrical activity passing along a nerve fibre. When a nerve is in its **resting state** it is positively charged on the outside and negatively charged on the inside. There is a potential difference of about 90 millivolts (mV) between the inside and the outside of the fibre.

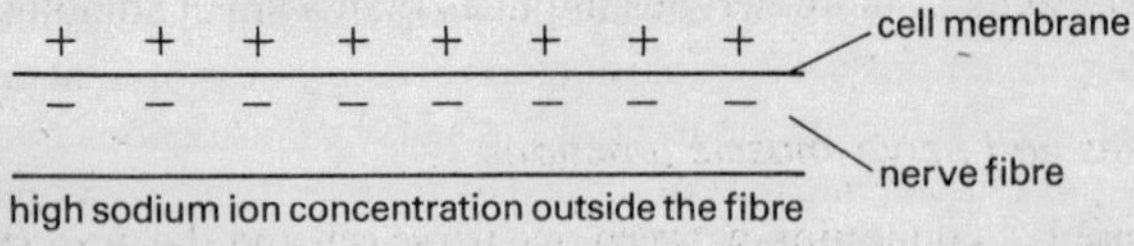

Fig. 11.3. *A nerve fibre in its resting state*

A nerve impulse can be triggered in a nerve fibre in a variety of ways – mechanically, electrically or chemically. Stimulation causes sodium ions to rush into the nerve fibre across the cell membrane. If the stimulation is strong enough it causes the charge across the membrane to become temporarily reversed. This is called **depolarization** and results in a nerve impulse being produced. Depolarization in one part of a membrane sets up an electric current which triggers depolarization in the membrane nearby. As a result, the nerve impulse travels along the fibre.

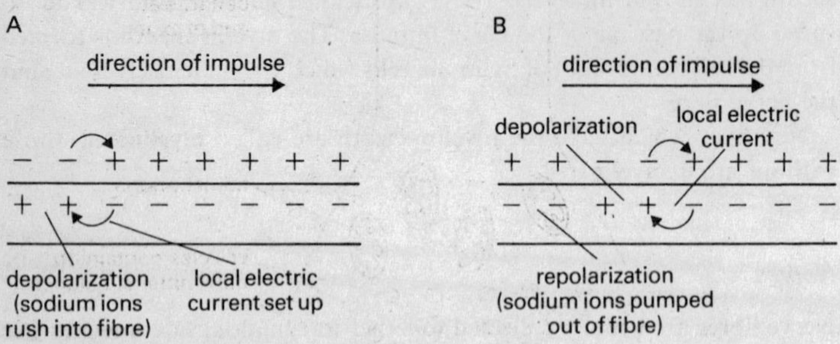

Fig. 11.4. *Transmission of a nerve impulse*

After the impulse has passed, the sodium ions are 'pumped' out of the fibre so bringing it back to its original resting state and restoring the potential difference. The 'pumping' action is an example of active transport (page 76), and requires energy from ATP. Nerve tissue always has a good blood supply bringing glucose and oxygen for respiration.

For a given nerve fibre, the speed and size of the nerve impulse are always the same. Impulses travel rapidly along myelinated fibres (those covered in a fatty myelin sheath). The depolarization jumps from one node of Ranvier to the next giving a speed of travel about one hundred times faster than in unmyelinated fibres.

Nerve fibres obey the **'all-or-none' rule**. If the stimulus is below the **response threshold**, no impulse is produced. Above the threshold, the impulse is always of the same intensity. Above the threshold, a strong stimulus results in more nervous impulses than a small stimulus.

Synapses and nerve–muscle junctions

A synapse is a connection between one nerve cell and the next. (See Fig. 11.5.) It is across the synapse that a nerve impulse is passed from one cell to another. The synapse allows transmission in only one direction so, as a rule, nerve impulses travel along a nervous pathway in one direction only. When a nerve impulse reaches a synapse it causes the release of a chemical **transmitter** substance. This substance diffuses rapidly across the gap in the synapse and triggers off a fresh impulse in the cell on the other side. The transmitter substance is then rapidly removed to allow new impulses to be transmitted across.

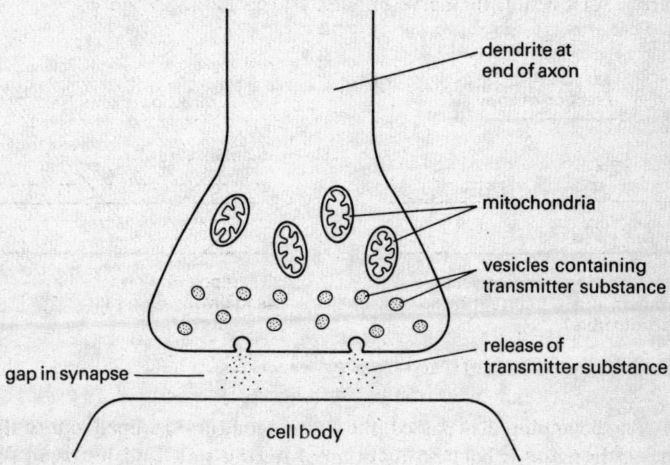

Fig. 11.5. *A synapse*

Chemical transmission is also found at the gap between a nerve cell and a muscle fibre. At a **nerve–muscle junction** the nerve cell axon is splayed out to form a **motor end plate** (see Fig. 11.6). There is a gap between the motor end plate and the muscle fibre. A transmitter substance, usually **acetyl choline**, is released when a nerve impulse arrives at

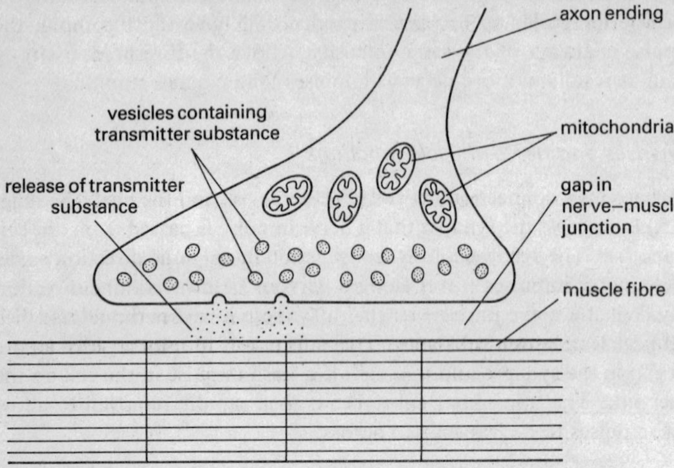

Fig. 11.6. *A nerve–muscle junction (structures not drawn to scale)*

the end plate. The substance diffuses across the gap and triggers contraction in the muscle fibre.

11.3. *Reflex Actions*

Simple reflexes

Definition: A reflex action *is a rapid, automatic (involuntary) response to a stimulus.*

Reflex actions are involved in homeostasis (keeping conditions in the body constant) and in preventing damage to the body. For example, changes in breathing rate during exercise occur automatically without conscious control. This reflex action is a homeostatic function: it serves to keep the blood carbon dioxide level roughly constant. The rapid removal of a hand from a hot object occurs without conscious control. If you waited to 'think' about what response to give, your hand could well be burnt. Instead, the brain is bypassed and preventative action taken before the brain 'decides'. Other examples of reflex actions which have a protective function include suddenly blinking when an object comes towards the eye, or coughing when the throat (pharynx) or windpipe (trachea) is irritated.

In reflex action, the nervous pathway between receptor and effector is known as a reflex arc. Simple reflex arcs normally have five components:

sensory receptor → sensory neurone →
intermediate (relay) neurone → motor neurone → effector

(the arrows show the direction of travel of the nerve impulses).

The reflex arc for the knee jerk reflex is unusual in having only four components: an intermediate (relay) neurone is not involved. The reflex arc for the hand withdrawal reflex is shown in Fig. 11.7.

Study this diagram carefully: in an exam you might have to draw this, or a similar reflex arc, or you may have to label or comment on one provided. Note the position of the different types of neurone and their cell bodies. The sensory neurone runs through the dorsal root of the spinal cord whereas the motor neurone runs through the ventral root. Cell bodies of the intermediate and motor neurones form the H-shaped zone of grey matter in the spinal cord. Cell bodies of the sensory neurones are collected together in the dorsal root ganglion.

The diagram is a simplification. Not one, but hundreds of reflex arcs are involved in the reflex withdrawal of a hand from a hot object.

Reflexes which involve the spinal cord only and not the brain, are called **spinal reflexes**. Although the brain is not directly involved in these reflex arcs, it does not mean the brain is not informed of these events. Although your hand may be removed automatically from a hot object, a short time later you will feel pain and may let out a cry. The intermediate neurone in the reflex arc has synapses with other intermediate neurones which convey nerve impulses up the spinal cord to the brain. Also, nerve impulses can be sent down from the brain via intermediate neurones to modify reflex actions. For example, the simple reflex response to picking up a very hot object might be to drop it. However, if the object is a pan of boiling water, the person may place the pan down safely rather than spill the contents all over him- or herself. Impulses from the brain have overridden the simple reflex. Connections between reflex arcs and the brain enable reflex actions to be modified by experience. Conditioned reflexes are examples of such modifications.

Conditioned reflexes

In most simple reflexes, the stimulus and response are related. For example, the chemical stimulus of food in the mouth triggers the salivary reflex (secretions of saliva). After a period of learning or training, however, it is possible for a different and often irrelevant stimulus to produce

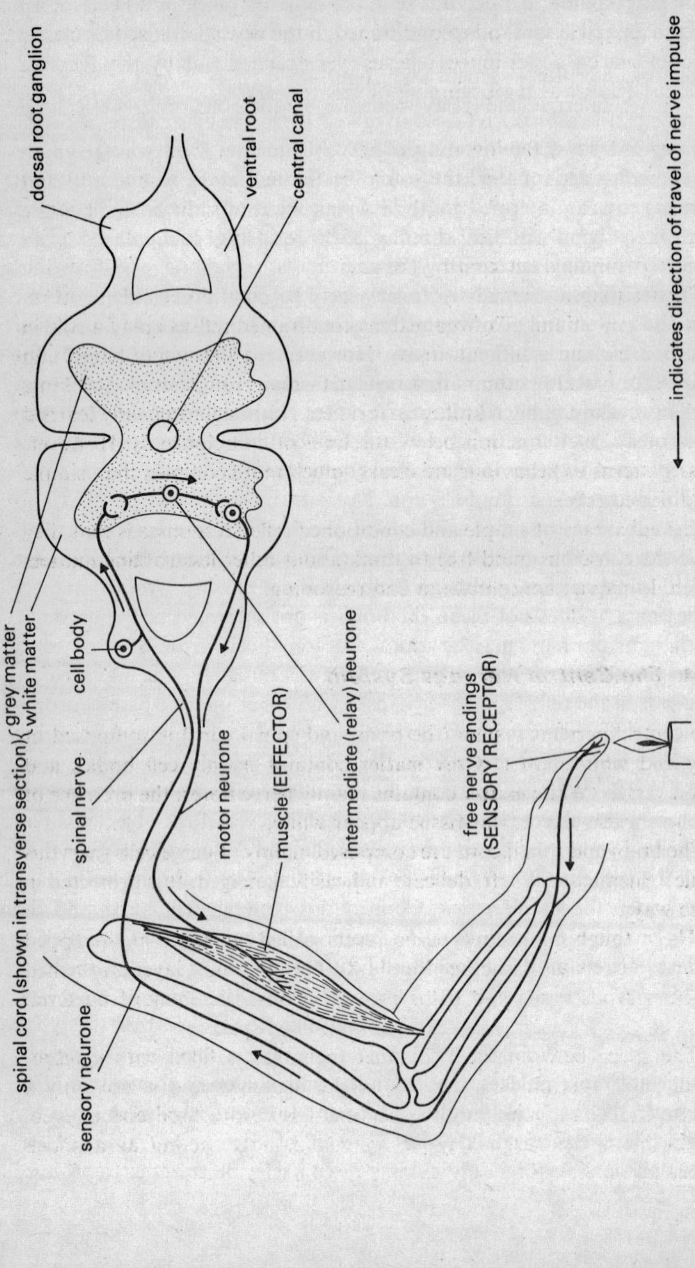

Fig. 11.7. *A reflex arc for the hand withdrawal reflex*

the same response. In such a case a 'conditioned reflex' has been set up and the animal is said to be conditioned to the new stimulus. The classic experiments on conditioned reflexes were carried out by the Russian biologist Pavlov at the beginning of this century.

In dogs, the salivary reflex is triggered by the smell or taste of food. For several days, Pavlov rang a bell at the time food was given to experimental dogs. Later, the sound of the bell alone was a sufficient stimulus to cause a dog's mouth to water, without sight or smell of the food. The original chemical stimulus of the food has been replaced by an unrelated stimulus detected by the ears.

The training of animals is done largely by conditioning them to respond to new stimuli. To what extent conditioned reflexes play a role in human behaviour is difficult to say. However, the learning of habits and basic skills probably occurs in a similar fashion. For example, walking, running, cycling, using a knife and fork, etc., although originally learned consciously, later function below the level of consciousness. However, these patterns of behaviour are clearly much more complex than simple conditioned reflexes.

The advantage of simple and conditioned reflex responses is that they leave the conscious mind free to think about other less routine matters which do require concentration and reasoning.

11.4. *The Central Nervous System*

The central nervous system (the brain and spinal cord) is composed of grey and white matter. **Grey matter** contains mainly cell bodies and blood vessels. **White matter** contains mainly nerve fibres; the presence of myelin sheaths makes this tissue appear white.

The brain and spinal cord are composed mainly of nerve cells (nervous tissue). Such tissue is soft, delicate and easily damaged. It is protected in three ways:

1. Three tough connective tissue layers called **meninges** are wrapped around the nervous tissue (see Fig. 11.8). The innermost layer is attached to the nervous tissue and helps protect against the entry of bacteria. Between this layer and the next is a fluid-filled space.
2. The space between the two inner meninges is filled with **cerebrospinal fluid**. This fluid is secreted by the meninges and is not only a nutritive medium, supplying the nervous tissue with food and oxygen, but cushions the nervous tissue against damage, acting as a shock absorber.

3. Outside the meninges, the nervous and connective tissue is encased in *bone*. The skull (page 215) encases the brain, while the vertebral column (page 216) encases the spinal cord.

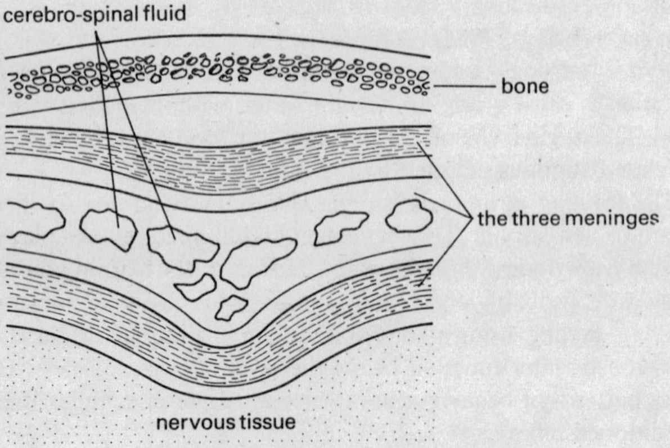

Fig. 11.8. *The protective layers encasing the central nervous system*

The spinal cord

The spinal cord in cross-section (see Fig. 11.7) comprises white matter (mainly nerve fibres) surrounding an H-shaped zone of grey matter (mainly cell bodies). There is a **central canal** which contains cerebro-spinal fluid. You should memorize this arrangement.

The spinal cord is surrounded and protected by the vertebral column. At regular intervals pairs of spinal nerves leave the spinal cord and run between the cartilage-filled gap between one vertebra and the next. Where the spinal nerve comes out of the spinal cord it is in two parts called roots. The **dorsal root** contains sensory nerve fibres which run into the CNS. The **ventral root** contains motor nerve fibres running out of the CNS. Soon after leaving the spinal cord, the dorsal and ventral roots join to form a spinal nerve. A spinal nerve is an example of a mixed nerve – it contains both sensory and motor nerve fibres.

The spinal cord has three main functions:

1. It contains the circuitry for reflex arcs involving the muscles or glands of the body, other than those of the head.
2. It provides connections between reflex arcs, both along and across the cord, so that a limited degree of coordination is possible.

3. It acts as a relay station for impulses passing between the brain and the lower parts of the body.

The brain

When the human foetus (page 244) is 2–3 weeks old, the brain develops as a swelling of the anterior (front) end of the spinal cord. This swelling is made up of three regions: the **fore-brain**, **mid-brain** and **hind-brain**. The hind-brain and mid-brain are the more primitive parts of the brain and are largely concerned with involuntary (automatic) activities. In the adult brain, the three regions are not clearly distinguishable due to the great expansion of the fore-brain to form the **cerebral hemispheres** or **cerebrum**. This is the largest part of the brain and spreads out and covers much of the rest of the brain.

The major parts of the human brain are as follows (see Fig. 11.9):

1. Derived from the **hind-brain**:

The **medulla oblongata** is the central part of the **autonomic nervous system** (see section 11.5). This system coordinates internal and mainly unconscious (involuntary) activities such as regulation of body temperature, blood pressure, and rates of heartbeat and breathing.

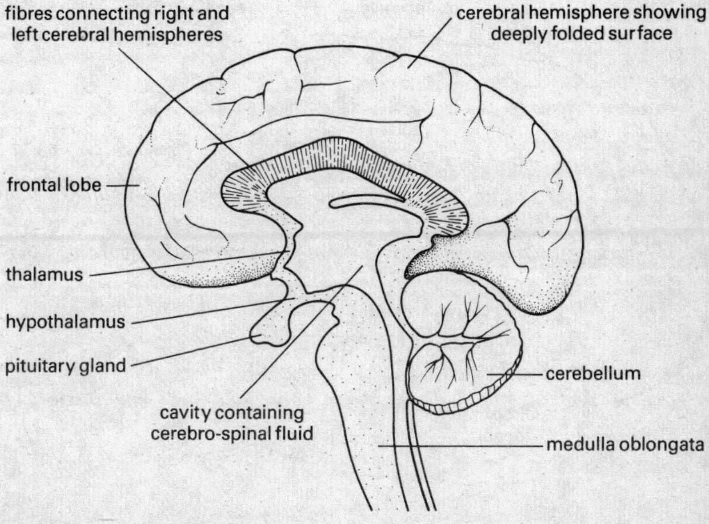

Fig. 11.9. *V.S. of the human brain*

The **cerebellum** is a reflex centre which receives nerve impulses from the organs of balance in the inner ear (page 200) and from stretch receptors in joints and muscles. The cerebellum coordinates the actions of skeletal muscles. This enables body balance and posture to be maintained and enables coordinated movement e.g. handling objects, walking, running or riding a bicycle.

2. Derived from the **mid-brain**:

The **thalamus** is a relay centre, directing sensory nerve impulses to appropriate parts of the cerebral hemispheres.

The **hypothalamus**, a small downfold below the thalamus, is a reflex centre concerned with homeostatic functions. It contains cells which act as sensory receptors in the reflex mechanisms which control body temperature (page 166), the O.P. of body fluids (page 162) and the glucose concentrations of blood (page 98). The hypothalamus also contains groups of cells which control sleep and wakefulness and appetite and thirst.

3. Derived from the **fore-brain**:

The **cerebrum** makes up the largest part of the human brain and consists of two **cerebral hemispheres**. These have a greatly folded sur-

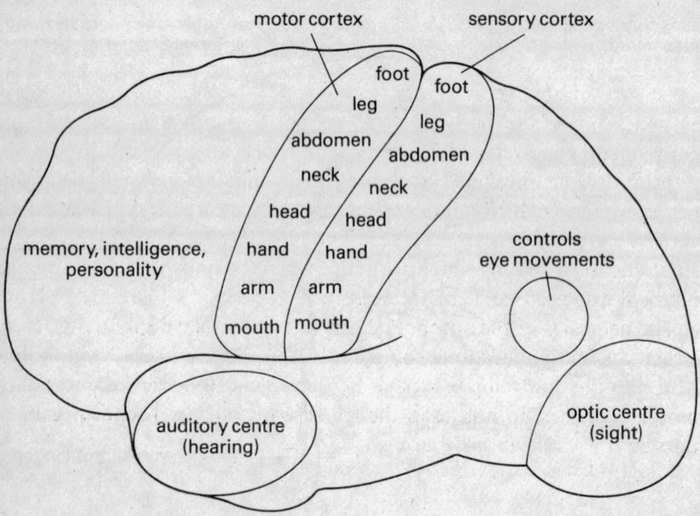

Fig. 11.10. *Functional areas of the cerebral cortex*

face which forms a complex outer layer called the **cerebral cortex**. This is richly supplied with blood vessels to provide food and oxygen.

Within the cerebral cortex, a layer of grey matter (mainly cell bodies and their connections) lies outside white matter (mainly nerve fibres). The cortex is deeply folded to increase the surface area of grey matter, so that many cell bodies and their connections can be packed together.

All parts of the cortex have nerve cells of similar appearance, yet different parts of the cortex have different functions. Using stimulation experiments (applying mild electric shocks to different parts of the brain), and by observing the effects of brain damage in accident victims, it is possible to plot a map of the brain's surface to show the functions of different areas. One region of each cerebral hemisphere is called the **motor area**, because shocks applied here result in contraction of muscles in various parts of the body. These regions have connections which pass down the spinal cord to motor neurones. **Motor areas** direct conscious movement of the body.

The lower parts of the brain (the medulla oblongata, cerebellum and hypothalamus) contain reflex centres for controlling many unconscious (involuntary) activities.

11.5. *The Autonomic Nervous System*

This part of the nervous system controls unconscious (involuntary) activities inside the body. It has two parts, the **sympathetic** and the **parasympathetic** systems. These systems work antagonistically (in opposition to one another). In general, the sympathetic system transmits nerve impulses which stimulate the organs concerned with immediate activity e.g. running away. Nerve impulses in the parasympathetic system stimulate those organs which are active when the body is not undergoing physical exercise (see Table 11.1).

The neurones of the autonomic nervous system have slightly different structures and connections compared with other neurones. Autonomic neurones are unmyelinated (page 177) and the cell bodies of autonomic motor neurones do not lie in the spinal cord but are found in ganglia outside it.

Table 11.1. *Summary of some of the antagonistic effects of sympathetic and parasympathetic nervous systems*

	Body physically active	*Body at rest*
Activity of autonomic system	Sympathetic system active	Parasympathetic system active
Effect	Speeds up heartbeat. Speeds up breathing rate. Effect is to prepare body for physical activity. Constricts arterioles of the gut and associated glands. Reduces peristalsis of the gut. Overall effect is to reduce digestive activity	Slows down heartbeat. Slows down breathing rate. Dilates arterioles of the gut and associated glands. Increases peristalsis of the gut. Overall effect is to increase digestive activity

11.6. *Voluntary Actions*

Voluntary actions require conscious thought and involve the cerebral cortex of the brain. Table 11.2 compares the key features of simple reflex actions with those of voluntary actions.

Table 11.2. *Comparison of a simple reflex and a voluntary action*

Simple reflex action	*Voluntary action*
1. Response is rapid	Response may be slow
2. Nerve impulses take the shortest route	Nerve impulses take a long route
3. Often the spinal cord is the only part of the CNS involved	The cerebral cortex is always involved
4. The response is involuntary and initiated by the original stimulus	The response is voluntary and initiated by the cerebral cortex
5. Effectors are muscles or glands	Effectors are muscles only

Consider what happens when you choose to pick up a pencil from a table top. The pencil is detected by **sensory cells** in the retina of the eye. These cells transmit nerve impulses via the optic nerve to the visual area of the cerebral cortex (see Fig. 11.10). Also, nerve impulses are directed to an **association area** for decision-making. The association area then passes nerve impulses to the motor area of the central cortex. From here, nerve impulses are sent along relay neurones, via the cerebellum, to the spinal cord. Finally, nerve impulses travel along motor neurones to the muscles of the hand and arm. These muscles contract in a coordinated fashion to enable you to pick up the pencil.

11.7. *Sensory Receptors: Sensory Cells and Sense Organs*

Sensory receptors are specialized cells which convert stimuli into nerve impulses. These cells are points of entry for information entering the nervous system. Sensory receptors may consist of isolated single cells e.g. pressure receptors in the skin (page 165), or they may be collected together to form a highly efficient sense organ e.g. the eye (page 190).

Nerve impulses travelling along sensory neurones are interpreted and identified in the brain.

1. **External receptors** detect stimuli arising from outside the body. The main ones are:

(a) **Skin receptors**, which detect heat, cold, touch, pressure and pain (see Fig. 10.4, page 164). Certain regions of the skin are more sensitive to particular stimuli than others. For example, the tip of the tongue, the lips and fingertips are very sensitive to touch. In these areas the appropriate sensory cells each have their own nerve fibre running to the CNS. In other, less sensitive areas, several sensory cells share the same nerve fibre.

(b) **Olfactory cells** in the roof of the nasal cavity have sensory cilia which extend above the surrounding epithelial cells. The olfactory cells are **chemoreceptors** and provide us with the sense of smell. They detect chemical substances which dissolve in the mucus covering their sensory cilia. Nerve impulses from the olfactory cells are transmitted to the olfactory lobe of the cerebral cortex where the sensation of smell is produced. Much of the so-called 'taste' of food is actually due to the detection of smells given off by food. Both taste and smell are much reduced during a heavy cold because of the thicker layer of mucus covering the sensory cilia.

(c) **Taste receptors** are grouped together in **taste buds** found along the sides of papillae on the surface of the tongue. Each taste receptor cell has an extension of protoplasm which extends into the overlying mucus. Foods dissolved in the mucus can be tasted. There are four types of taste bud, each sensitive to a different primary taste sensation: sweet, sour, salt and bitter. 'Sweet' and 'salt' buds are found at or near the tip of the tongue, 'bitter' at the back, and 'sour' at the sides. For taste, see also olfactory cells (above).

(d) In the retina of the eye, **light receptors**, rods and cones, are sensitive to different wavelengths and intensities of light (see page 194).

(e) In the inner ear (see page 200) **sensory hair cells** in the **organ of Corti** are sensitive to vibrations coming from sound waves. **Sensory hair cells** in the **sacculus**, **utriculus** and **semicircular canals** are sensitive to the orientation and movement of the body.

2. **Internal receptors** respond to stimuli within the body and are often linked with homeostatic mechanisms (page 207):

(a) **The hypothalamus** detects changes in blood temperature (see page 209).

(b) **The hypothalamus** detects changes in blood osmotic pressure (see page 208).

(c) **Chemoreceptors** in the aorta, carotid arteries and respiratory centre are sensitive to carbon dioxide level (see page 208).

(d) **Proprioreceptors** respond to stimuli from muscles and joints. One type, stretch receptors, are embedded in every skeletal muscle in the body, and similar receptors are found in muscle tendons, and in the ligaments of joints (page 221). These receptors provide the brain with information about the degree of tension in each part of the muscular system, and the angle to which each joint is bent. Without proprioreceptors, muscular coordination and locomotion would be impossible.

On all syllabuses, you are required to know in detail the functioning of the external sense organs, the eye and ear.

11.8. *The Eye*

The eye is a remarkable device for focusing light rays and converting them into nerve impulses. These impulses are carried along nerve fibres in the optic nerve to the brain. In the optic centre of the cerebral cortex an image of remarkable precision is produced.

You are unlikely to be asked to draw a detailed fully labelled diagram of the eye (see Fig. 11.11). However, you may well be a given a diagram which you must label. Alternatively, you may have to draw simplified diagrams to illustrate how the eye works (see Figs. 11.13 and 11.14), or

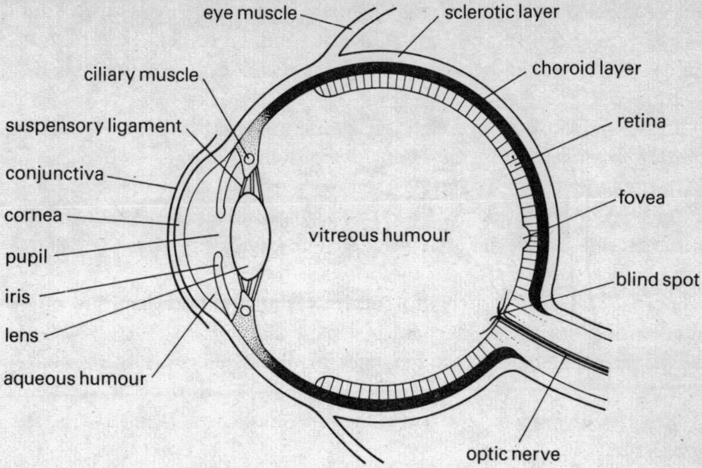

Fig. 11.11 *V. S. of the human eye*

to illustrate how visual defects are caused and how they can be corrected (Figs. 11.15a and b).

The eyes are made up of delicate soft tissues. It is essential that they are protected from mechanical or chemical damage:
– the outer layer of the eyeball, the sclerotic layer, is covered with fatty tissue to provide padding.
– the eyeballs are situated in the orbits (sockets) of the skull and are surrounded by bone.

Movement of the eyelids (blinking) occurs by reflex action in response to any sudden movement towards the eye. The eyes blink routinely every few seconds to distribute tears over the surfaces of the eyes.

The **tear (lachrymal) glands** are situated above the eye (Fig. 11.12) and secrete tears **(lachrymal fluid)**. Tears are slightly salty and contain the anti-bacterial enzyme **lysozyme**. Tears keep the **conjunctiva** moist, so preventing drying and cracking, and wash away dust. Tears are produced continuously and drain into the **tear (lachrymal) ducts**, which open into the nasal cavity (see Fig. 11.12).

The eye functions by focusing an image on the light-sensitive layer, the retina, at the back of the eye. Light entering the eye takes the following path:

conjunctiva → cornea → aqueous humour
→ pupil → lens → vitreous humour → retina

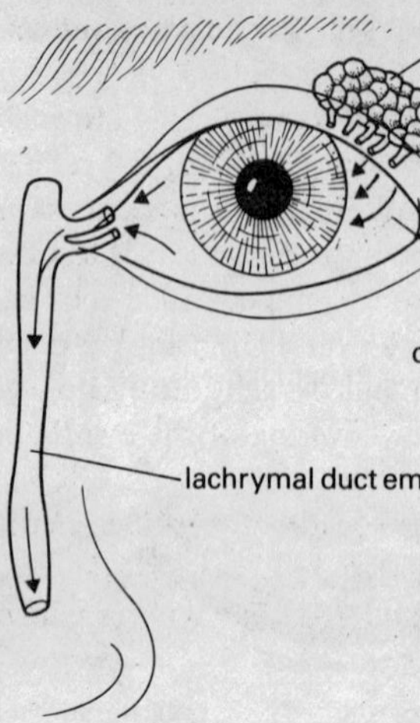

Fig. 11.12. *Position of the lachrymal gland and duct*

To help you remember the structure of the eye, you can think of it as a number of layers. The conjuctiva (the outer covering of the front of the eye) is joined to the eyelids; the cornea and sclerotic layer form a continuous ring; the choroid layer, iris, ciliary body and lens form another ring, while the retina forms the inner lining.

Here are the parts of the eye with a brief mention of their function:

Conjunctiva: a thin layer of transparent epithelial cells protecting the cornea.

Cornea: the transparent part of the sclerotic layer which refracts (bends) light rays towards the retina.

Pupil: the dark spot in the centre of the eye as seen from the front. It is the hole in the iris through which all light enters the eye.

Iris: the coloured part of the eye. It is a muscular diaphragm which alters the size of the pupil and thus adjusts the amount of light entering the eye. It is made up of two sets of involuntary muscles – the radial and circular muscles (see Fig. 11.13).

Aqueous humour: a clear watery fluid which supports the lens and provides the lens and cornea with food and oxygen.

Lens: made up of transparent living cells. It is elastic and focuses light rays on to the retina to form an image.

Ciliary muscle: circular muscles which alter the shape of the lens during focusing (accommodation).

Suspensory ligaments: which hold the lens in place and are attached to the ciliary muscles. They are non-elastic.

Retina: contains the light-sensitive sensory cells, the rods and cones.

Fovea (yellow spot): the most sensitive part of the retina where most light rays are focused. It contains colour-sensitive cones only.

Blind spot: the point where the optic nerve leaves the eye and blood vessels enter and leave. There are no light-sensitive cells here.

Choroid layer: a dark layer which stops light being reflected. It contains blood vessels which supply food and oxygen to other parts of the eye.

Sclerotic layer: the tough outer covering of the eye. It maintains the shape of the eyeball.

Eye muscles: six of these are attached between the sclerotic layer and the skull. They move the eyeball.

Optic nerve: this contains the bundle of nerve fibres which carry nerve impulses to the brain.

Controlling the amount of light entering the eye

The pupil size is adjusted by reflex action according to the prevailing light conditions (light intensity).

In bright light, the circular muscle of the iris diaphragm contracts and the pupil becomes smaller (see Fig. 11.13). This prevents too much light entering the eye and damaging the retina.

In dim light, the radial muscles of the iris diaphragm contract, and the pupil becomes larger, allowing more light to enter. Under these conditions maximum use is made of available light.

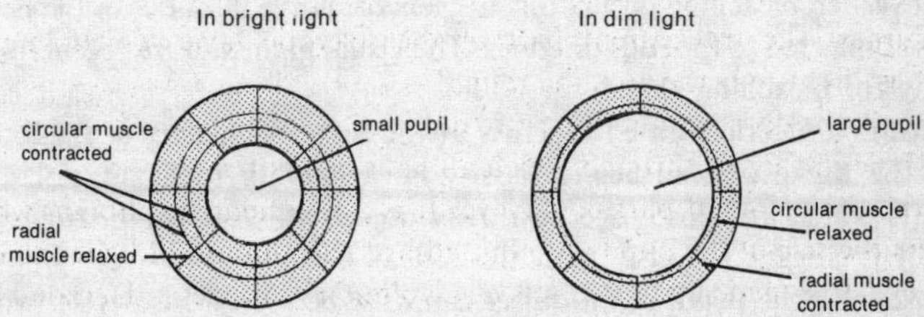

Fig. 11.13. *Altering the amount of light entering the eye: the iris/pupil response to light*

Forming the image on the retina

When light passes from a medium of one density to a medium of another density (e.g. from air to water) the light is normally **refracted** (bent).

Light rays entering the eye are refracted to a large extent by the cornea and to a lesser extent by the lens and aqueous and vitreous humours. This causes the light rays to be focused at a point on the retina. The image so formed on the retina is upside down (inverted). However, within the optic centre of the cerebral cortex of the brain (page 187) the image is 'corrected' and is interpreted as 'right way up'.

The retina

The retina is the part of the eye where light is converted into nerve impulses. The retina is made up of two types of sensory cell, rods and cones.

Rods respond to light even at low light intensity. However, rods do not discriminate between light of different wavelengths (colour). The information rods transmit to the brain is interpreted as black, white or shades of grey.

Cones respond only to bright light but they can discriminate between light of different wavelengths i.e. they can detect colour. There are thought to be three types of cone cell, each responding to one of the primary colours, red, green and blue. Light of other colours stimulate varying proportions of the three different cones. For example, orange light will stimulate red-sensitive cones strongly and green-sensitive cones to a lesser extent. Impulses from the cones pass along the optic nerve to the brain. In the optic centre of the cerebral cortex the sensation of colour is produced.

Both rods and cones contain **visual pigments** which are bleached by light. When bleaching occurs this triggers off nerve impulses in the nerve cells connected to the rods or cones. The visual pigments are regenerated, ready for bleaching again.

Cones are concentrated together at the **fovea**. This part of the retina has the highest **visual acuity** (acuity is the ability to distinguish two points which are close together). Any object which is being studied in detail is always focused upon the fovea. Because the fovea contains only cones, the detail of an object can only be seen in relatively bright light.

Rods are most abundant at the edge of the retina and decrease in number towards the fovea. Since rods are more sensitive to light, a dim object can be seen more clearly by gazing slightly to one side of the object, so that its image falls on the retina some distance from the fovea. Rods provide us with vision at night and under poor light conditions. They do not provide detail or colour vision.

Stereoscopic (binocular) vision

Stereoscopic or three-dimensional vision occurs when both eyes focus on the same object. Each eye receives a slightly different view of the object and from these the optic centre in the brain forms a three-dimensional impression. Stereoscopic vision enables distance and depth to be judged accurately.

Focusing (accommodation)

The eye is able to focus on objects at different distances by altering the shape (curvature) of the lens.

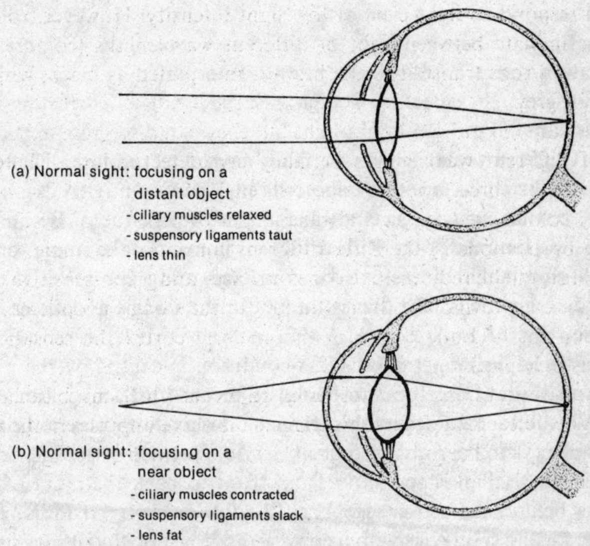

Fig. 11.14. *The human eye: focusing (accommodation)*

Adaptation for distant vision

When an object is a long distance away, the light rays reflected from it are almost parallel when they enter the eye. They have to be refracted (bent) by a small amount to be focused on the retina. A flattened (thin) lens shape is required. This is brought about as follows:

1. The ciliary muscles relax and the pressure of the vitreous humour pushes them outwards.
2. This causes the suspensory ligaments to be pulled taut.

3. The lens is pulled out into a flattened (thin) shape (see Fig. 11.14a).

Adaptation for near vision

When an object is close to the eye, the light rays reflected from it are diverging (moving apart) when they enter the eye. They need to be refracted to a larger degree to be focused on the retina. A rounded (fat) lens shape is required. This is brought about as follows:

1. The ciliary muscles contract.
2. The suspensory ligaments slacken.
3. The elastic lens springs back to a more rounded (fatter) shape (see Fig. 11.14b).

For technical reasons, the pupil size tends to be smaller when focusing on a close object.

Defective vision

Questions on sight defects, together with the means of correcting them, are popular.

1. **Short sight (myopia)**: This is normally caused by the eyeball being too long (from front to back). A short-sighted person can focus on near objects, but far-away objects always appear out of focus. Because the eyball is too long the point of clear focus is in front of the retina (see Fig. 11.15a). Short-sightedness can be corrected using spectacles (glasses) with a diverging lens; one that is thinner in the middle and fatter at the sides (see Fig. 11.15a).

2. **Long sight (hypermetropia)**: This condition is caused by the eyeball being too short (from front to back) or because the lens is not elastic enough. A long-sighted person can focus on far-away objects but near objects always appear out of focus.

When the eyeball is too short from front to back the point of clear focus is behind the retina (see Fig. 11.15b). Long-sightedness can be corrected using spectacles with a converging lens; one that is fatter in the middle and thinner at the edges (see Fig. 11.15b).

Later in life, a person may become long-sighted, not because the eyeball is too short, but because the lens has lost its elasticity. The lens remains thin for distant vision and does not fatten for close-focusing. For close-up work older people usually require 'reading glasses' which have converging lenses.

3. **Night blindness**: This is a deficiency disease caused by lack of vitamin A (page 82). Vitamin A is needed to make rhodopsin, the visual pigment found in rod cells. Shortage of the vitamin can thus affect night vision.

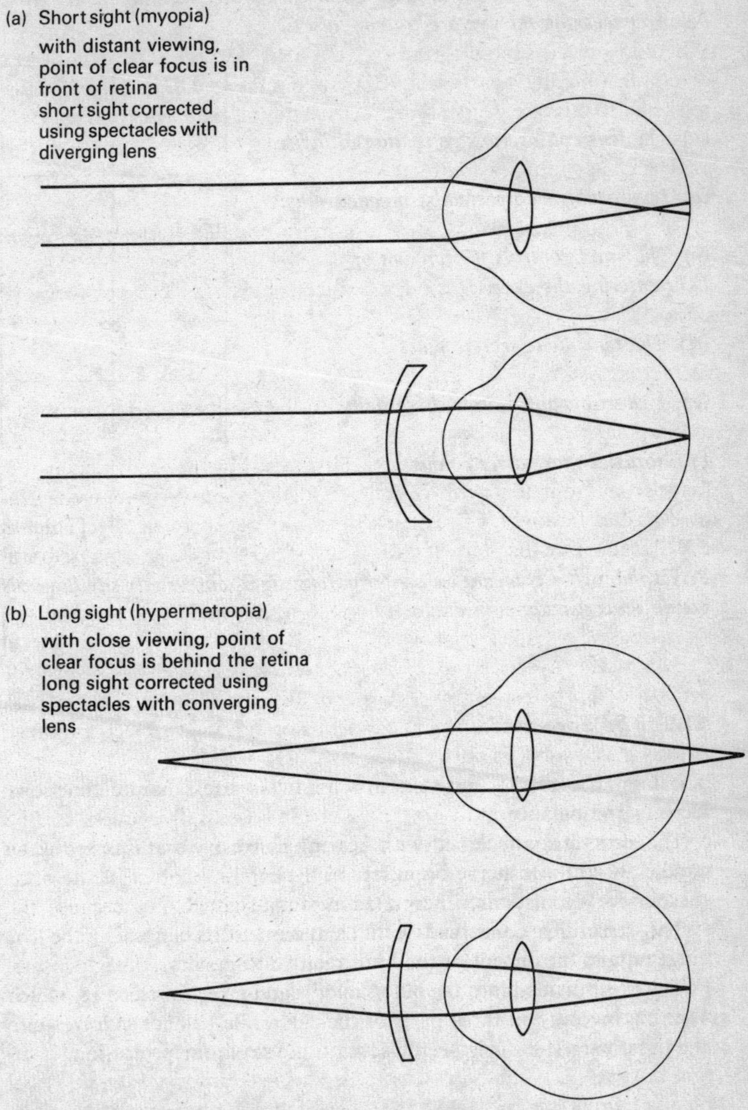

Fig. 11.15. *The human eye: sight defects and their correction*

Now try the following questions:

1. Indicate, by ticking the appropriate box, whether the statements given below concerning the eye are true or false.

	TRUE	FALSE
(*a*) *The lens causes most refraction of light.*		
(*b*) *Long sight is corrected by a concave lens.*		
(*c*) *The pupil controls the amount of light entering the eye.*		
(*d*) *The tear ducts secrete tears.*		
(*e*) *A short eyeball causes short sight.*		
(*f*) *Rods cannot detect colour.*		

[Total 6]

[JMB]

2. Explain what is meant by the term 'long sight' and briefly say how this condition is usually corrected. [4]

[SUJB]

11.9. *The Ear*

The human ear is a sense organ with two quite separate functions: hearing and balance.

The structures concerned with hearing convert vibrations in the air (sound waves) into nerve impulses. In the cerebral cortex of the brain these nerve impulses are interpreted as sound.

The structures concerned with balance detect changes in the orientation and movement of the head relative to gravity.

The ear is divided into the outer, middle and inner ear (see Fig. 11.16). Hearing involves all three parts of the ear, while balance involves only the inner ear. The ear is deeply set into the skull, for protection.

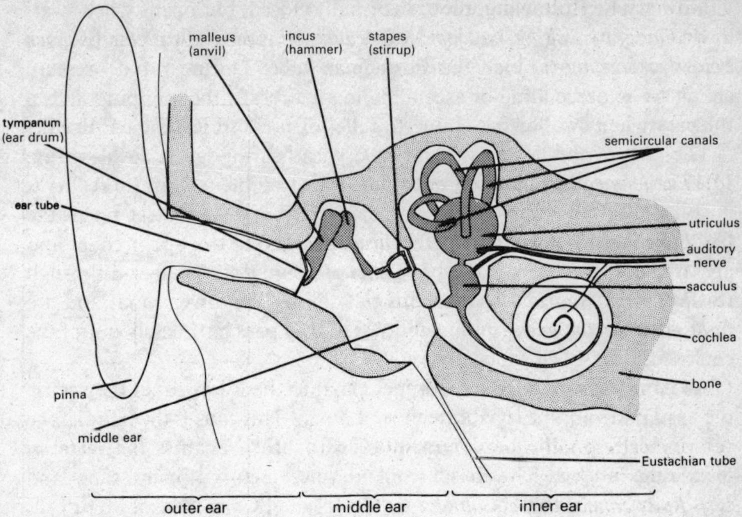

Fig. 11.16. *The human ear*

Hearing

The **outer ear** consists of the **pinna** which collects soundwaves and channels them down the **ear tube** to the **tympanum (ear drum)** which is caused to vibrate. The ear drum is protected and to some extent waterproofed by wax secreted by the lining of the ear tube. Small hairs lining the tube help to keep out insects and dust.

The **middle ear** is an air-filled cavity separated from the outer ear by the ear drum. Opposite the ear drum is a membrane called the **oval window**. Vibrations of the ear drum (caused by sound waves) are transmitted to the oval window by three tiny bones, the **ear ossicles** (the malleus, incus and stapes). The ossicles are held in place by muscles and tendons. They act as a system of levers. They magnify the force of vibrations about twenty times so as to set up vibrations in the fluid of the inner ear.

(NOTE: A greater force is required to set up vibrations in fluid than in air.)

The **Eustachian tube** connects the middle ear to the pharynx. It helps ensure that the air pressure inside the middle ear is the same as that of the outer ear. A large pressure difference between the two can burst the ear drum. A slight pressure difference between the two causes the ear drum to be stretched taut under pressure. This prevents the drum from vibrating. The Eustachian tube is normally closed, but opens when swallowing or yawning. A bad cold can cause temporary deafness because excess mucus may block the Eustachian tube. During rapid pressure changes e.g. descending or ascending in an aircraft, the 'popping' felt in the ears when swallowing is due to relief of pressure on the ear drum.

The part of the **inner ear** concerned with hearing is the **cochlea**. Fig. 11.17 is a simplified diagram of the cochlea straightened out (in reality it is coiled). When the oval window moves, vibrations are set up in the fluid called **perilymph**. These vibrations pass along the upper canal and are transmitted through the **endolymph** of the middle canal and through to the lower canal. The vibrations pass along the lower canal and are dissipated through the round window i.e. they pass harmlessly out of the enclosed, fluid-filled inner ear.

As vibrations pass from the upper canal to the lower canal they cause the **basilar membrane** to vibrate up and down. This causes the hairs of the sensory cells on the basilar membrane to brush against the **tectorial membrane** above. The basilar membrane, tectorial membrane and sensory hair cells together make up the **organ of Corti**. Sensory hair cells brushing against the tectorial membrane trigger nerve impulses in connected sensory neurones. The impulses are transmitted along the **auditory nerve** to the brain where they are interpreted as sound.

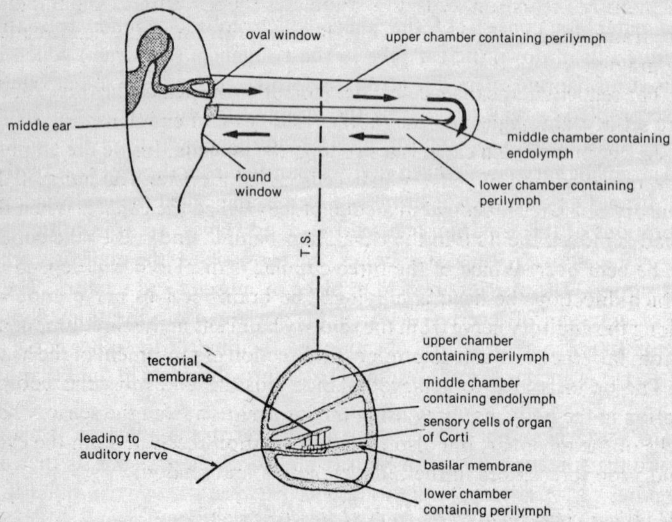

Fig. 11.17. *Detail of inner ear showing the cochlea straightened out*

The basilar membrane becomes thicker further away from the two windows and it is thought that the membrane here is sensitive to lower pitch (lower frequency) sounds. Nearer the windows the basilar membrane is sensitive to higher pitched (higher frequency) sounds. The nerve impulses generated by the sensory hair cells are transmitted along the auditory nerve to the brain. Impulses from low and high pitched notes are sent to different parts of the cerebral cortex.

Clearly the hearing mechanism must be extremely sensitive. It can detect differences in pitch and loudness and also in the quality of sound. A person can distinguish, for example, different musical instruments playing at the same time.

Balance

The **utriculus**, **sacculus** and the three **semicircular canals** are the structures of the inner ear concerned with balance (see Fig. 11.18).

The utriculus and sacculus are two swellings filled with endolymph. They detect the position of the head relative to the pull of gravity. Within these two structures are sensory hair cells, the hairs of which are embedded in a jelly-like mass containing granules of chalk called **otoliths**. Any tilting of the head tends to displace the otoliths and alter the pull on the hairs of the sensory cells; this stimulates the nerve fibres and impulses are transmitted to the brain giving the new position of the head relative to gravity.

The semicircular canals detect movement of the head. The three canals are set at right angles to one another and contain endolymph.

At one end of each canal is a swelling, the **ampulla**. Inside the ampulla is a raised mound of sensory hair cells called a **crista**. The hairs of the sensory cells are embedded in a cone of jelly called the **cupula**. When the head is moved the fluid in the canal 'lags behind' and causes the cupula to be bent over. Which of the three cupulae is displaced will depend on which direction the head is moving. The brain receives nerve impulses along the auditory nerve from the sensory hair cells in the three ampullae. From this, the brain can determine the direction of movement of the head.

The brain is able to achieve balance, posture and muscular coordination in the body, not only using the information from the sensory hair cells of the inner ear, but also from information received from the eyes, and proprioreceptors in the muscles, joints and tendons.

Q1. What part is played by each of the following?
(*a*) *Ear ossicles*

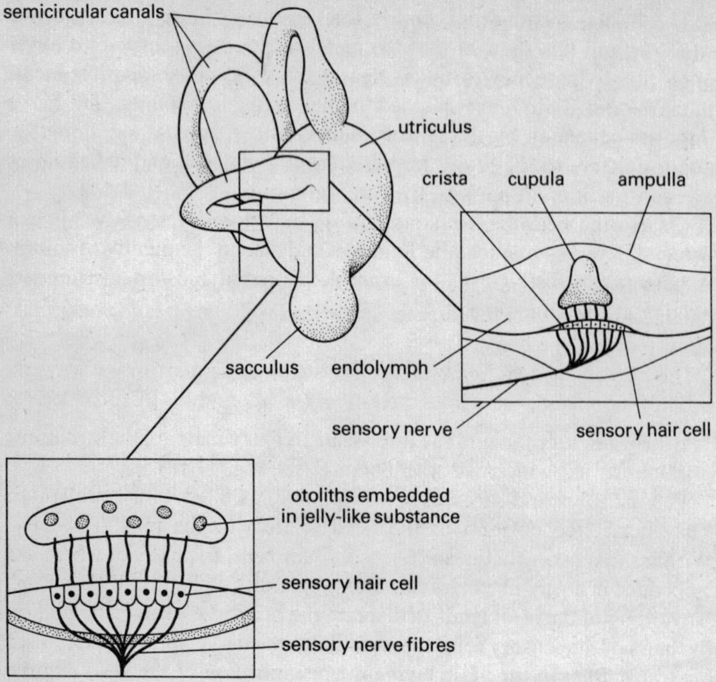

Fig. 11.18. *Detail of inner ear showing the structures concerned with balance*

(*b*) *Auditory (Eustachian) tube*
(*c*) *Cochlea*
(*d*) *Semicircular canals*

[AEB]

Q2. (*a*) *Make a large labelled diagram to show the structure of the ear* [10]
(*b*) *Explain how the ear functions when we listen to music* [11]
(*c*) *What are the other functions of the ear?* [4]

[OXF]

11.10. *The Endocrine System*

The endocrine system is made up of **endocrine (ductless) glands** which secrete 'chemical messengers' called **hormones**. These chemicals are released in minute quantities directly into the blood, rather than through tubes (ducts). Hormones travel through the bloodstream and exert an effect on particular **target organs** or tissues, speeding up or slowing down their activity.

Endocrine glands should not be confused with exocrine glands. **Exocrine glands**, e.g. sweat glands, possess tubes (ducts) which lead out of the body onto the skin or into the digestive system. Their products are secreted onto the surface of the skin or into the lumen of the gut, and *not* into the circulatory system.

The endocrine system, sometimes working together with the nervous system, controls and coordinates growth, development and metabolic activity within the body.

The nervous system and endocrine system are similar in two ways:

1. They are both set into action by a stimulus to produce a response.
2. They both involve chemical transmission. In the case of the nervous system this occurs only across synapses or nerve-muscle junctions, whereas in the endocrine system the chemical, a hormone, travels considerably further.

More usually, the *differences* between nervous and hormonal action are stressed (Table 11.3). In general, the endocrine system controls long-

Table 11.3. *Differences between nervous and hormonal action*

	Nervous	*Hormonal*
1. Method of transmission	Electrical impulse passing along nerve fibre (chemical transmission across synapses)	Chemical passing through bloodstream
2. Speed of transmission	Rapid	Slow
3. Speed of response	Immediate	Usually slow e.g. thyroxine, but may be fast e.g. adrenalin
4. Duration of response	Short-lived	Longer-lasting
5. Localization of response	Response very localized	Response usually widespread e.g. adrenalin

term bodily functions e.g. growth, while the nervous system controls rapid, short-term activities e.g. movement.

The main endocrine glands in the human body are the pituitary, thyroid, parathyroids, adrenals, pancreas and the reproductive organs. The positions of these glands are shown in Fig. 11.19. The pituitary gland, sometimes called the 'master gland', coordinates and controls the activity of the other glands. It releases hormones which stimulate other glands to release their own hormones.

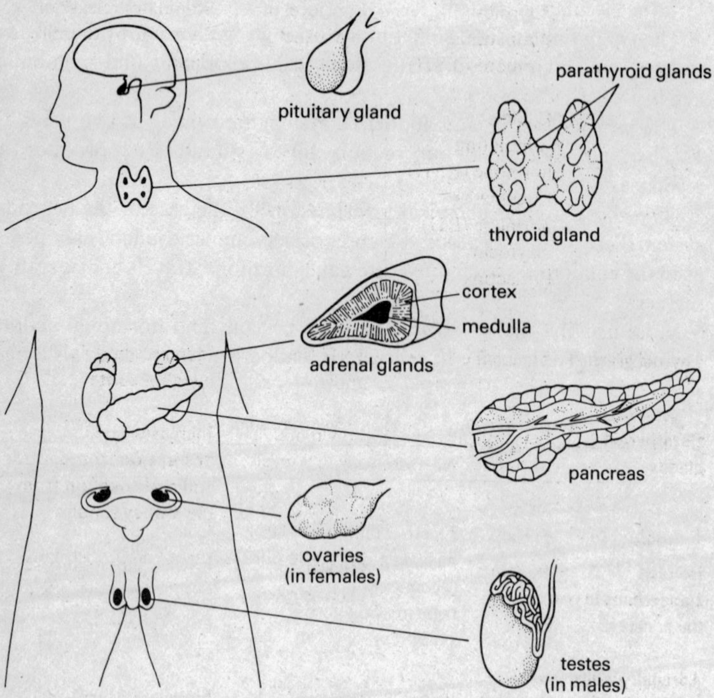

Fig. 11.19. *The main endocrine glands*

The various endocrine glands are listed in Table 11.4 together with their hormones, the stimulus which triggers release of the hormone, and the effect of the hormone on target tissue. Knowledge of these glands, their hormones and their effects is frequently demanded in short-answer papers.

The level of circulating hormone is controlled by a **'feedback'** process;

Table 11.4. *Summary table of human endocrine glands and hormones*

Endocrine gland	*Hormone*	*Stimulus*	*Effect*
Pituitary gland (master gland)	Anti-diuretic hormone (ADH)	High blood O.P.	Increases reabsorption of water from the kidney tubule (see page 160)
	Growth hormone		Stimulates cell division and protein synthesis
	Thyroid-stimulating hormone (TSH)	Low level of thyroxine (feedback)	Stimulates release of thyroxine by thyroid gland
	Follicle-stimulating hormone (FSH) Luteinizing hormone (LH) Oxytocin Prolactin	See pages 238, 239, 248, 249	
Thyroid gland	Thyroxine	TSH (see above)	Increases body's metabolic rate
Parathyroid glands	Parathyroid hormone	Low blood calcium level	Increases calcium absorption from the gut and reabsorption from the kidney tubules
Islets of Langerhans in the pancreas	Insulin	High blood glucose level	Lowers blood glucose level, stimulates glucose uptake by cells
Adrenal glands			
Medulla	Adrenalin (fight or flight hormone)	Danger, fright, stress	Increases heart beat Increases breathing rate Diverts blood flow from gut to brain and muscles. Raises blood glucose level
Cortex	Aldosterone	Low blood O.P.	Increases reabsorption of mineral salts from the kidney tubule

Endocrine gland	*Hormone*	*Stimulus*	*Effect*
	Cortisone	Shock or stress	Stimulates the conversion of proteins to glucose
Ovaries (females only)	Oestrogen	See page 238	Stimulates development and maintenance of secondary sexual characteristics. See also page 255
	Progesterone	See page 238	See page 238
Testes (males only)	Testosterone	See page 235	Stimulates development and maintenance of secondary sexual characteristics. See also page 253

a hormone adjusts its own output by influencing the endocrine glands that cause its secretion. The hypothalamus and pituitary gland monitor hormone levels in the blood. If the level of a particular hormone is too high, the pituitary gland is blocked from releasing the appropriate stimulating hormone. If the hormone level is too low, more stimulating hormone is released. Feedback control provides an effective means of monitoring and maintaining suitable hormone levels in the body. An example is:

Pituitary gland ⟶ TSH ⟶ Thyroid gland

↑ Thyroxine level (feedback) ←

If the thyroxine level in the blood is too high, it blocks the pituitary from releasing TSH. This causes the production of thyroxine to fall, causing the thyroxine level in the blood to fall.

If the thyroxine level in the blood is too low, this stimulates the pituitary to release TSH. The thyroid gland is stimulated to produce more thyroxine, so the thyroxine level in the blood increases.

In this way, the level of thyroxine is kept relatively constant.

In the female menstrual cycle (page 238), feedback between several hormones generates cyclical changes.

Several hormones often affect the level of a substance or an activity in the body. For example, blood glucose level is affected by four hormones: cortisone, adrenalin, thyroxine and insulin. Blood glucose level is raised by the action of cortisone stimulating the conversion of proteins to glucose, and by the action of adrenalin stimulating the conversion of glycogen to glucose. Blood glucose level falls through the action of insulin, stimulating the conversion of glucose to glycogen, and through the action of thyroxine, increasing basal metabolic rate (page 20), so accelerating the breakdown of glucose in respiration.

11.11. *Homeostatic Mechanisms*

In Chapter 10 we looked at homeostasis – keeping conditions constant within the body. The mechanisms involved in homeostasis all follow the same basic plan and involve either nervous or hormonal action, or a combination of the two. This basic plan can be represented as follows:

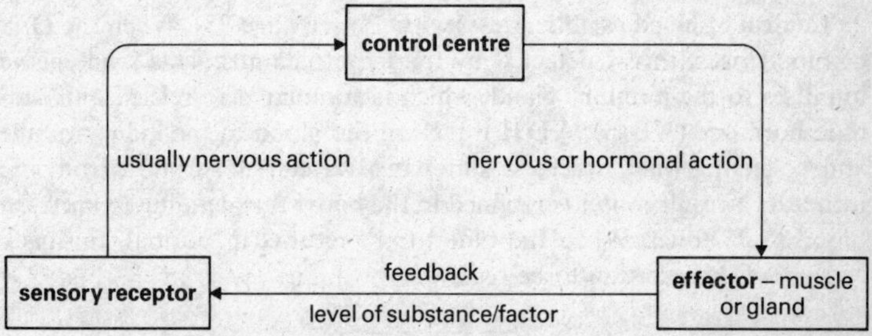

As with the control of hormone levels in the blood, the level of other substances and factors in homeostasis is controlled by feedback.

To understand the above scheme it is best to apply it to a few examples. Once understood, this scheme is very useful in checking your knowledge and understanding of different homeostatic mechanisms. It is also a convenient way of remembering them.

1. **Control of breathing** (see page 119). If the level of carbon dioxide rises, this is sensed by chemoreceptors in the respiratory centre and in the aorta and carotid arteries. These chemoreceptors send nerve impulses to the respiratory centre which responds by increasing the number of nerve impulses to the intercostal and diaphragm muscles. These contract more frequently and more strongly, increasing the ventilation rate (page 119). As a result, excess carbon dioxide in the blood is more rapidly

removed from the body. When the level of carbon dioxide returns to normal, this is sensed by the chemoreceptors. As a result, the respiratory centre sends out fewer nerve impulses to the diaphragm and intercostal muscles and the ventilation rate returns to normal.

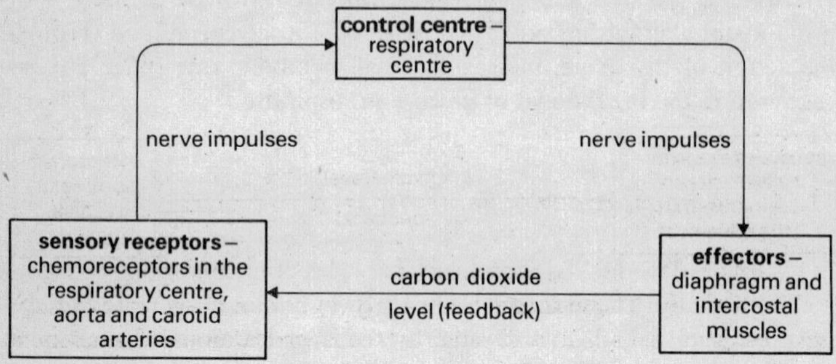

2. **Control of blood osmotic pressure** (O.P.; see page 75). When the O.P. of blood rises, this is detected by the hypothalamus. This sends nerve impulses to the pituitary gland, which is stimulated to release anti-diuretic hormone (ADH). ADH travels in the blood to the kidney tubule and collecting duct, where it stimulates water reabsorption from the urine. As a result, water is retained in the body, thus tending to keep the blood O.P. down. When the blood O.P. returns to normal, feedback causes ADH secretion to be reduced.

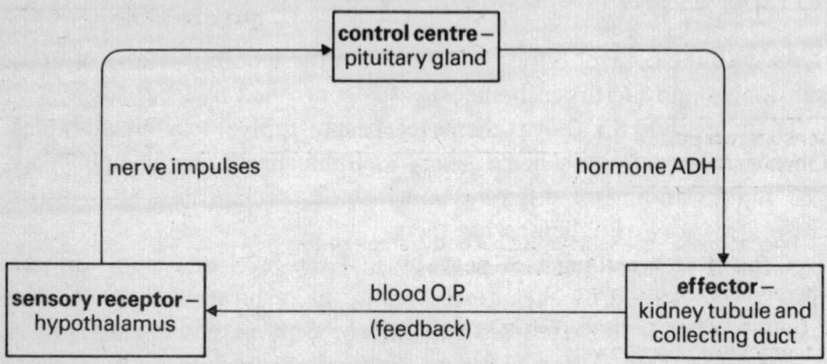

3. **Control of blood glucose level** (see page 98). When blood glucose levels are high, the hormone insulin is released by the islets of Langerhans in the pancreas. This stimulates the uptake of glucose by cells in the

body, and the conversion of glucose to glycogen by the liver and muscles.

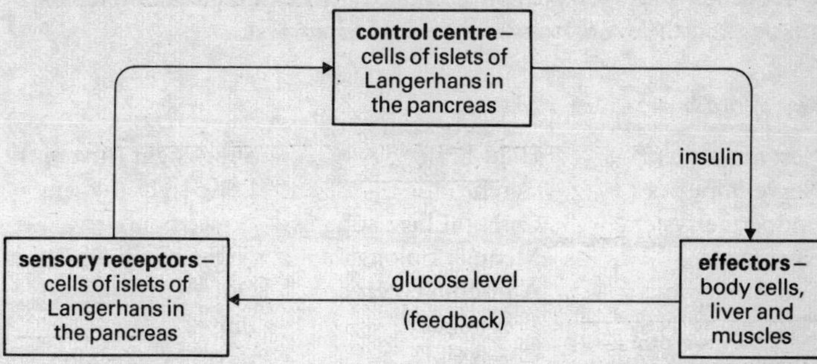

4. **Control of body temperature** (see page 166). When body temperature rises above normal this is detected by the hypothalamus which sends nerve impulses to various effectors in the skin. These respond to increase heat loss through the skin and thus lower body temperature (page 167). When body temperature drops below normal, the hypothalamus sends nerve impulses to effectors in the skin which respond to reduce heat loss. At the same time skeletal muscles may be stimulated to contract (shivering).

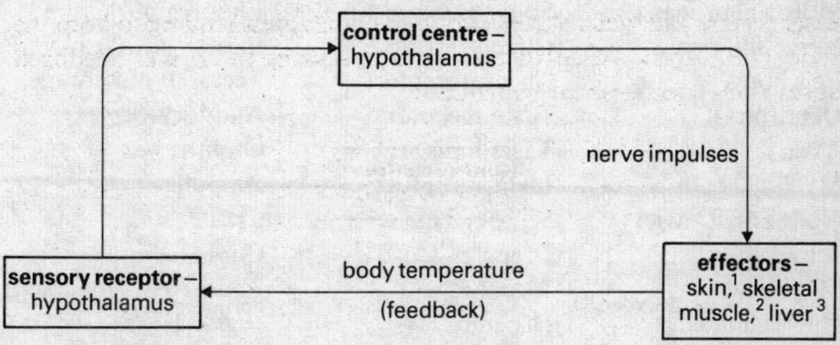

1 The response is vasoconstriction if body temperature is too high, or sweating and vasodilation if body temperature is too low.

2 The response is contraction (shivering) if body temperature is too low.

3 Metabolic rate is increased if body temperature is too low, or decreased if body temperature is too high. Metabolic rate is controlled by the hormones thyroxine and adrenalin.

Definition

Reflex action

Key Words

Nervous system
Nerve impulses
Endocrine system
Hormones
Central nervous system (CNS)
Peripheral nervous system (PNS)
Sensory receptors
Sensory nerve cells
Motor nerve cells
Effectors
Sensory neurones
Intermediate (relay or connector) neurones
Motor neurones
Nerve fibre
Cell body
Dendron
Axon
Myelin sheath
Nodes of Ranvier
Schwann cells
Myelinated
Unmyelinated
Nerve
Sensory (afferent) nerves
Motor (efferent) nerves
Mixed nerves
Resting state
Depolarization
'All-or-none' rule
Hind-brain
Cerebrum
Cerebral hemispheres
Medulla oblongata
Autonomic nervous system
Cerebellum
Thalamus
Hypothalamus
Cerebral cortex
Motor area
Sensory areas
Association areas
Sympathetic
Parasympathetic
External receptors
Skin receptors
Olfactory cells
Chemoreceptors
Taste receptors
Taste buds
Light receptors
Sensory hair cells
Organ of Corti
Sacculus
Utriculus
Semicircular canals
Proprioreceptors
Lachrymal glands
Lachrymal fluid
Lysozyme
Lachrymal ducts
Conjunctiva
Cornea
Pupil
Short sight (myopia)
Long sight (hypermetropia)
Night blindness
Outer ear
Pinna
Ear tube
Tympanum (ear drum)
Middle ear
Oval window
Ear ossicles
Eustachian tube
Inner ear
Cochlea
Perilymph
Endolymph
Basilar membrane
Tectorial membrane
Auditory nerve
Otoliths
Ampulla
Crista
Cupula
Endocrine (ductless) glands
Hormones
Target organs
Exocrine glands
Pituitary gland
Feedback
ADH
Growth hormone
TSH
FSH

Response threshold	Iris	LH
Transmitter	Aqueous humour	Oxytocin
Nerve–muscle junction	Lens	Prolactin
	Ciliary muscle	Thyroid gland
Motor end plate	Suspensory ligaments	Thyroxine
Acetyl choline	Retina	Parathyroid hormone
Spinal reflexes	Fovea (yellow spot)	Islets of Langerhans
Conditioned reflex	Blind spot	Insulin
Grey matter	Choroid layer	Adrenal gland
White matter	Sclerotic layer	Adrenalin
Meninges	Eye muscles	Aldosterone
Cerebro-spinal fluid	Optic nerve	Cortisone
Central canal	Refraction	Ovary
Dorsal root	Rods	Oestrogen
Ventral root	Cones	Progesterone
Fore-brain	Visual pigments	Testis
Mid-brain	Visual acuity	Testosterone

Exam Questions

1. The diagram shows a motor neurone.

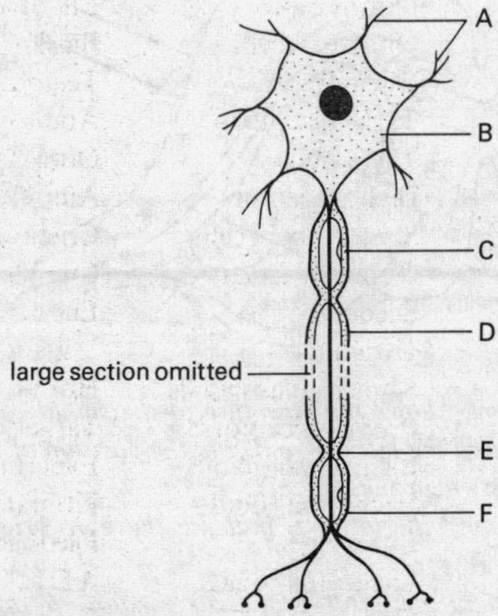

(*a*) *Label the diagram using the guide lines* A–F. [3]
(*b*) *What is the function of a motor neurone?* [1]

(*c*) *State two ways in which the structure of a motor neurone differs from that of a sensory neurone.* [2]

[JMB]

2. *The diagram represents the junction of two nerve cells.*

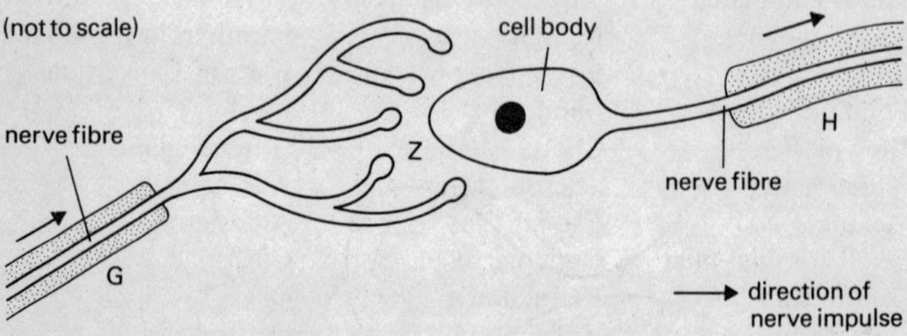

(*a*) *What is the name of the junction, labelled* Z, *between the two nerve cells?* [1]

(*b*) *State the form in which the nerve impulse travels:*

(*i*) *across the gap* Z; [1]

(*ii*) *along the nerve fibres* G *and* H. [1]

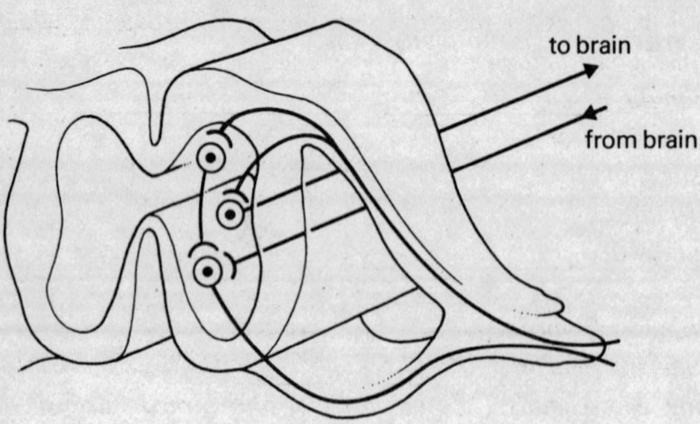

3. *The diagram above shows the structure of the spinal cord.*

(*a*) *With an arrow and the letter* R *indicate the position of the cell body of the sensory (afferent) neurone.* [1]

(*b*) *With an arrow and the letter* S *indicate the fibre originating from a receptor.* [2]

(*c*) *With an arrow and the letter* T *indicate the fibre to an effector.* [2]

(*d*) *In the diagram draw in the spinal canal and label it with the letter* U. [1]

(*e*) (*i*) *Name the fluid contained in the spinal canal.*
(*ii*) *Give* one *function of the fluid.* [2]
(*f*) *State a physiological reaction by the body to the detection of pain.* [2]
(Total 10)
[LON]

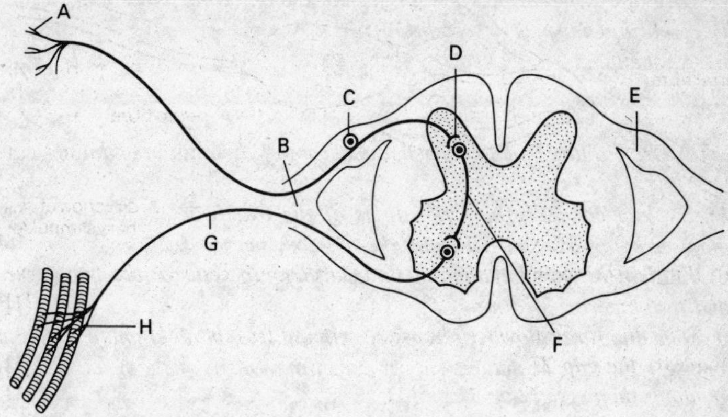

4. *The diagram above shows part of the human nervous system, showing a spinal nerve. Write down the letter, in the space provided, which labels each structure given below.*
(*a*) (*i*) *a ganglion . . .*
(*ii*) *a sensory receptor . . .*
(*iii*) *a dorsal root . . .*
(*iv*) *an end-plate . . .*
(*v*) *a mixed nerve . . .*
(*vi*) *a synapse . . .*
(*vii*) *a motor nerve fibre . . .*
(*viii*) *a connector neuron . . .*
(*b*) *By using arrowheads* (>) *on each of the three neurons, show the direction of an impulse in the reflex arc.*
(*c*) *What is found in a ganglion?*
[Total 10]
[CAM]

5. *Explain how the body is able to carry out the following functions:*
(*a*) *the detection of colour;* [6]
(*b*) *the maintenance of balance;* [8]
(*c*) *the protective withdrawal from a painful stimulus.* [6]
[JMB]

6. (*a*) *Describe the nervous pathway involved in the simple reflex action which causes a person to rapidly remove the hand from a hot object.* [10]
(*b*) *Explain briefly what is meant by:*
(*i*) *conditioned reflex action;*
(*ii*) *voluntary action.* [3]
(*c*) *Give* one *different function for each of the following parts of the brain:*
(*i*) *cerebral hemispheres (cerebrum);*
(*ii*) *cerebellum;*
(*iii*) *medulla.* [3]
[WJEC]

7. (*a*) *Draw a large clearly labelled diagram of the* middle *and* inner ear. [7]
(*b*) *Explain concisely how vibrations of the oval window lead to nerve impulses being transmitted along the auditory nerve.* [6]
(*c*) *Explain why an infection in the auditory tube (eustachian tube) may lead to temporary deafness.* [4]
(*d*) *The diagram below represents a sectional view of an ampulla. Explain concisely how the structures shown detect movement of the head.* [3]

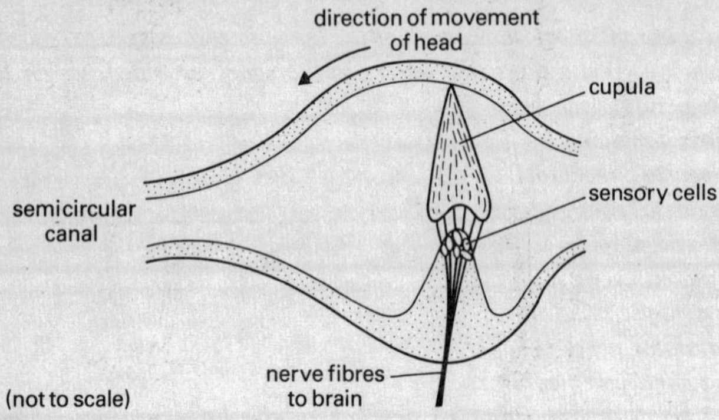

[AEB]

12. *Support and Movement*

12.1. *The Human Skeleton*

Vertebrates have a skeleton that is inside the body, that is, an **endoskeleton**. This skeleton is made of bone and cartilage. The main bones of the human skeleton are shown in Fig. 12.1.

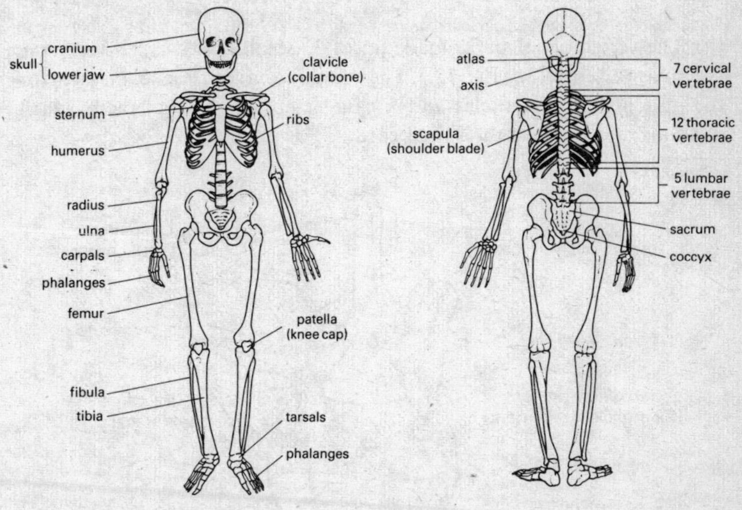

Fig. 12.1 *The human skeleton*

The mammalian skeleton has two parts:

1. **The axial skeleton.** This is made up of the skull, vertebral column (backbone), ribs and sternum.

(a) The **skull** is composed of the cranium and the jaws (see Fig. 12.2). The cranium is actually made of several bones fused together. The joints between these bones are called **sutures**. The upper jaw is fixed in place by its attachment to the cranium. The lower jaw is able to move up and down.

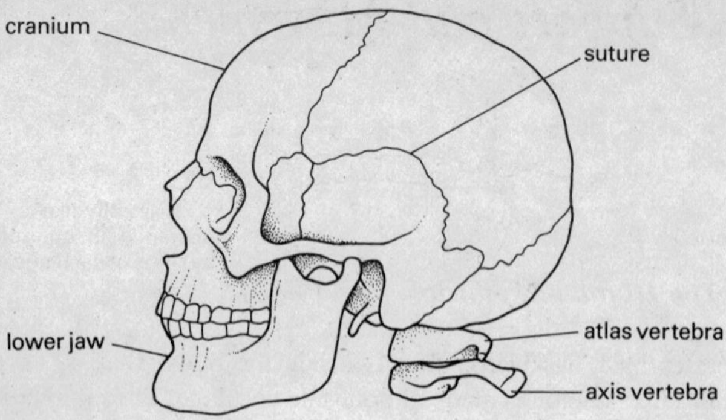

Fig. 12.2. *The human skull*

(b) The **vertebral column** is made up of 33 small bones called **vertebrae** (singular vertebra). See Fig. 12.3. The vertebrae have processes on them for the attachment of muscles and a canal running through them which contains and protects the spinal cord.

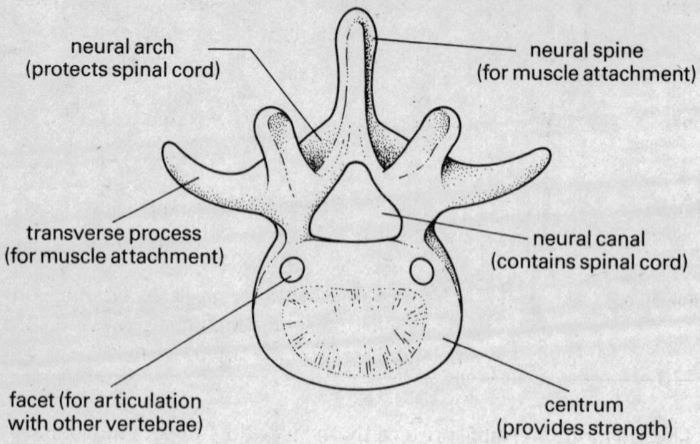

Fig. 12.3. *Basic structure of a vertebra*

The vertebrae are separated from each other by discs (Fig. 12.4) which act as shock absorbers and allow some movement.

There are several types of vertebrae (see Fig. 12.1) which perform different functions. These functions are summarized in Table 12.1.

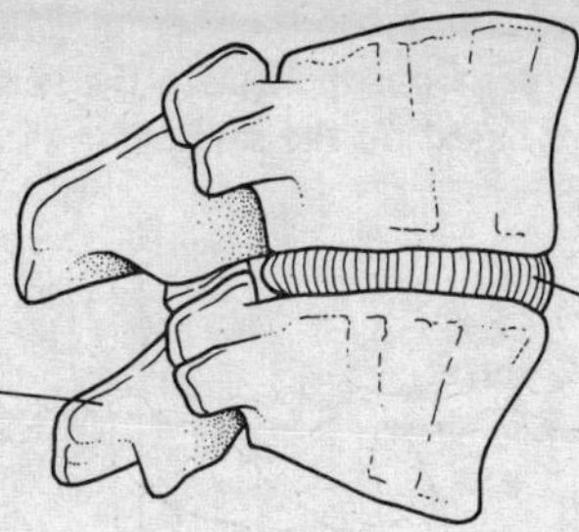

Fig. 12.4. *A disc between vertebrae*

Table 12.1. *Functions of the vertebrae*

Type of vertebra	*Number*	*Function*
Cervical	7	The first (atlas) supports head and allows nodding movements. Second (axis) allows swivelling of head. Other five allow twisting of head, also have holes to allow blood vessels to reach brain
Thoracic	12	Support ribs and allow trunk to bend and rotate. Provide attachment for shoulder and back muscles
Lumbar	5	Provide support for trunk and withstand stress. Allow movement of trunk
Sacral	5	Fused together to form **sacrum** which forms part of pelvis
Caudal	4	Fused together to form **coccyx**. No function in humans, most other mammals have more than 4 and these form the tail

(c) The **ribs** and **sternum** protect the heart and lungs. The ribs are also involved in breathing (see Chapter 8).

2. **The appendicular skeleton.** This is made up of the pectoral and pelvic girdles and the limbs (arms and legs).

(a) The **pectoral** (shoulder) **girdle** connects the arms to the axial skeleton. It is made up of two shoulder blades (scapulas) and two collar bones (clavicles).

(b) The **pelvic girdle** (pelvis) consists of several bones which are fused

together. The whole structure is fused to the sacrum. The pelvis is rigid and helps to transmit the forces from the legs to the vertebral column.
(c) The **limbs** of humans are based on the same plan (see Fig. 12.5).

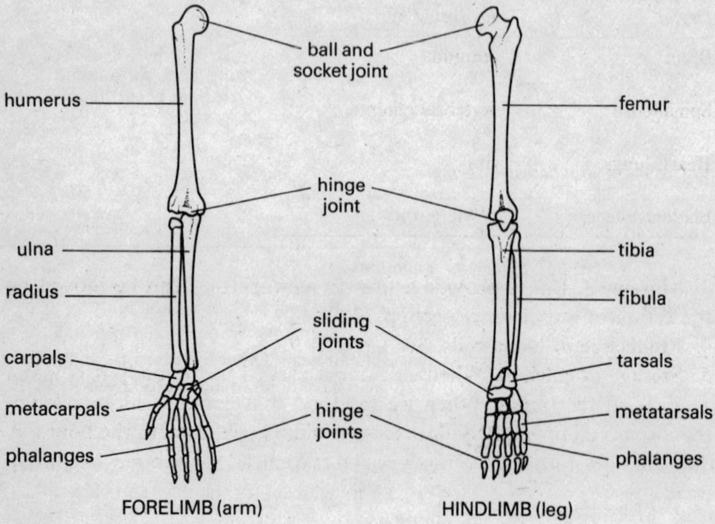

Fig. 12.5. *Arrangement of the limbs*

All limbs are attached to the girdles by ball and socket joints which allow a wide range of movement. They also have a hinge joint approximately halfway along their length, joining an upper bone to two lower bones. Hands and feet are made up of smaller bones arranged in a similar pattern.

The presence of five **digits** (fingers and toes) is called the **pentadactyl** arrangement. This basic plan is modified among the vertebrates according to the functions of the limbs.

12.2. *The Functions of the Skeleton*

1. **Support.** Without a skeleton our bodies would be just a floppy mess on the floor. As well as holding the body up the skeleton provides a framework to hang the organs from, preventing them from squashing each other.

2. Protection. The skeleton provides a strong casing to protect the soft organs inside (see Table 12.2).

Table 12.2. *Protection of organs by the skeleton*

Organ	*Protected by*
Brain	cranium
Spinal cord	vertebral column
Heart, lungs	ribs
Bladder, uterus	pelvic girdle

3. **Movement.** Bones provide a firm framework that can be moved by the action of muscles (see section 12.6).
4. **Production of blood cells.** See Chapter 9.
5. **Storage of calcium.** When calcium is needed in the body it is taken away from the bones. When we eat food that contains more calcium than we need immediately the excess calcium is returned to the bones. A diet that does not contain enough calcium can lead to the bones becoming weak.

12.3. *The Structure of Bone and Cartilage*

Bone

The basic structure of a bone is shown in Fig. 12.6.

The **periosteum** is a tough, fibrous layer surrounding the whole bone. This helps to protect the bone and repair any damage.

The **bone tissue** itself is partly living and partly non-living. The living bone cells produce a non-living matrix made up of calcium, phosphate, carbonate and fluoride salts, together with a protein called **collagen**.

An experiment to show the function of collagen in bone

If a bone is left in dilute acid for a few days the mineral salts are dissolved out and the bone goes rubbery. This is because only the collagen is left. This experiment demonstrates that collagen gives the bone flexibility.

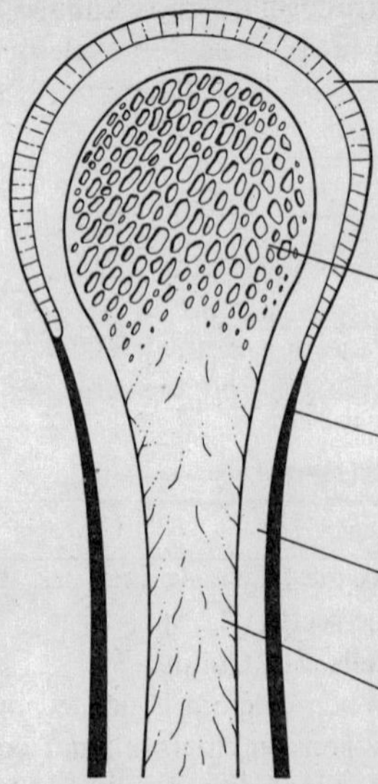

Fig. 12.6. *Structure of a bone*

An experiment to show the function of the mineral salts in bone

If a bone is heated strongly the collagen will be burnt off leaving only the minerals salts. The remains can be crumbled into dust, showing that the salts give the bone its hardness.

Spongy bone contains many tiny cavities and is found mainly at the heads of the long bones. The materials in compact bone are packed closely together, making this type of bone harder than spongy bone. Most bones contain bone marrow at the centre, which is involved in the production of blood cells (see Chapter 9).

All of the living parts of bones are supplied with the materials they need by a rich supply of blood vessels.

Cartilage

Cartilage, or gristle, is closely associated with bone throughout the skeleton. It is made up of cells called **chondroblasts** which are surrounded by a hard, smooth, flexible matrix.

When the embryo is forming most of the skeleton is made of cartilage.

Gradually, as the foetus develops the cartilage is replaced by bone, a process called **ossification**. In the adult skeleton most of the cartilage that remains is found on the articulating surfaces of the bones at the joints.

12.4. *Joints*

Where two bones meet a joint is formed. There are basically three classes of joint: fixed (immovable), slightly movable and freely movable.

Table 12.3. *Types of joint in the body*

Type of joint	*Examples*	*Characteristics*
Fixed (immovable)	Bones of cranium, where ribs meet sternum, pelvic girdle	Bones are joined by tough fibres of collagen
Slightly movable	Between vertebrae	Bones are separated by cartilage and held tightly together by ligaments
Freely movable (synovial)	Shoulder, elbow, hip, knee	Bones held together by ligaments and separated by synovial fluid. Ends of bones covered by cartilage (see Fig. 12.7)

You are required to know the structure of a freely movable or **synovial** joint, the structure of which is shown in Fig. 12.7.

The functions of each part are:
ligament – holds the bones together;
synovial membrane – secretes synovial fluid;
synovial fluid – acts as a lubricant to reduce friction;
cartilage – shiny and slippery to reduce friction.

There are basically four groups of synovial joint:

1. In a **ball and socket** joint the round head of one bone fits into a cup-shaped socket e.g. between femur and pelvis or between humerus and pectoral girdle (Fig. 12.8).
2. In a **hinge** joint movement is limited to one plane, like the hinge on a door, e.g. knee and elbow (Fig. 12.9).
3. In **sliding** or **gliding** joints the flat surfaces of two bones slide across

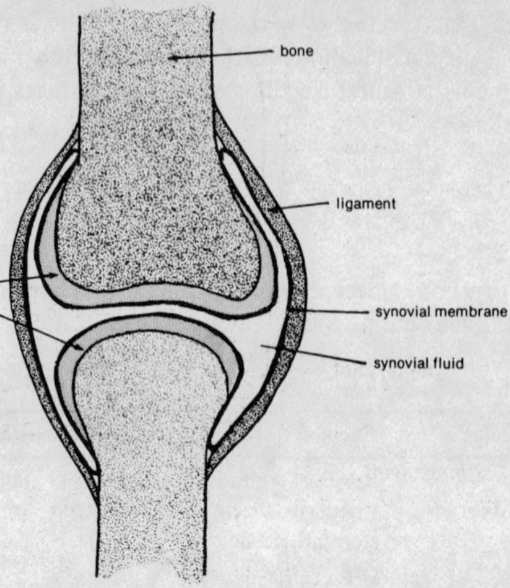

Fig. 12.7. *Structure of a synovial joint*

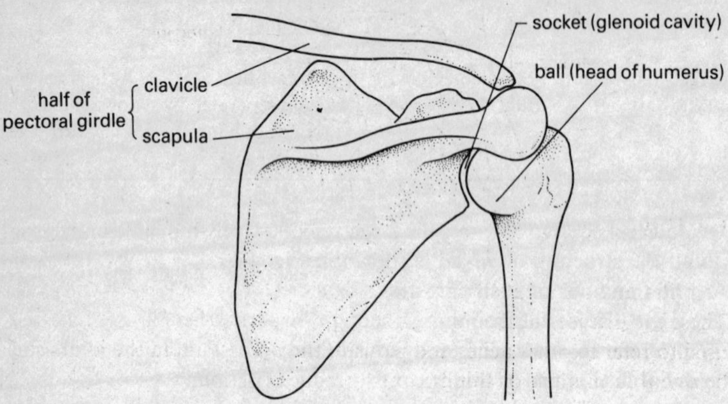

Fig. 12.8. *A ball and socket joint*

each other, e.g. the twisting movement of the vertebrae and the wrist and ankle joints (Fig. 12.10).

4. In a **pivot** joint one bone twists against another, e.g. between the atlas and axis vertebrae.

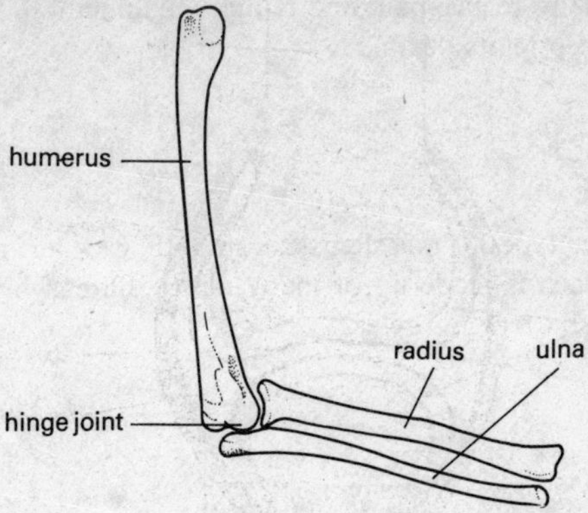

Fig. 12.9. *A hinge joint*

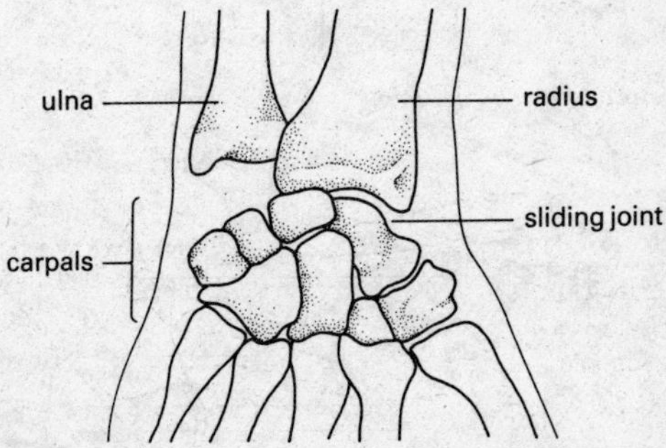

Fig. 12.10. *A sliding joint*

Arthritis and rheumatism

These are diseases of the joints, although the term 'rheumatism' is often used to refer to other aches and pains in the body. Pain in the joints can be due to a number of things.

1. Degeneration – when general wear and tear on the joint is not repaired properly and the joint no longer articulates smoothly.
2. Inflammation due to infection (e.g. rheumatic fever).
3. Inflammation due to other causes (e.g. rheumatoid arthritis).
4. The presence of uric acid crystals in the joint (gout).

Although there is no cure for arthritis and rheumatism there are many drugs available to relieve pain and reduce inflammation. Physiotherapy can help to keep joints flexible.

12.5. *Muscle*

There are three types of muscle tissue: smooth, cardiac and striped (see Fig. 12.11). Each is made up of many **muscle fibres** which are able to contract (get shorter) and relax.

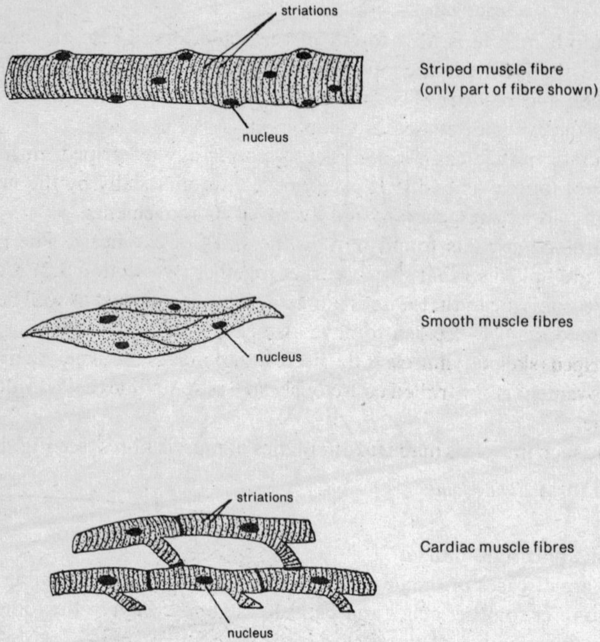

Fig. 12.11. *Types of muscle fibre*

1. **Smooth (involuntary) muscle** fibres have no markings. They are found in the walls of internal organs e.g. the bladder, gut and blood vessels. In the walls of tubes such as the intestine and blood vessels contraction of smooth muscle makes the **lumen** (space) inside the tube narrower (see Fig. 12.12).

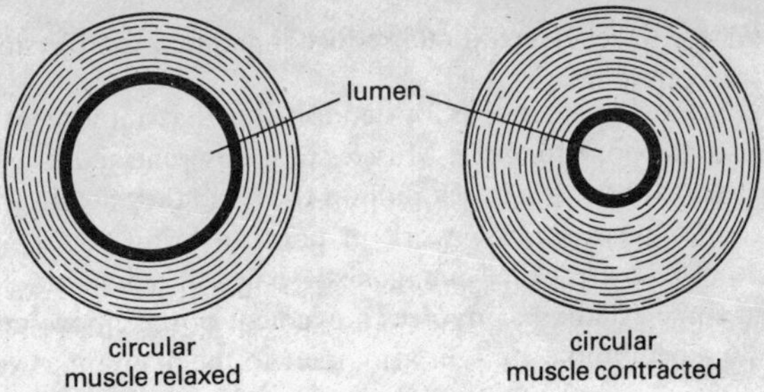

Fig. 12.12. *The action of circular muscle*

Smooth muscle is also found in the **sphincters**. These are bands of muscle that control the opening and closing of organs such as the stomach and bladder. The role of smooth muscle in the control of the iris of the eye is discussed in Chapter 11.

Smooth muscle cannot contract as powerfully as striped muscle but does not fatigue as easily. It is controlled automatically by the nervous system and we are generally not aware of its movements.

2. **Cardiac muscle** is found only in the walls of the heart. The muscle fibres are linked so that they contract together (see section 9.2). Cardiac muscle is unique in that it does not get tired (which is just as well because we would die if it decided to have a rest).

3. **Striped** (skeletal) **muscle** is the muscle that moves the skeleton around. Its movement is controlled consciously so it is sometimes called **voluntary** muscle.

One such muscle is made up of bundles of muscle fibres (see Fig. 12.13).

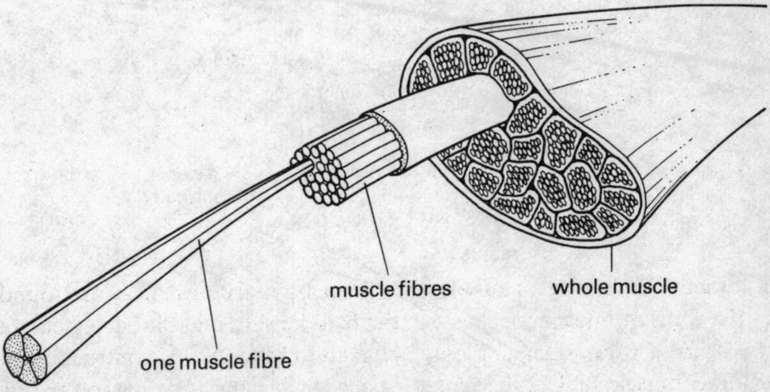

Fig. 12.13. *The action of striped muscle*

12.6. *How Muscles Cause Movement*

Muscles are attached to bones by tendons so that movement of the muscle causes the bone to move. Muscles move by **contracting** or getting shorter. When they contract they pull on the bone they are attached to. Muscles cannot push so they work in pairs to bring about opposite movements. These are called **antagonistic pairs**. A common example, specified in some syllabuses, involves movement of the elbow joint. Fig. 12.14 shows a bent and a straight arm: refer to the diagram as you read on.

The muscle that bends (flexes) a limb is called the **flexor**, in this case it is the biceps. The triceps straightens or extends the limb so it is the **extensor**.

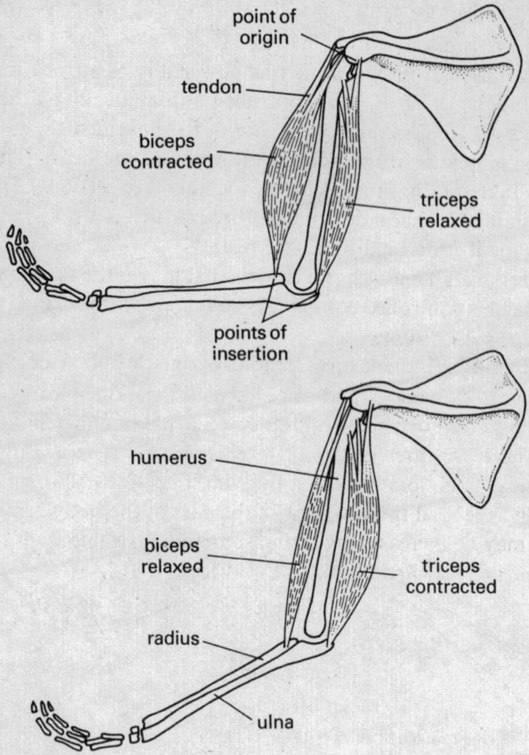

Fig. 12.14. *Antagonistic muscles*

Note the following points:

1. The muscles are attached to the bones at both ends by **tendons**. These do not stretch, so all of the force from the muscle is transmitted to the bone.
2. Each muscle has a point of **origin** and a point of **insertion**. The origin is at the end of the bone that does not move, the insertion is at the end of the bone that does move.
3. The position of the point of insertion causes a big movement of the bone with only a small movement of the muscle.
4. As the biceps contracts it gets shorter and fatter. At the same time the triceps is relaxed, getting longer and thinner.
5. Similarly, the contracted triceps is shorter and fatter and the biceps relaxes at the same time.
6. The biceps is bigger than the triceps because it generally lifts things against gravity and therefore does more work.
7. If both muscles contracted at the same time they would be pulling against each other and there would be no movement. This is prevented by the nervous system; when one member of the pair is stimulated the other is automatically prevented from contracting.

Contraction of muscles uses energy so all of our muscles have a good blood supply to carry oxygen and food to them. There is also usually a store of glycogen in the muscles that can be converted to glucose when needed.

12.7. *Bones as Levers*

The interaction of bones and muscles uses the principles of levers to produce efficient movement. A lever has a **load**, an **effort** and a **fulcrum** (pivot). There are three orders of lever and each is represented in the human body. Each joint acts as a fulcrum, the effort is provided by the muscles and the load is the weight of the part of the body being moved. The load may be increased by lifting something. Examples of each type of lever in the body are shown in Fig. 12.15.

12.8. *Posture and Lifting*

Posture

At any time, even in a seemingly relaxed muscle, some of its fibres remain slightly contracted producing **muscular tone** which holds the body in position. The muscle fibres in each muscle take it in turns to remain

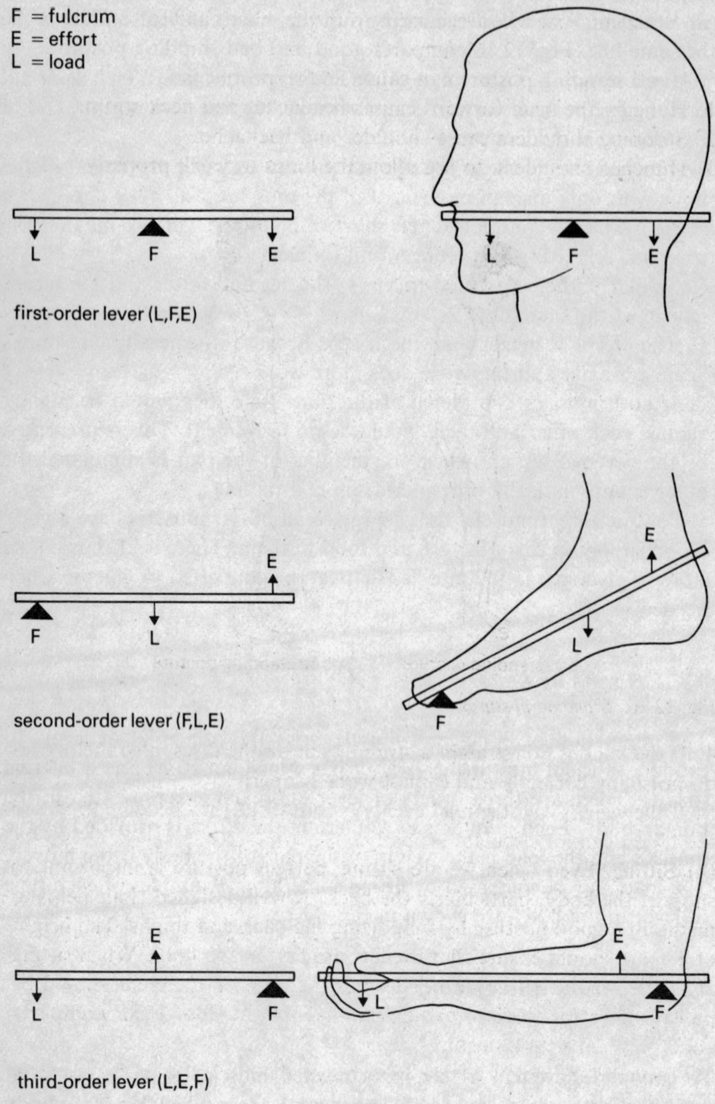

Fig. 12.15. *Levers in the body*

contracted so that none of them get too tired. Maintaining muscle tone helps us to adopt the correct **posture** which is very important for health.

(a) **Standing.** When we are standing our ears, hands and feet should be in the same line. Fig. 12.16 compares good and bad standing postures.

A bad standing posture can cause several problems:

1. Hanging the head forward causes headaches and neck strain.
2. Stooping shoulders cause shoulder and backache.
3. Hunched shoulders do not allow the lungs to work properly.

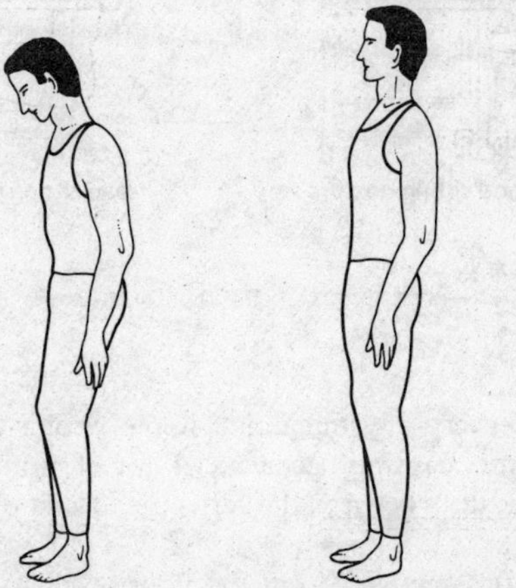

Fig. 12.16. *Standing postures*

4. If the back is not straight a strain is put on the discs, also the organs do not hang correctly and cannot work properly.
5. If the weight is not spread evenly on both legs they become tired and the blood cannot circulate properly.

(b) **Sitting.** Even when we are sitting, correct posture is important to support the body, particularly the back. A well-designed chair helps to maintain a good posture by supporting the back and thighs. The height of a chair should ensure that the feet are flat on the floor. When sitting at a desk, the desk should be at elbow height and the chair should be pulled under the desk to avoid leaning forward. Fig. 12.17 compares good and bad sitting postures.

(c) **Lying down.** When we are lying down the back should be properly supported so the backbone is not strained. The head should be slightly raised to keep it in line with the backbone.

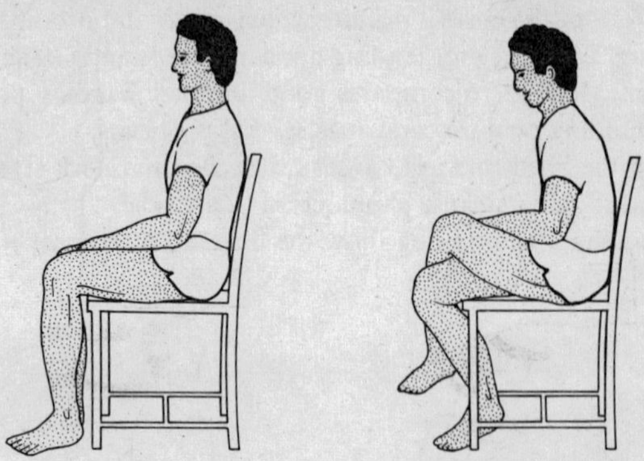

Fig. 12.17. *Sitting postures*

Lifting

We lift things every day but doing it the wrong way can strain the vertebral column, causing backache. A lot of strain on the back can cause one of the discs between the vertebrae to split open. This is called a **slipped disc**.

When we lift something from the floor, even if it is not especially heavy:

1. the back should be nearly straight;
2. the body should be lowered by bending the legs *not* the back;
3. the body should be close to the object;
4. the load should be supported by the muscles of the shoulders, hips and legs.

Fig. 12.18 shows the correct way to lift.

Carrying bags and cases puts a different strain on the back, twisting it to one side. Distributing the load evenly in two bags, one either side of the body, helps to keep the back straight.

12.9. *Looking After Feet*

The bones in our feet do not become completely ossified (see page 221) until we are about 25 years old. Until then the bones are easily squashed. So, if our socks and shoes do not fit properly the bones in our feet grow

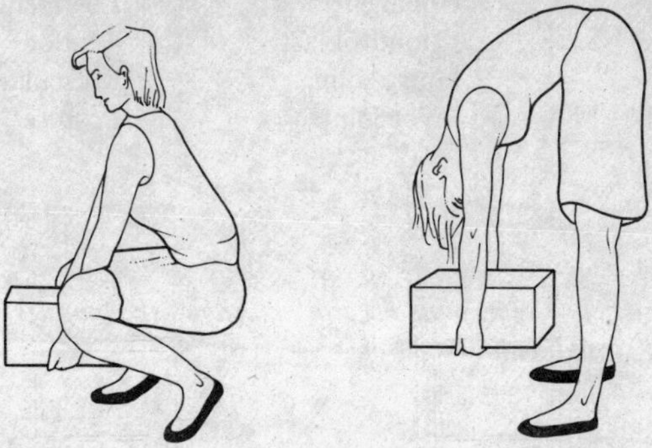

Fig. 12.18. *Lifting*

out of shape, that is they become **deformed**. Badly fitting shoes can also cause corns, bunions, blisters and callouses. High-heeled shoes force the heel bone upwards and if they are worn regularly the ankle will not develop correctly.

Caring for the feet

1. Socks, stockings and tights should never be tight.
2. Shoes should not be tight or rub and should provide support for the feet. Childrens' shoes should allow room for growth.
3. Heels should not be high.
4. Whenever possible, walk around in bare feet to ensure the feet get enough exercise.
5. Feet should be kept clean and dried properly after washing.
6. Socks, tights or stockings should be changed every day.
7. Toenails should be cut straight across.

Key Words

Skeleton	Pectoral girdle	Sliding joint
Endoskeleton	Vertebral column	Muscle
Axial	Digits	Synovial membrane
Sutures	Bone	Synovial fluid flexor
Appendicular	Ball and socket joint	Extensor
Ribs	Cartilage	Periosteum

Sternum	Collagen	Ligament
Pelvic girdle	Chondroblast	Tendon
Limbs	Hinge joint	Muscular tone
Pentadactyl	Pivot joint	Posture

Questions

1. The figure below represents an arm and shows the muscles involved in bending and straightening it.

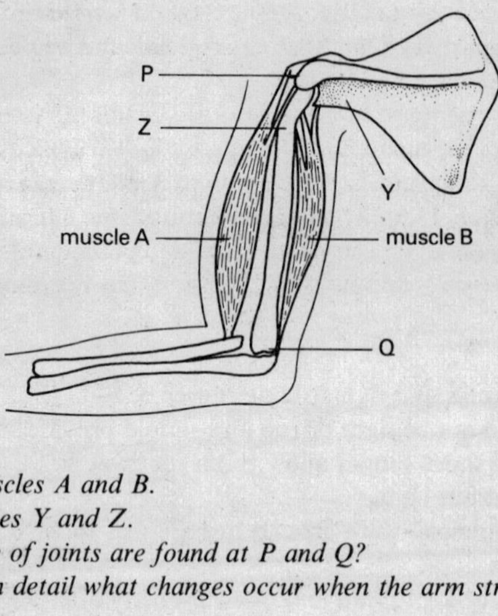

(*a*) *Name muscles A and B.*
(*b*) *Name bones Y and Z.*
(*c*) *What type of joints are found at P and Q?*
(*d*) *Explain in detail what changes occur when the arm straightens.*

2. The basic structure of a synovial joint is shown in the figure on page 233.
(*a*) *The type of joint shown is a:*
A. hinge joint; B. ball and socket joint;
C. sliding joint; D. pivot joint.
(*b*) *Name two places in the human body where you would find this sort of joint.*
(*c*) *Name the parts labelled A, B, C and D and state the function of each.*
(*d*) *What properties must tissue A possess?*

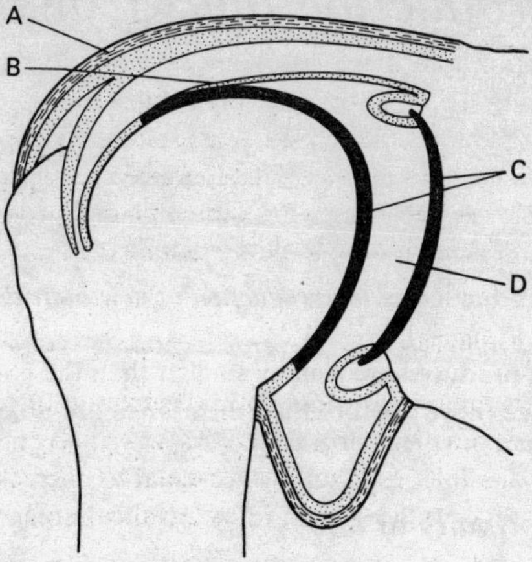

3. Why is correct posture important to health?

4. American supermarkets give their customers strong paper bags to carry their shopping in. Most English supermarkets provide carrier bags. A recent study has shown that American shoppers are less likely to develop back problems from carrying their shopping home. Explain why this should be.

13. Reproduction and Growth

Definition: Reproduction *is the production of new individuals (offspring) from existing individuals (parents).*

The offspring produced are usually smaller than the parents and have to increase in size (grow) before they themselves are able to reproduce.

13.1. *The Continuity of Life*

All organisms die eventually but each species continues because offspring are produced by reproduction. Reproduction may be **asexual** or **sexual**.

Asexual reproduction involves only one parent and the offspring are identical to the parent. Asexual reproduction has certain advantages:

1. When conditions are good an organism can produce many offspring in a short time.
2. If conditions remain good the offspring are likely to survive because they are genetically identical to the parent.

The disadvantage of asexual reproduction is that if conditions change the offspring have no better chance of survival than the parents. If the offspring were different to the parents some of them might be able to survive.

Many simple organisms, such as protozoa and bacteria are capable of sexual reproduction, as are some of the higher plants.

Sexual reproduction produces offspring by the fusion of two cells. These two cells usually come from different individuals of the same species. The offspring contain a mixture of the characters of both parents.

Each parent produces sex cells called **gametes**.

Definition: Fertilization *occurs when a gamete from one parent fuses with a gamete from another parent and a zygote is formed.*

The **zygote** develops into a new individual that is different from both of its parents.

The nucleus of each cell contains structures called **chromosomes** which carry information. The zygote must have the same number of chromosomes as the parents; the gametes contain half the normal number of chromosomes so that when they fuse the resulting cell (zygote) has the full number. Gametes with half the number of chromosomes are produced by **meiosis** which is discussed in Chapter 14.

13.2. *Human Reproductive Organs*

Male

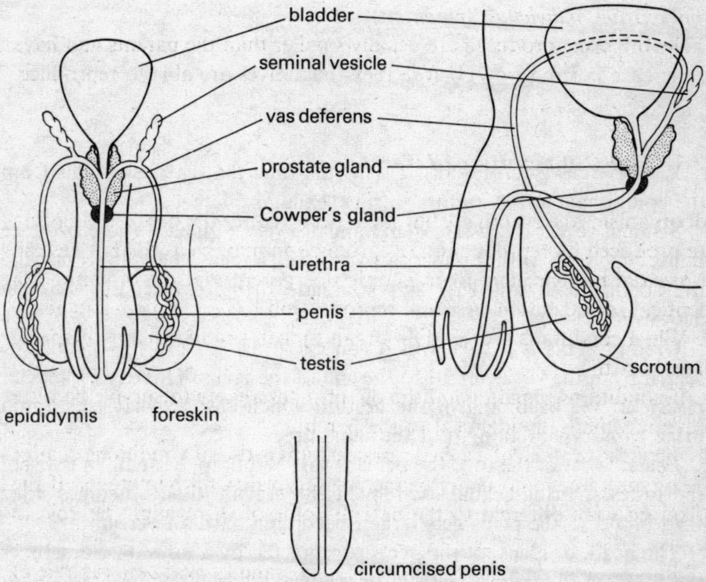

Fig. 13.1. *Male reproductive system*

Testes (singular **testis**). There are two testes which hang outside the body inside a pouch called the **scrotum**. The testes first develop inside the body and descend into the scrotum just before birth. Each testis contains many tiny tubes (**seminiferous tubules**) which produce the male gametes or **sperms** (see Fig. 13.2).

There is also a special tissue in testes that produces a hormone called **testosterone**.

Epididymis. This is attached to the testis and is a long coiled tube where sperms are stored.

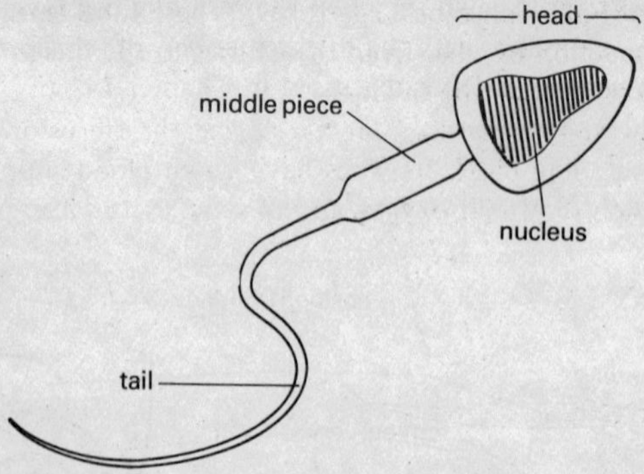

Fig. 13.2. *A sperm*

Vas deferens (sperm duct). This is the tube that carries sperms from the epididymis to the urethra during sexual excitement.

Seminal vesicles, **prostate gland** and **Cowper's glands**. These produce fluids which mix with the sperms to produce **semen**. These fluids provide the sperms with nutrients and stimulate them to start a swimming action.

Urethra. This is a tube which can carry urine from the bladder or semen from the vas deferens to the end of the penis. There is a **sphincter muscle** at the beginning of the urethra which ensures that semen and urine cannot pass along it at the same time.

Penis. Most of the time the penis is soft and limp, hanging in front of the testes. During sexual excitement the **erectile tissue** becomes filled with blood so the penis gets larger, becoming hard and erect.

The head, or **glans**, of the penis is protected by a **foreskin**. Sometimes the foreskin is removed, either for medical or religious reasons; this is called **circumcision**.

The penis has two functions:

1. To carry urine out of the body when limp.
2. To carry sperms out of the body when erect.

Female

Ovaries. The two ovaries are held in place by ligaments at the back of the abdomen. They produce the female gametes or **ova** (singular **ovum**). The ovaries also produce the hormones **oestrogen** and **progesterone**.

Oviducts (Fallopian tubes, egg tubes). These tubes carry the ova, by the beating action of cilia, from the ovaries to the uterus. Fertilization usually takes place in the oviducts.

Uterus (womb). If fertilization takes place, the uterus provides a place for the developing baby. Its walls have a rich blood supply to provide the baby with food and oxygen and to remove its waste products. The

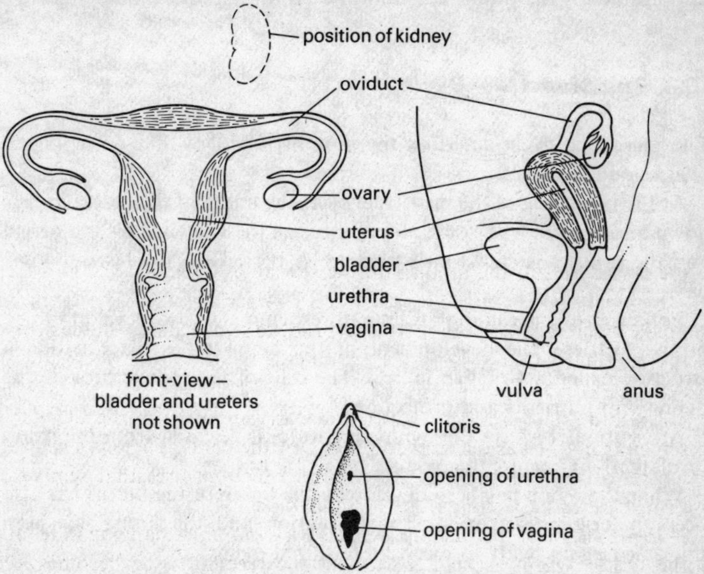

Fig. 13.3. *Female reproductive system*

walls of the uterus contain muscles which contract during birth to push the baby out.

Cervix. This is a ring of muscle at the lower end of the uterus which separates it from the vagina.

Vagina. The vagina is a muscular-walled tube about 8 cm long which leads from the vulva to the cervix. Mucus glands in the walls provide a lubricant for sexual intercourse and help to keep the vagina clean. There are also 'friendly' bacteria in the vagina that help to kill other bacteria and fungi that might cause disease. The walls are very folded and allow the vagina to stretch during birth.

The opening of the vagina is partly covered by a thin membrane called the **hymen**. When young women did not take part in sport the hymen remained intact until the first time a girl had sexual intercourse. An intact hymen was considered proof of virginity. Nowadays the hymen is often broken during exercise long before the girl has sex.

Vulva. The openings of the vagina and urethra are covered by two folds of skin called the vulva. Within these folds of skin there is also a small organ called the **clitoris** which is very sensitive and is largely responsible for the pleasure a women feels during sexual intercourse.

13.3. *The Menstrual Cycle*

The menstrual cycle describes the monthly changes that occur in the ovaries and uterus.

At the beginning of the menstrual cycle the lining of the uterus breaks down and is shed, with some blood, through the vagina. This is a **period** and the process is called **menstruation**. A period usually lasts about 5 days.

Following menstruation an immature ovum starts to develop in one of the ovaries. The development of the ovum takes place within a structure called a **Graafian follicle**. The cells of the follicle provide the ovum with nutrients and protection.

After about 14 days the ovum is mature, is released from the ovary (**ovulation**) and enters the oviduct.

While the ovum has been developing the lining of the uterus has also been undergoing repair after menstruation and the lining has been thickened again ready to receive a fertilized ovum.

If the ovum is fertilized it implants in the wall of the uterus and develops into the embryo. If the ovum is not fertilized the lining of the uterus breaks down and the cycle starts again.

Control of the menstrual cycle

NOTE: Check your syllabus to see whether you need to know about the hormones involved in the menstrual cycle.

All of the events in the menstrual cycle are controlled by hormones (see Fig. 13.4).

Following menstruation the **pituitary gland** at the base of the brain produces a hormone called **follicle stimulating hormone** (FSH) which has two functions:

1. It causes the follicle to develop in the ovary.
2. It stimulates the ovary to produce another hormone, called **oestrogen**.

Oestrogen controls the repair and build up of the uterus lining. Gradually over the next 12–14 days the level of oestrogen in the blood rises. When it reaches a certain level it *inhibits* the production of F S H by the pituitary gland and *stimulates* the pituitary to produce **luteinizing hormone** (L H).

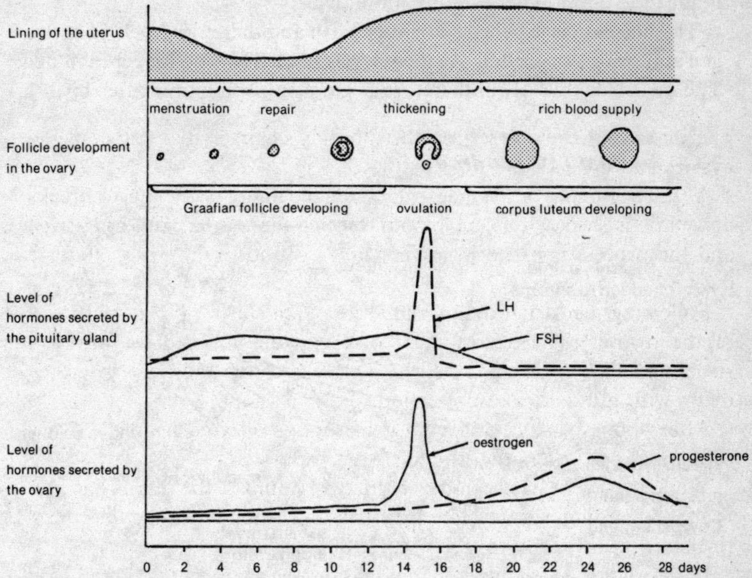

Fig. 13.4. *The menstrual cycle*

L H causes ovulation (about 14 days after menstruation). The Graafian follicle then develops into the **corpus luteum** which produces **progesterone**. This hormone builds up and maintains the lining of the uterus so that it is ready to receive a fertilized ovum. Progesterone also continues the inhibition of F S H production.

If the ovum is not fertilized the corpus luteum breaks down and, therefore, production of progesterone falls. This causes the uterus lining to break down (menstruation). Also, in the absence of progesterone, F S H production is no longer inhibited so increases and the cycle starts again.

Changes in the cycle during pregnancy

If the ovum is fertilized the embryo that is formed **implants** in the uterus wall. This causes messages to be sent to the corpus luteum, which persists and continues to produce progesterone.

Later in pregnancy the placenta takes over the production of progesterone and oestrogen. These hormones maintain the uterus wall and inhibit the development of any more ova.

The placenta is expelled soon after birth and therefore levels of oestrogen and progesterone fall. As these levels fall FSH is no longer inhibited. The menstrual cycle will therefore begin again some time after birth.

13.4. *Sexual Intercourse*

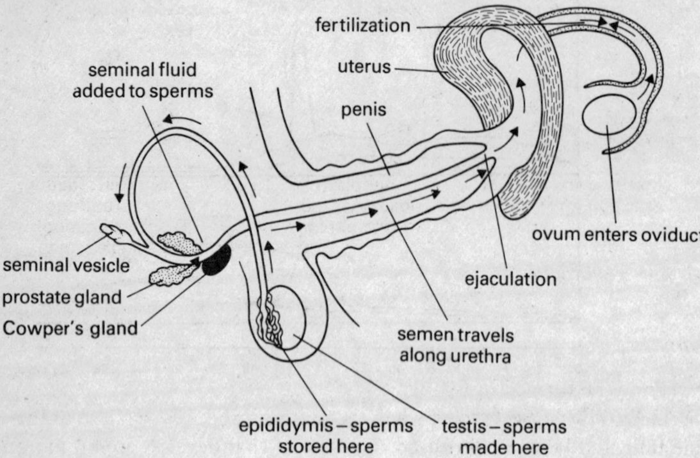

Fig. 13.5. *Sexual intercourse*

During sexual intercourse (copulation) the erect penis is inserted into the vagina, its passage aided by lubricating fluids from the walls of the vagina.

The penis is moved up and down the length of the vagina. This movement stimulates sensory cells in the glands of the penis and in the clitoris. Muscular contractions of the epididymis and vas deferens move sperms to the base of the urethra where they mix with secretions from the seminal vesicles, prostate gland and Cowper's glands, forming **semen**. Contractions of the urethra expel the semen from the end of the penis into the vagina. This is called **ejaculation**.

The pleasant feelings associated with the climax of sexual intercourse are called **orgasm** in both males and females.

13.5. *Fertilization*

Sperms ejaculated into the vagina enter the uterus through the cervix and swim towards the oviducts. Of the 100 million or so sperms in each ejaculation only a few will reach the oviducts.

If there is an ovum in one of the oviducts it may be fertilized by *one* of the sperms, forming a **zygote** (see Fig. 13.6).

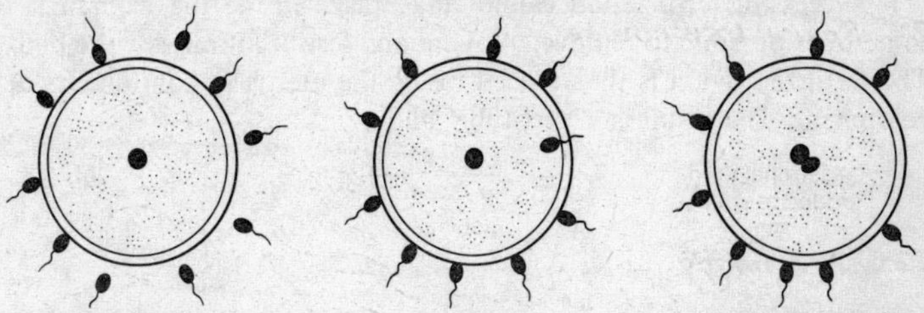

Fig. 13.6. *Fertilization*

Twins

Twins may be formed in two ways:

1. **Fraternal** twins are formed when the mother produces two ova at the same time and both are fertilized. The babies that develop are no more similar than normal brothers and sisters because they were formed from different ova.
2. **Identical** twins are formed when *one* fertilized ovum splits into two. These then develop into two separate babies which are genetically identical because they come from the same ovum and sperm.

Infertility

There are several causes of infertility. Some are given here:

1. Sperms need to be produced at a temperature lower than normal body temperature, which is why the testes hang outside the body. Tight

underpants can cause infertility by keeping the testes too warm to produce fertile sperms.
2. The testes may produce sperms that are not formed properly.
3. The vas deferens may be blocked, preventing sperms reaching the urethra.
4. The ovaries may not be able to produce fertile ova.
5. The oviducts may be blocked, preventing sperms reaching the eggs.

Some women are given fertility drugs to help them produce ova. This may lead to the production of several ova at the same time, leading to multiple births (e.g. quintuplets, sextuplets).

If successful fertilization cannot take place inside the woman it is sometimes possible to remove an ovum and fertilize it outside the body. The fertilized ovum is then placed inside the uterus to continue its development. The result is a 'test tube' baby.

13.6. *Pregnancy*

A fertilized ovum, or zygote, will divide several times by **mitosis** (see Chapter 14) to form a hollow ball of cells. It is now called an **embryo**. Four to seven days after fertilization the embryo will reach the uterus and embed itself in the uterine wall (**implantation**).

As the embryo develops, finger-like projections, called **villi** (singular **villus**) grow from it into the uterus wall. Here, they come into close contact with blood-filled spaces in the wall of the uterus and form the **placenta**.

The placenta has four functions:
1. Dissolved food substances and oxygen diffuse from the mother's blood to the embryo. Diffusion is fast because the blood of the mother comes into close contact with that of the embryo. Also the villi provide a large surface area over which diffusion can take place.
2. Waste products, such as carbon dioxide and urea, pass from the embryo into the mother's blood.
3. The placenta can prevent some harmful substances from the mother's blood reaching the embryo.
4. The placenta produces oestrogen and progesterone. These hormones maintain the blood supply in the uterine wall and prevent production of further ova.

After about two months the developing baby is called a **foetus**. It has

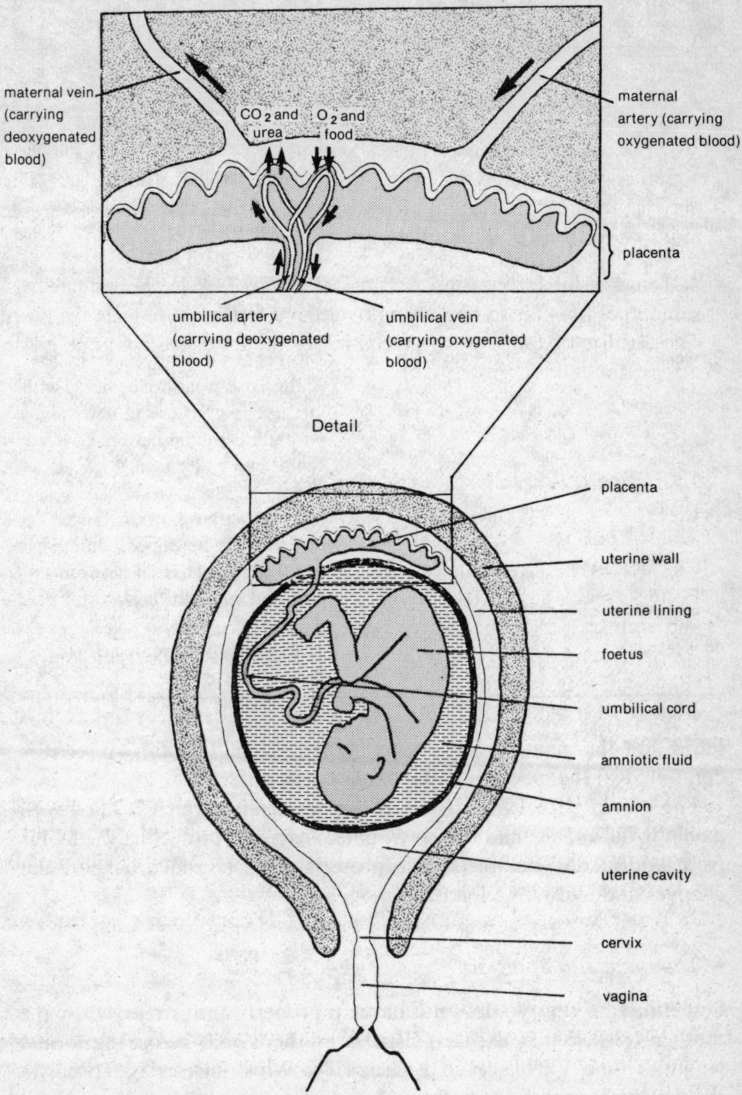

Fig. 13.7. *The foetus a few weeks before birth, with detail showing placenta*

Table 13.1. *Development of the human embryo*

Time after fertilization	*Approximate size*	*Detail*
50 hours	Just visible using a microscope	Ball of cells
5 weeks	0.5 cm	Head beginning to develop. Simple heart. Limb buds visible
10 weeks	3.5 cm	Placenta formed. Now called a foetus. Clearly human in appearance, most internal organs fully formed
20 weeks	25 cm	Mother can feel movement of limbs. Heartbeat can be heard with stethoscope. Sex can be determined with ultrasound. Foetus is covered in fine hair called **lanugo**
28 weeks	35–38 cm	Head now above cervix. Finger and toenails developed. Thin film of fat provides barrier between skin and amniotic fluid
40 weeks	50 cm	Lanugo has disappeared. Ready for birth

limbs and the main organ systems have developed by this stage. It is connected to the placenta by the **umbilical cord**.

The growing foetus is enveloped by the **amnion** which is filled with **amniotic fluid**. This fluid acts as a shock absorber, protecting the foetus from knocks and bumps. It also protects against sudden temperature changes and allows the foetus to move.

Miscarriage and abortion

Sometimes an embryo does not develop properly and is rejected by the mother. It will then be expelled from the mother's body before the normal length of time. This is called a **miscarriage**. Most miscarriages occur in the first three months of pregnancy.

Abortion is the correct term for miscarriage but in recent years has been used more often to refer to the deliberate termination of pregnancy. There are several reasons why a woman may have a pregnancy terminated:

1. The pregnancy may be the result of rape.
2. The foetus may have abnormalities or may not be developing properly.
3. The health or welfare of the woman or her family may suffer as a result of having a baby.

The method of terminating a pregnancy will depend on how long the woman has been pregnant.

1. 'Morning-after' pills can prevent a pregnancy if taken very soon after sexual intercourse. They contain high doses of progesterone which may cause unpleasant side-effects. For this reason they are only used for emergencies.
2. In the first 14 days of pregnancy the contents of the uterus can be sucked out through a small tube inserted through the cervix.
3. If the woman is between 2 and 12 weeks pregnant the cervix has to be opened to allow the insertion of a syringe to remove the embryo. This method causes some discomfort and therefore the woman is anaesthetized.
4. After 12 weeks the woman is injected with chemicals which cause her to give birth prematurely. Abortions are only performed this late under special circumstances.

Care during pregnancy

A pregnant woman needs to take certain precautions to ensure the health of her baby.

1. **Diet.** Her diet must be well balanced and contain plenty of protein, calcium, phosphates, vitamins and iron. **Protein** is needed for growth of cells. **Calcium** and **phosphates** are required for growth of the skeleton. If the mother's diet does not contain enough calcium it may be removed from her teeth, thus weakening them. **Vitamins** are needed to work with the enzymes involved in growth and development of the baby. During pregnancy the mother's blood may increase by half to supply the baby with its requirements. **Iron** is needed to make extra haemoglobin for the mother and for the development of the baby's red blood cells.
2. **Rest.** During the later stages of pregnancy the extra effort of carrying the baby can be very tiring and a pregnant woman needs to rest regularly.

3. **Smoking.** The chemicals from tobacco are able to pass across the placenta and can affect the development of the baby. In addition, smoking reduces the ability of the mother's blood to carry oxygen. This can lower the amount of oxygen reaching the foetus and retard its growth, both physically and mentally.
4. **Alcohol.** Alcohol can pass across the placenta. Drinking can therefore raise the concentration of alcohol in the foetal blood thus affecting its development.
5. **Disease.** Some diseases that infect the mother may also affect the foetus. **Rubella** (German measles) is caused by a virus that can cross the placenta. Although it is not a serious illness in adults it can cause heart disease, blindness, deafness and other deformities in a foetus. Women who contract rubella while pregnant often have an abortion because of the risk of abnormality in the baby.

Syphilis can also interfere with the development of the foetus.

6. **Drugs.** During pregnancy the mother should try to avoid taking *any* drugs and should certainly never take drugs without consulting her doctor. Some years ago a drug called **thalidomide** was prescribed to pregnant women to relieve nausea. The drug crossed the placenta and interfered with the development of limbs, causing deformed babies.

Babies born to heroin addicts are often addicted to heroin themselves.

7. **X-rays.** X-rays can affect the development of a foetus by causing mutations of the chromosomes. X-rays of pregnant women are only taken when absolutely necessary and the mother is exposed to only the minimum of radiation. Whenever possible the woman's abdomen is covered with a lead shield to prevent the radiation reaching the foetus.

The ante-natal clinic

'Ante-natal' means before birth. At an ante-natal clinic a pregnant woman will undergo several tests:

1. **Weight.** She will be weighed regularly. During the later stages of pregnancy she will be expected to put on about 0.5 kg per week. Excessive weight gain could mean she is retaining too much fluid (**oedema**). Oedema can occur to some extent in normal pregnancies but may be the result of raised blood pressure and kidney problems. Therefore further investigations may be necessary.

The average weight of a baby at birth is 3.5 kg but the mother's weight may increase by as much as 12.5 kg. This is because the mother's breasts become larger and she stores more fat than usual. This increase in weight also includes the weight of the amniotic fluid.

2. **Blood.** The woman's blood pressure will be tested regularly and samples of blood will be taken for testing:
(a) Blood group. It is important to know the mother's blood group in case she will need a transfusion. It is also important to know whether the mother is rhesus positive or negative (see section 9.6).
(b) Haemoglobin. The level of haemoglobin is important because it determines the amount of oxygen that can be carried by the mother's blood.
(c) Syphilis. This disease is rare in pregnant women but is so dangerous to the foetus that all pregnant women are tested for it.
(d) Rubella. A blood test can determine whether the women has had rubella (German measles) before. If so, she is unlikely to catch it again.
(e) Spina bifida. When the foetus has an abnormality called spina bifida a substance called alpha foetoprotein appears in the mother's blood in increased amounts and can be tested for. Spina bifida is a condition caused by abnormal development of the vertebral column leading to a variable section of the spinal cord being exposed on the skin surface.
(f) Sickle cell disease and thalassaemia. Sickle cell disease may affect women of African or Asian origin and thalassaemia may affect women of Mediterranean origin. If these conditions are detected special precautions will have to be taken during the pregnancy.

When abnormalities, such as spina bifida, are detected by blood tests the mother may be offered a termination of pregnancy (abortion).

3. **Urine.** A sample of urine is taken at every visit to the clinic and tested for protein and glucose. The presence of protein may indicate **toxaemia**, a condition in which the blood pressure is raised and oedema is often present. Glucose in the urine is not unusual but sometimes indicates the development of diabetes.

The hormones produced by the placenta and foetus can also be detected in the urine and used to monitor their functioning.

4. **Cervical smear.** Cancer of the cervix is rare in pregnant women but a smear is usually taken at the first visit to the clinic just to make sure.

5. **Genetic counselling.** Some abnormalities in babies are inherited. A genetic counsellor will take details of the family history from the parents. This information may identify a possible problem so that further tests can be made.

6. **Ultrasound.** A picture of a foetus may be obtained using high frequency sounds which echo from the foetus and are detected on a screen. This technique can be used to monitor the development of the foetus.

Abnormalities of the foetus will show up on an ultrasound scan, as will the position of the foetus and placenta. A new type of ultrasound detector can monitor the heart beat and breathing rate of the foetus.

7. **Amniocentesis.** If foetal complications are suspected a needle may be inserted into the amniotic sac to remove a sample of amniotic fluid. Before inserting the needle the positions of the foetus and placenta are determined by an ultrasound scan so that they are not damaged by the needle.

Amniotic fluid can be tested for mongolism (Down's syndrome) by observing the chromosomes in foetal cells floating in the fluid. If the blood test for spina bifida is positive it may be confirmed by a similar test on the amniotic fluid.

In late pregnancy the presence of **bilirubin** in the amniotic fluid may indicate the baby has developed jaundice due to rhesus incompatibility.

When a baby is born its lungs must contain certain substances that allow them to open for the baby to take its first breath. Premature babies do not always have enough of these substances for the lungs to work properly. When a woman goes into labour prematurely an amniocentesis test will show whether these substances are present. If they are not present the delivery may be delayed if possible, or the levels of the substances may be increased medically.

Ante-natal classes

At ante-natal classes the mother will do exercises to strengthen and train the muscles she will use in giving birth. This will make the birth easier. Parents are also given advice on care of the baby.

13.7. *Birth* (*Parturition*)

Pregnancy lasts around 40 weeks; this is the **gestation period**. When the foetus has reached the end of this time it is said to be at **full term**. During the last 6–8 weeks of pregnancy the foetus usually turns so the head is pointing downwards towards the cervix. About 3 per cent of babies do not turn and are born feet first; this is a **breech birth**.

Birth occurs in 3 stages:

1. The pituitary gland produces a hormone called **oxytocin** which causes contractions of the muscles in the wall of the uterus. At first the contractions are mild and the mother feels twinges about every half hour. Gradually the contractions increase in strength and frequency until they

occur about every 5 minutes. At this point the baby's head is being pushed against the cervix, which gradually dilates. The amniotic sac breaks and the amniotic fluid is released through the vagina.

At the end of this first stage of labour the mother is advised to take short, sharp breaths.

2. The cervix is now open and the uterus contracts strongly to push the baby out through the vagina. The mother helps by pushing with her abdominal muscles, taking deep breaths as she does so.

Once the head has passed through the vagina the rest of the baby soon follows.

3. Soon after the birth of the baby the uterus contracts a few more times to expel the placenta and umbilical cord; this is the **afterbirth**.

Induction

Sometimes it is decided that mother and baby will benefit from the baby being born sooner than if it happened naturally. In such cases the birth will be **induced** by artificial means.

Changes at birth

In the uterus the baby receives its oxygen from the placenta. As soon as it is born it needs to use its lungs to get oxygen. This requires certain changes in the circulation of blood in the baby (see Fig. 13.8).

In the foetus the pulmonary artery and vein are not used. At birth the **foramen ovale** and the **ductus arteriosus** close up. Blood from the right ventricle then goes to the lungs.

13.8. *Post-natal Care*

Breast feeding

During pregnancy the breasts get larger and the ducts and glands inside them develop (see Fig. 13.9).

After the birth of the baby the pituitary gland produces a hormone, **prolactin**, which stimulates **lactation** – the production of milk in the mammary glands. The sucking action of the baby stimulates the pituitary to continue secreting prolactin so the production of milk is maintained.

For the first few days the milk is a thick yellow fluid called **colostrum**. This is rich in protein and salts but contains less fat and carbohydrate

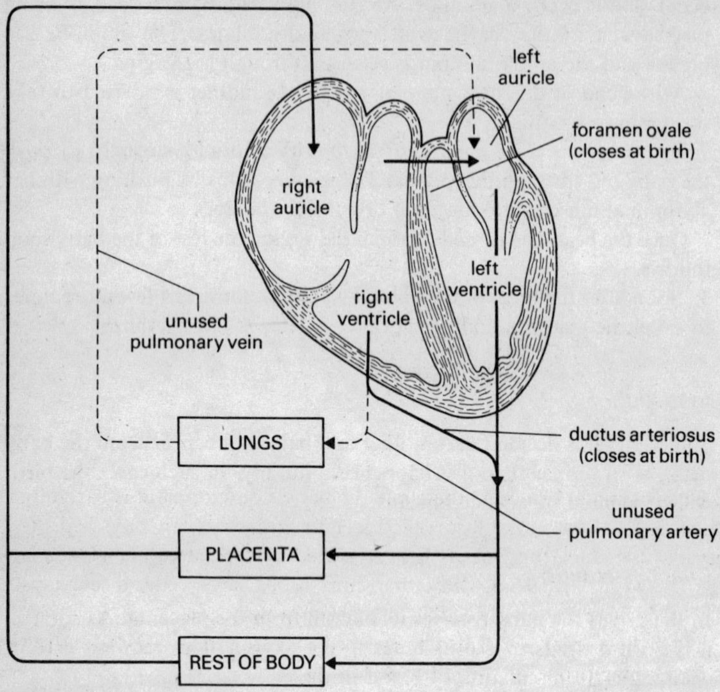

Fig. 13.8. *Foetal circulation*

than breast milk later. Colostrum also contains antibodies to protect the baby against infection.

At one time it was fashionable to bottle-feed babies but doctors now advise mothers to breast-feed if possible. This is because breast milk contains the exact requirements for the baby. As the baby's requirements change so does the milk. The antibodies that the baby receives from its mother's milk also help it to stay healthier.

Breast-feeding also helps to establish the bond between mother and child.

Sometimes mothers are unable to breast-feed and have to use dried milk. Dried milk is cow's milk that has been modified so that its constituents are as similar as possible to those of human milk. When bottle-feeding great care must be taken in sterilizing the equipment used.

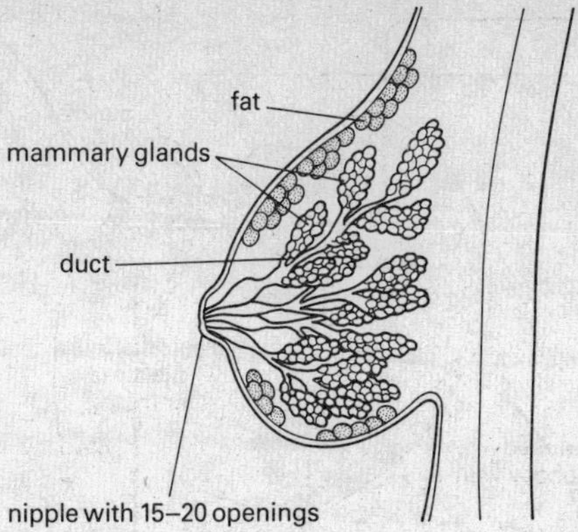

Fig. 13.9. *The breast*

The post-natal clinic. At the clinic the baby's development is carefully monitored. Most babies lose a little weight in the first few days. This is because the colostrum that is first produced by the mammary glands is less rich in fat or carbohydrate than breast milk later. After a few days the baby should show a regular increase in weight.

The baby's reflexes will also be checked to ensure that its coordination is developing properly.

The baby will also be tested for certain hereditary diseases. One such disease is **phenylketonuria**, which does not allow the baby to metabolize phenylalanine, an amino acid present in milk. This condition can be treated with a special diet.

If any of the health checks give cause for concern the baby will be examined further by a **paediatrician**.

At the clinic the mother will be shown how to exercise to restore the muscle tone lost during pregnancy.

Just as important as any of its medical roles, the clinic gives mothers a chance to meet and discuss their new babies.

13.9. *Growth and Development*

Many changes occur between birth and death. The most obvious of these is growth. This increase in size is brought about by an increase in the number of cells by **mitosis**.

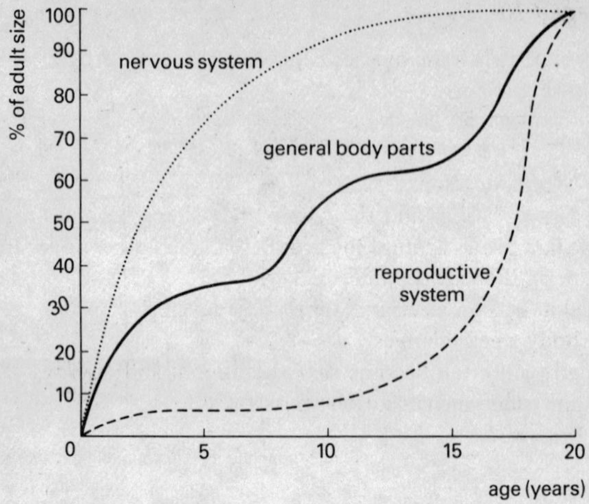

Fig. 13.10. *Development of different parts of the body*

Fig. 13.10 shows how different parts of the body grow at different rates.

Babies' heads are about ¼ of the height of the body. In an adult the head is only about ⅛ of the height of the whole body. This is because the brain is well developed at birth, allowing the baby to learn quickly and to control its movements.

Gradually the muscles in the neck, back and shoulders strengthen allowing the baby to sit up. Later, the legs will become more developed and the baby will start to walk.

Growth comes in spurts. An increase in height is an indication of the growth of the skeleton. This will be followed by a period of filling out when there is little height change.

Growth spurts occur during the first year, between years 5 and 7 and at puberty. Girls tend to grow faster than boys and reach puberty at an earlier age.

Puberty. This describes the changes that occur when the body becomes sexually mature. Puberty is triggered by hormones from the pituitary gland. The reproductive organs mature and secondary sexual characteristics develop, (these are features associated with the sex of the person but not directly involved in reproduction).

Girls (aged 10–15)

Puberty starts when the ovaries begin to produce oestrogen which causes the following changes:
1. The nipples and the area around them get larger and darken in colour.
2. The breasts develop.
3. The hips get wider and the whole body shape becomes rounder.
4. Pubic hair grows around the groin area, hairs grow under the armpits and hairs on the legs become thicker.
5. The skin gets greasier and spots may develop.
6. The body smell changes.
7. The girl will often become more emotional and moody.
8. At some stage menstruation starts.

Boys (aged 11–16)

The testes begin to produce testosterone which causes the following changes:
1. The body grows faster, muscles get bigger, shoulders get broader.
2. The penis gets bigger, the testes get larger and heavier. The scrotum gets darker and more wrinkled.
3. Pubic hair grows around the groin region.
4. The hair under the arms and on the legs gets thicker, hair may also grow on the chest and the back. Facial hair will grow between the ages of 14–18.
5. The voice gets deeper.
6. The skin gets greasier and spots may develop.
7. The body smell changes and there is more sweating.
8. Very often the boy becomes more emotional and moody.

As the reproductive organs develop the boy will have frequent erections and may occasionally have 'wet dreams'.

Menopause

The menopause (change of life) occurs at about the ages of 48–52 in women. but this varies from woman to woman. The woman stops ovulating because the ovaries no longer produce sex hormones. Her periods cease and the reproductive organs decrease in size.

Men can be fertile throughout their life but generally an older man's sperms are less healthy. Sometimes testosterone production in men drops as they get older. This causes emotional changes and occasionally a decrease in the size of the sex organs.

Senescence (ageing)

It is not known why we age but it is probably because the replacement of cells becomes less efficient. As a result the general wear and tear on the body produces the following changes:

1. The skin becomes thinner, less elastic and wrinkled.
2. The hair grows slower and turns white. Hair may be lost, causing baldness.
3. The arteries become less elastic and the circulation becomes less efficient.
4. There is a loss of calcium from the bones and they break more easily. Broken bones take longer to mend.
5. The kidneys are less efficient.
6. Eyesight deteriorates as the lenses harden and cannot focus so well.
7. Hearing and balance deteriorate.
8. Some old people find it harder to remember things and they get confused easily (senility).
9. The control of the body temperature becomes less efficient and it is harder to keep warm in cold weather.

Death. Eventually we all die; the body becomes less efficient and more things go wrong. Women usually live longer than men but the life expectancy of everybody has been increased by improved eating habits and health care.

13.10. *Growth of Populations*

The increase in the size of the population of any organism follows a certain pattern (see Fig. 13.11).

The growth of the population is slow at first but as the number of reproducing individuals increases the population grows faster. This type of increase is known as **exponential**. Eventually the population levels off because of limiting factors e.g. space and food available, predation and disease.

Fig. 13.12 shows how the population of Britain has grown.

The early growth of the population was very slow. At this time humans were hunter-gatherers, and numbers were limited by the amount of food occurring naturally.

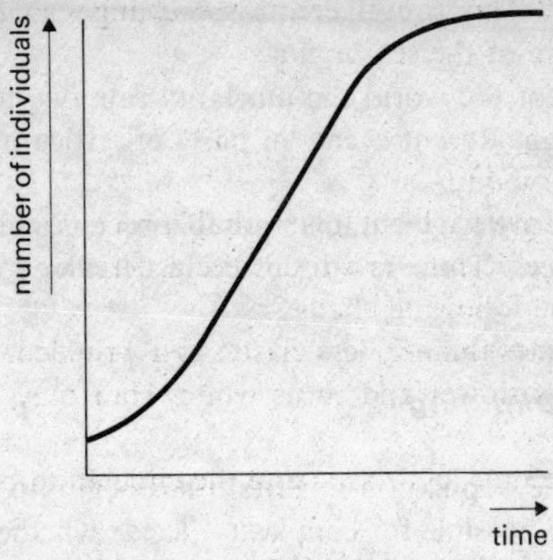

Fig. 13.11. *Population growth*

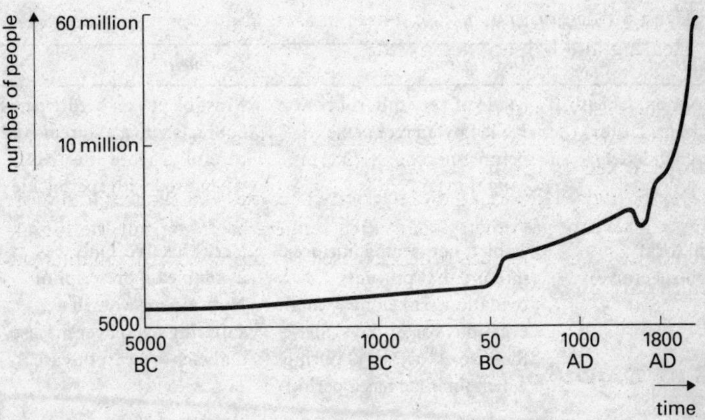

Fig. 13.12. *Growth of Britain's population*

The development of agriculture allowed humans more control over their food supply and the population was able to grow faster. Since the late 19th century the population has increased dramatically. This is due to a number of factors:

1. Health care has improved, more babies survive and people live longer.
2. The standards of housing and sanitation have improved so there is less disease.
3. Improved diet has led to better health.

4. Food production is more efficient, nobody in Britain dies of starvation any more.

In some parts of the world the mortality rate due to starvation and disease is still high. Recent events in parts of Africa have brought this fact home to everybody.

The massive growth of the human population has had dramatic effects on the environment. These are discussed in Chapter 15.

13.11. *Family planning*

The growth of the population in Britain has begun to level off. This is because it is now possible for couples to decide whether or not to have children and how many to have.

Table 13.2. *Methods of birth control*

Method	*Description*	*Comments*
Condom (sheath, rubber, Durex, French letter)	Made of very thin rubber. Rolled over erect penis before intercourse. Sperms caught in end	Must be put on before penis contacts vulva and removed carefully. More effective when used with spermicide
Pill (oral contraceptive)	Tablets containing hormone mixture that prevents ovulation. Taken by woman every day for 21 days. She then stops for 7 days during which time she has a period	Very effective. Only available on prescription. Not safe for women suffering from liver disease, diabetes or heart disease
Intra-uterine device (I.U.D.) (coil or loop)	Piece of plastic or metal placed in uterus by doctor. Prevents implantation	Very effective. Not suitable for all women. May cause heavier periods in some younger women
Diaphragm (Dutch cap)	Dome-shaped disc of thin rubber placed at top of vagina before intercourse. Smeared with spermicide before fitting	Very effective when fits cervix properly. Should not be removed before 6–8 hours after intercourse

Method	*Description*	*Comments*
Spermicides	Chemicals in cream, jelly, foam or tablet form that kill sperms. Cream may be put in sheath or around diaphragm. All forms may be placed high in vagina not more than 10 minutes before intercourse	Not very effective on their own. Best when used to improve safety of condom or diaphragm
Sterilization	Woman – oviducts are cut to prevent ova reaching uterus. Man – vas deferens is cut to prevent sperms reaching urethra (vasectomy)	Extremely effective. Only suitable for couples who already have a family as is not usually reversible. Men may continue to produce live sperms for up to 6 months
Rhythm method (mucothermic or calendar method)	Woman records body temperature daily and looks to see when thin, clear mucus is discharged from vagina. Mucus becomes clear just before ovulation and there is a slight temperature increase at the time of ovulation. The woman must then avoid sex around the time of ovulation	Not very effective because the temperature increase is very small and requires accurate measurements. Also the safe period varies with the individual. Sperms and ova can stay fertile for varying lengths of time
Withdrawal	The penis is removed from the vagina before ejaculation	Not at all reliable as a small amount of semen leaves the penis as soon as it erects

There are many methods of birth control available. The most commonly used methods involve the use of **contraceptives**. These are devices or drugs that prevent conception.

The various methods of birth control are described in Table 13.2.

Table 13.3. *Sexually transmitted diseases*

Disease	*Cause*	*Early symptoms*	*Late symptoms*	*Treatment*
Syphilis (pox)	Spirochaete bacteria	Sores on or inside sex organs	Heart disease, insanity, paralysis and death	Antibiotics, cure may take 2 years
Gonorrhoea (clap)	Gonococcus bacteria	Men – pus from penis, burning pain on passing water. Women – extra mucus from vagina. 70 per cent have no symptoms	Scars form inside sex organs, tubes may become blocked causing sterility	Antibiotics
Vaginitis	Protozoa *Trichomonas vaginalis*	Women only. Sore, itchy vulva and vagina; yellow, smelly discharge	Early symptoms continue	Chemicals to kill protozoa
Pelvic inflammatory disease (P.I.D.)	Bacteria	Women only. Burning pain in abdomen	Oviducts may become blocked by scar tissue	Antibiotics
Non-specific urethritis (N.S.U.)	Not known	Men only. Pus from penis, pain when urinating	Arthritis. Infections of skin, eyes and mouth	Antibiotics. May recur

Thrush	Fungus	Rare in men, penis red and sore at tip Women – sore, itchy vagina. Thick discharge. Not always transmitted sexually	Discharge may worsen, other symptoms continue	Fungicide applied as pessaries, ointment or tablets
Herpes	Virus	Sores like 'cold sores' on penis or vagina	Possibly causes other damage in body. Can pass to baby in uterus	Different methods, very difficult to cure
A.I.D.S. (acquired immune deficiency syndrome)	Virus	Frequent illness due to suppression of immune system	Body worn down by illnesses, eventually death	None
Crab lice (crabs)	Lice	Itchiness. Lice visible on pubic hair	Lice spread to rest of body. Blood loss can weaken body, leading to secondary infection	Washing in special shampoo

13.12. *Sexually transmitted diseases*

There are a number of diseases that can be passed from one person to another during sexual intercourse. These are known as **venereal diseases** (V.D.) or sexually transmitted diseases (S.T.D.) and are described in Table 13.3.

Definitions

Reproduction
Fertilization

Key Words

Sexual	Mitosis	Vas deferens
Asexual	Testes	Seminal vesicles
Chromosomes	Seminiferous tubules	Prostate gland
Zygote	Scrotum	Cowper's glands
Gametes	Urethra	Oestrogen
Sperm	Penis	Progesterone
Ovum	Oviducts	Menstrual cycle
Ovaries	Vagina	Menstruation
Cervix	Ovulation	Graafian follicle
Vulva	Foetus	Follicle stimulating hormone (FSH)
Placenta	Lactation	Luteinizing hormone (LH)
Embryo	Senescence	Corpus luteum
Puberty	Exponential	Amniotic fluid
Menopause	Contraceptive	
Venereal	Testosterone	
Meiosis	Epididymis	

Questions

1. (a) The diagram below shows a front view of the female reproductive system.

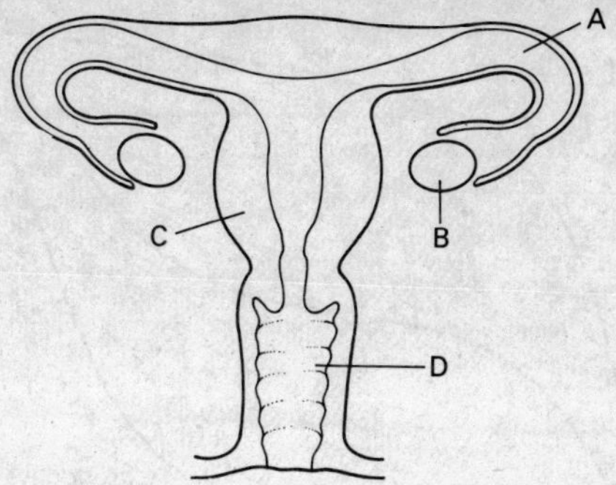

Complete the table below by naming each of the labelled parts and giving one *function for each.*

Part	*Name of part*	*One function of part*
A		
B		
C		
D		

(*b*) *The diagram below shows the structure of a sperm.*

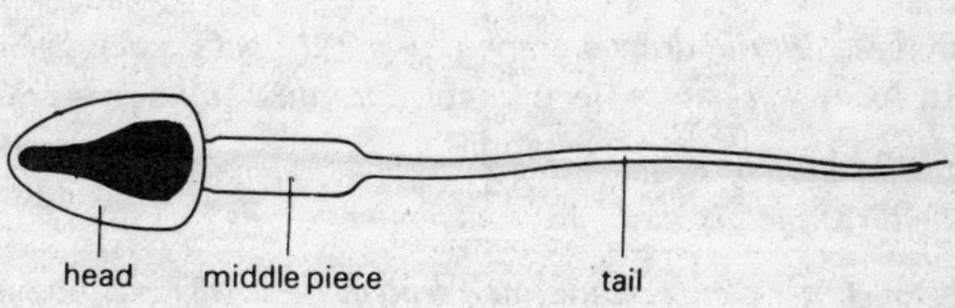

(*i*) *The middle piece of the sperm is able to produce a great deal of energy. What importance does this have for the sperm?*
(*ii*) *How many chromosomes are there in the nucleus of a sperm?*

2. *The graph below shows the development of certain parts of the body.*

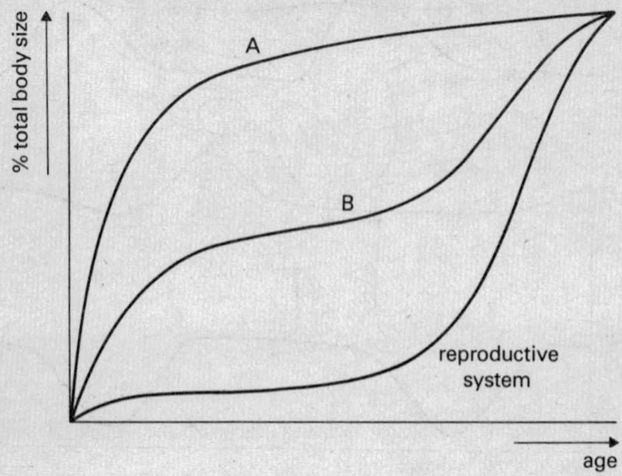

(*a*) *Which parts of the body are represented by line A?*
(*b*) *Explain why there is a difference in the rate of development of parts A and the reproductive system.*

3. The table below shows the changes in weight of a developing baby.

Weeks after fertilization	*5*	*10*	*15*	*20*	*25*	*30*	*35*	*40*
Weight (kg)	*0.1*	*0.15*	*0.2*	*0.45*	*0.75*	*1.5*	*2.5*	*3.5*

(*a*) *Use these data to draw a graph showing the baby's development.*
(*b*) *How many weeks after fertilization does the baby weigh 2.0 kg?*

4. The population of Britain has grown rapidly since the late 19th century. Describe three factors that have contributed to this.

5. Items A–C are contraceptives and sentences (i)–(iii) are descriptions of contraceptives. Match the contraceptive with the description.

A. condom	(i) prevents implantation
B. pill	(ii) prevents ovulation
C. I.U.D.	(iii) prevents sperms entering vagina

6. The figure below shows the levels of two hormones and the changes in the thickness of the uterus lining.

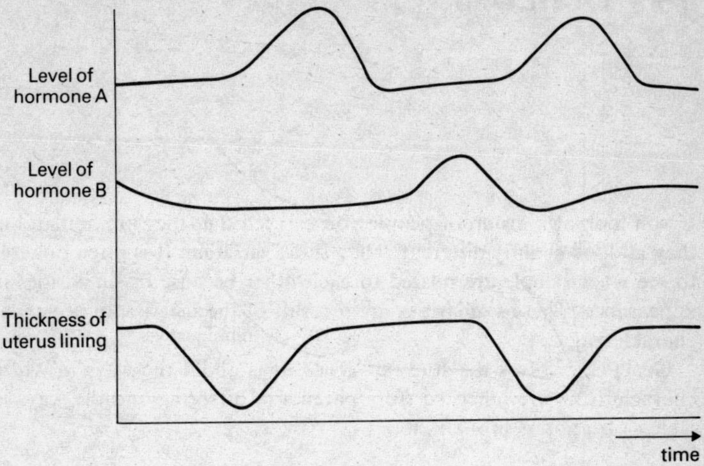

Name the hormones A and B and describe the functions of each.

14. Genetics

If you look at a group of people you can tell that they are human but they all look slightly different. They show **variation**. It is often possible to see when people are related to each other because of similarities in appearance. These similarities are a result of the **inheritance** of similar characteristics.

Genetics involves the study of **genes**. It is about the ways in which characteristics are inherited from parents to offspring and the ways in which variation is brought about.

14.1. *Chromosomes and Genes*

A. **Chromosomes.** These are tiny, threadlike structures in the nucleus of a cell. In the human body cells there are 46 chromosomes arranged into 23 **homologous** pairs (homologous chromosomes carry genes for the same characters – except the sex chromosomes). In the gametes there are only 23 chromosomes, half the normal number.

The letter n is used to represent the number of homologous pairs of chromosomes. In humans n = 23.

As there are 46 chromosomes in the body cells these have 2n number of chromosomes. Gametes have n number of chromosomes.

Body cells, with 2n chromosomes, are called **diploid**.

Gametes, with n chromosomes, are called **haploid**.

Chromosomes are made of protein and a large molecule called deoxyribonucleic acid (DNA). Each chromosome carries many **genes**.

B. **Genes**. A gene is a segment of a chromosome that carries the instructions for one activity in the cell.

Genes are arranged in matching pairs, situated on the matching (homologous) pairs of chromosomes. Each gene has its own position (**locus**) on the chromosome.

Copies of the genes are passed on from parents to offspring so that their cells are controlled in a similar way. These copies are made during **cell division**.

14.2. *Cell Division*

There are two types of cell division.

Most cell division provides new cells for growth or to replace cells which have died. These cells are provided by **mitosis**, the type of cell division occurring in non-reproductive (somatic) cells.

When gametes are made they must have only half the normal number of chromosomes. This is so that when two gametes fuse the resulting zygote has the normal number of chromosomes. Gametes are produced by **meiosis**, the type of cell division associated with sexual reproduction.

A. **Mitosis.** Daughter cells are produced with the same number of chromosomes as the parent cell (diploid). The stages of mitosis are shown in Fig. 14.1.

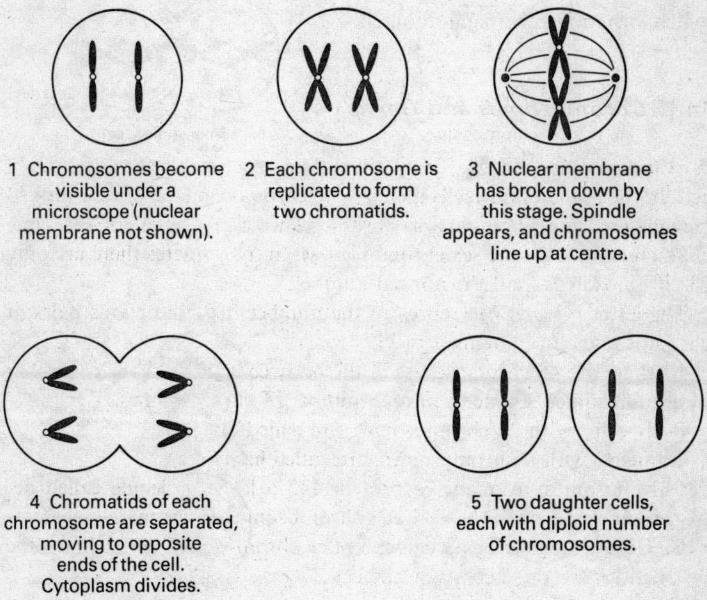

Fig. 14.1. *Mitosis (for simplicity, only two chromosomes are shown)*

B. **Meiosis.** This only occurs in the testes and ovaries and produces haploid gametes. There are two divisions in meiosis, the stages of which are shown in Fig. 14.2.

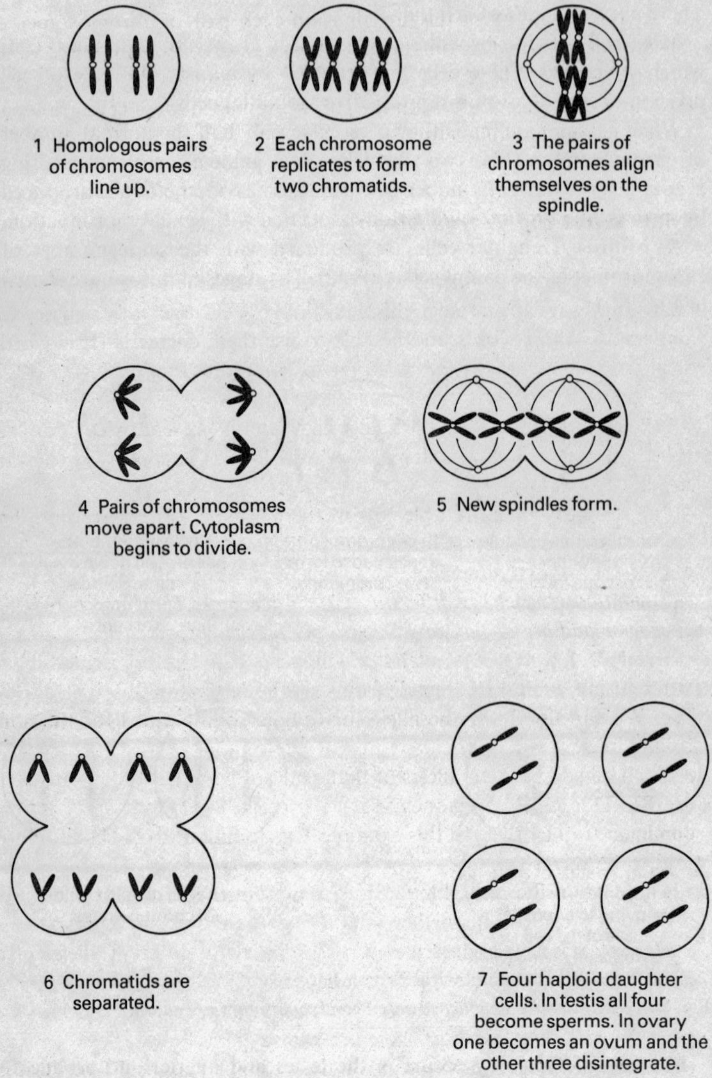

Fig. 14.2. *Meiosis (for simplicity, only two chromosomes are shown)*

Note the following important points about meiosis.

1. Daughter cells are haploid.
2. At the beginning of the first division each pair of chromosomes replicates itself. These chromatids are then separated, forming cells which are still diploid.
3. During the second division the chromosomes in these cells are separated, forming haploid cells.

14.3. *What the Words Mean*

One of the biggest problems with genetics is that there are lots of words that sound similar but mean different things. Unfortunately you need to understand these words and be able to use them correctly. It is worthwhile, therefore, spending some time learning the terminology to avoid confusion. The next section should help you.

Alleles. Each gene for a particular character is present twice in diploid cells, one on each chromosome of a homologous pair. These genes are not always identical.

E.g. Some people are able to roll their tongue, others are not. The same gene is involved but there are two different versions, one for rolling and one for non-rolling. These different versions are **alleles** of that gene.

Definition: Alleles *are different types of one gene. They affect the same character and are at the same site* (*locus*) *on the chromosome.*

Symbols for different alleles. Each gene can be represented by a letter, using capital and small forms of the letter for different alleles. E.g. We can use T for the allele for tongue rolling and t for the non-rolling allele.

Each person has two alleles of that gene so the possible combinations are TT, Tt, and tt. When one of each is present, i.e. Tt, one allele may be **dominant** to the other. In this example T is dominant to t. Therefore t is said to be **recessive** to T.

REMEMBER the capital letter must represent the dominant allele. So, a Tt person can roll his or her tongue because there is a T present.

Heterozygous. This describes a person carrying different alleles of a gene, e.g. Tt. A person with Tt is a **heterozygote**.

Homozygous. This describes a person carrying the same alleles of a gene, e.g. TT or tt. Both of these are **homozygotes**.

Phenotype. A person who can roll their tongue may be TT or Tt, it is impossible to tell just by looking. The ability to roll their tongue is their **phenotype**.

Definition: Phenotype *is the character of the organism that can be observed.*

Genotype. Two tongue-rollers TT and Tt have the same phenotype but their genetic make-up is different; that is they have different **genotypes**.

Definition: Genotype refers to the genetic make-up of the individual.

14.4. *Single Factor (Monohybrid) Inheritance*

Although all of our genes are inherited at one time, to avoid confusion we need only consider how one gene is inherited. This is what we mean by single factor or monohybrid inheritance.

Consider a cross between a TT woman and a tt man. Fig. 14.3 shows what gametes are formed and how they may combine.

REMEMBER that each gamete carries only one of the genes.

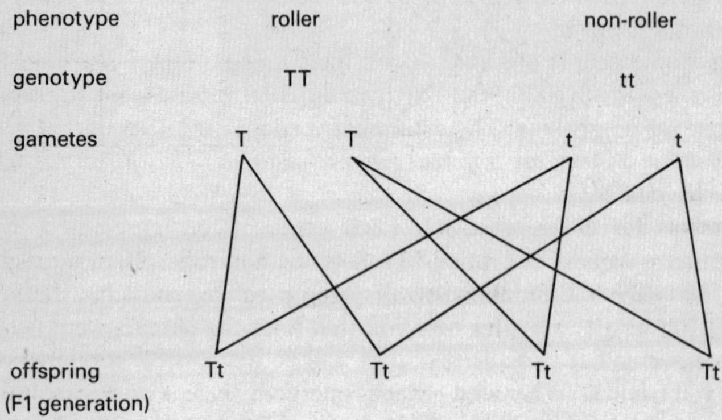

Fig. 14.3. *TT × tt*

Note that the offspring are called the F1 generation. F1 stands for the 'first filial' generation (but just remember F1).

All of the offspring from this cross are heterozygous.

When working these things out the first step is to decide what alleles are carried by the gametes. Then sort out how they will combine. The method shown above is one way. An alternative is to use a punnet square (see Fig. 14.4).

	t	t
T	Tt	Tt
T	Tt	Tt

Fig. 14.4. *Using a punnet square*

You can experiment with both methods to see which you prefer. Let's consider another cross.

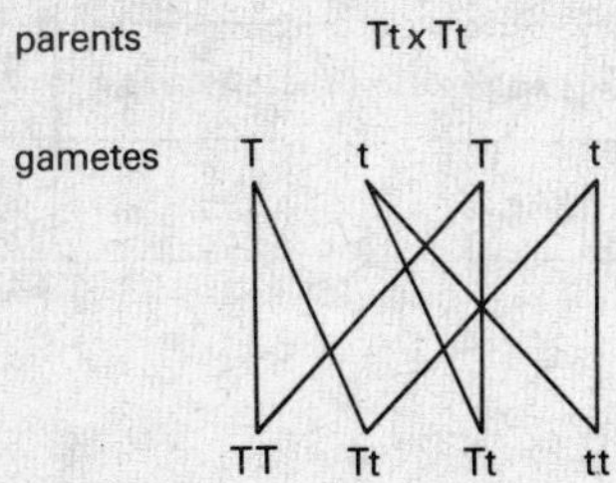

	T	t
T	TT	Tt
t	Tt	tt

Fig. 14.5. *Tt* × *Tt*

This cross produces a ratio of 3 rollers to 1 non-roller. If, in a question, you are given the numbers of offspring produced and they show an approximate 3:1 ratio this tells you that both the parents were heterozygotes.

If you have difficulty with genetics questions there is no easy solution. All you can do is get as much practice at answering questions as possible.

Look at the worked examples below to get an idea of how to go about it.

Example question

Albinism (being albino) in humans is caused by a recessive gene which we will call a.

This first sentence is information. It tells you that albinism is recessive and that you must use a as the symbol for the albino allele. The symbol A must therefore represent the normal allele.

(*a*) *How can normal parents produce an albino child?*

There is only one way in which this can happen. Normal parents may be either AA or Aa.

The possible crosses are:

AA × AA AA × Aa Aa × Aa

Only one of these crosses can produce an albino child (see Fig. 14.6).

AA x AA

	A	A
A	AA	AA
A	AA	AA

AA x Aa

	A	a
A	AA	Aa
A	AA	Aa

Aa x Aa

	A	a
A	AA	Aa
a	Aa	aa
		albino

Fig. 14.6. *How albinism is inherited*

So both parents must be Aa to produce an albino child.

(*b*) *If a couple have had one albino child, what is the chance of their second child being albino?*

If you look at the square on the right of Fig. 14.6 you can see that the chances of producing an albino child are 1 in 4. This will be the case for every child these parents have.

The chance of producing an albino child is therefore 25 per cent.

Remember to try the questions at the end of this chapter.

14.5. *Incomplete Dominance* (*Co-dominance*)

The examples used so far show complete dominance. T is dominant to t, a person with the Tt genotype only shows the T phenotype.

In some cases different alleles of a gene may both be expressed in the phenotype. An example is blood groups in humans.

The four blood groups A, B, AB and O are described in section 9.6. The phenotypes and corresponding genotypes are shown below.

Phenotype	*Genotype*
A	AA or AO
B	BB or BO
AB	AB
O	OO

O indicates that there is no allele for that antigen present.

As you can see from the genotypes, O is recessive to both A and B but A and B are co-dominant. That is, if both are present the person will be AB.

14.6. *Sex Determination*

Of the 23 pairs of chromosomes in human cells, one pair are known as the sex chromosomes. There are two types of sex chromosomes, called X and Y.

Females have 2 X chromosomes so their genotype is XX.

Males carry one of each so their genotype is XY.

We can now see how sex is inherited. Each ovum produced by a woman contains an X chromosome. Of the sperms produced by a man, half carry an X chromosome and half carry a Y chromosome (see Fig. 14.7).

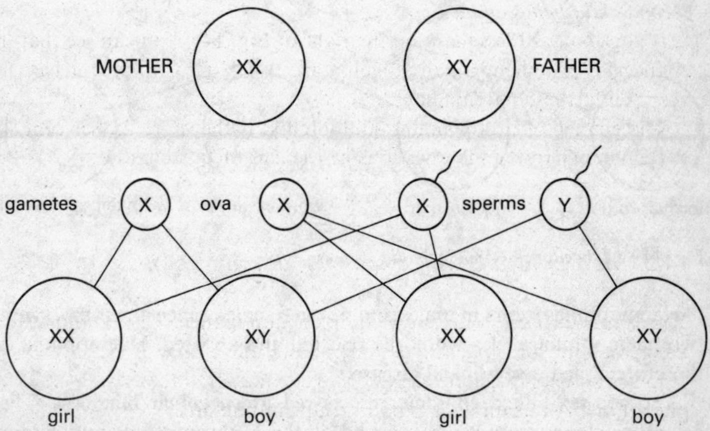

Fig. 14.7 *Inheritance of sex*

14.7. *Sex-Linked Inheritance*

Check your syllabus to see whether you need to know about this.

The Y chromosome does not carry as many genes as the X chromosome. One example is the gene for blood clotting which is carried on the X chromosome. This gene has a normal allele and another allele that causes a disease called **haemophilia**. The blood of haemophiliacs does not clot properly.

We will use the following symbols:

X^H = X chromosome with normal allele
X^h = X chromosome with haemophilia allele

A woman whose genotype is X^HX^h is normal although she carries the haemophilia allele which is masked by the normal allele. In a man the haemophilia allele cannot be masked because there is no corresponding gene on the Y chromosome. Fig. 14.8 shows how haemophilia can be inherited.

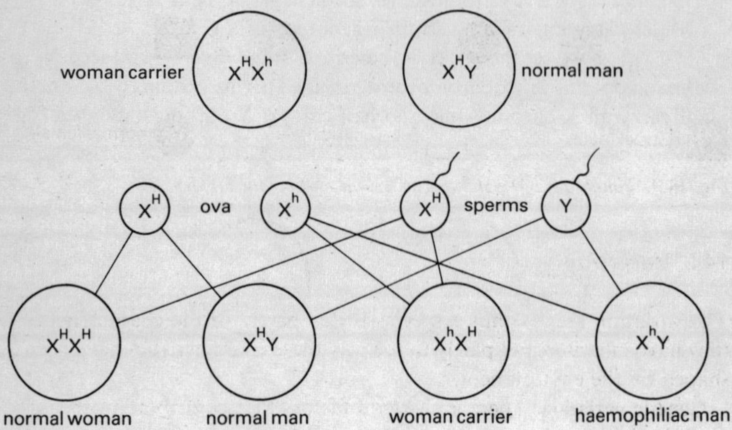

Fig. 14.8. *Inheritance of haemophilia*

Haemophilia occurs in males and not in females, since an embryo with two haemophilia alleles would be rejected and aborted. Haemophilia is therefore called a **sex-linked disease**.

Another sex-linked characteristic is **red–green colour blindness**. The gene for colour vision is only carried on the X chromosome and colour blindness is caused by a recessive allele. It is most common in men because there is no gene on the Y chromosome to mask the effects of the recessive allele.

14.8. *Pedigrees*

The way in which a characteristic is inherited over several generations can be seen by looking at the family pedigree. Fig. 14.9 is a family pedigree showing the inheritance of colour blindness.

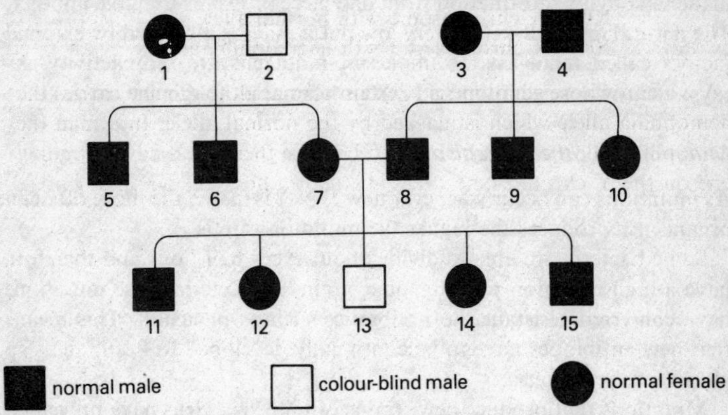

Fig. 14.9. *Family pedigree showing inheritance of colour blindness*

14.9 *Variation*

The variation seen within a species is due partly to the characteristics they have inherited and partly to the way these characteristics have been shaped by the environment.

Genetic variation. There are several factors that contribute to this:
1. Offspring produced by sexual reproduction receive a mixture of parental genes.
2. During meiosis some genes may be swapped between the homologous chromosomes, this is called **crossing over**. This means that one chromosome may end up with genes that were originally on another chromosome.
3. A **mutation** is a sudden change in the genetic material. There are two kinds of mutation:
(a) A change in the structure of the gene. An example is a disease called

sickle cell anaemia, in which the gene that controls the manufacture of haemoglobin has slightly changed its structure. The result is a change in the shape of the haemoglobin molecule. Haemophilia is also the result of a mutant gene.

(b) A change in the number of chromosomes. Down's syndrome (mongolism) is caused by a mutation which results in the ova carrying an extra chromosome. The child then inherits 47 chromosomes instead of 46.

Causes of mutations. Mutations occur naturally when a mistake is made in copying information from one piece of DNA to make another. The natural **mutation rate** is very low but it may be increased by external factors called **mutagens**. Examples of mutagens are radioactivity, X-rays, ultra-violet radiation and certain chemicals (e.g. mustard gas).

Mutations in other organisms

As mutations can occur whenever new DNA is made, the more often an organism reproduces the higher the mutation rate is.

Some bacteria are able to divide about every half hour and therefore have a high mutation rate. In some strains of bacteria these mutations have conferred resistance to antibiotics such as penicillin. This means that new antibiotics have to be continually developed to keep 'one step ahead' of the bacteria.

Mutations that produce new strains of influenza virus have prevented the development of an effective vaccine against flu. Similarly, many species of insect have acquired resistance to certain insecticides through mutations.

Continuous and discontinuous variation

Genetic variation is usually one of two types:

1. **Continuous variation.** Examples are height, weight and intelligence which have a continuous range rather than being split into separate categories.

Such factors are usually controlled by several genes and can be influenced by environmental factors.

2. **Discontinuous variation.** These types can be separated into different categories. For example, people are either male or female, they can either roll their tongue or they cannot, their ear lobes may be attached to the side of the head or not.

Such factors are usually controlled by one or two genes and cannot be influenced by environmental factors.

Environmental variation

Some factors can be affected by the environment. Height and weight are affected by food, exercise and disease.

Drugs (e.g. thalidomide) or viruses (e.g. rubella) that can cross the placenta may affect the development of the foetus. These are also examples of environmental factors which cause variation.

Melanin is a dark pigment in the skin which protects us from ultraviolet rays in sunlight. When exposed to sunlight the skin becomes darker because the amount of pigment increases.

Variation and selection

Variation in organisms is acted on by **natural selection** (described in Chapter 4). Humans have been able to make use of naturally occurring variation to increase the amount of food we get from the animals and plants used in agriculture. This **artificial selection** is discussed in more detail in Chapter 15.

Definitions

Allele
Phenotype
Genotype

Key Words

Chromosome	Gene	Diploid
Homologous	DNA	Haploid
Dominant	Locus	Mitosis
Recessive	Meiosis	Variation
Mutation	Haemophilia	Inheritance
Mutagen		

Questions

1. Refer to the family pedigree in Fig. 14.9.
(a) What are the genotypes of persons 7, 13, and 15?
(b) From which parent did person 13 inherit the gene for colour blindness?

2. The diagram below represents the combination of the gametes of a man and woman to produce three children.

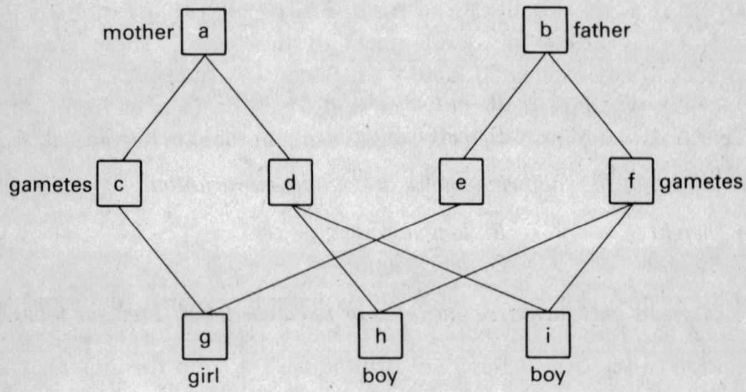

For each stage, labelled a–i, state which of the sex chromosomes would be present.

3. The diagram below shows the inheritance of blood groups.

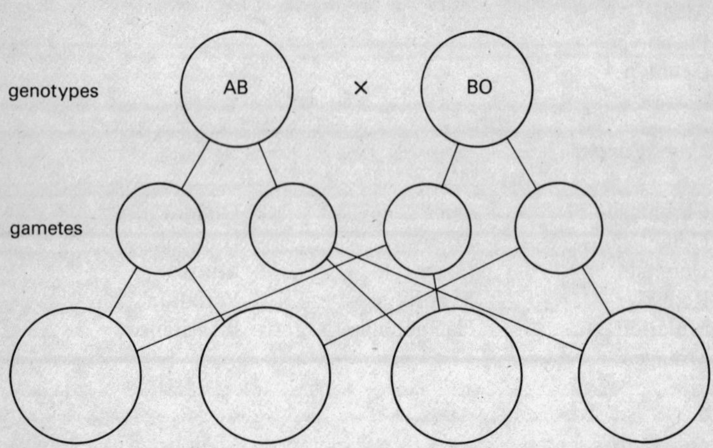

Put the correct symbol in the circles that have been left blank.

4. (*a*) *State* two *ways in which mitosis and meiosis differ.*
(*b*) *Why is meiosis important in the production of gametes?*

5. *Which of the following may be damaged by mustard gas to cause genetic mutation?*

A. *cell wall* B. *mitochondria*
C. *DNA* D. *cell membrane*

6. *Which of the following shows discontinuous variation?*

A. *height* B. *tongue rolling*
C. *weight* D. *hair length*

7. *Humans may have free ear lobes or fixed ear lobes. Free ear lobes* (*E*) *are dominant to fixed ear lobes* (*e*).
(*a*) *If two heterozygotes marry, what is the chance of their first child having free ear lobes?*
(*b*) *A very prolific couple had 16 children; 11 children had free ear lobes and 5 had fixed ear lobes. What were the genotypes of the parents?*
(*c*) *What combination of genotypes would give a 50 per cent chance of each child having fixed ear lobes?*
(*d*) *What would the ears of the parents in* (*c*) *look like?*

15. Humans and the Environment

Environment is a word used to describe our surroundings. The activities of humans have affected the environment in many ways. Over the last few hundred years the human population has increased dramatically (see section 13.10). With more people there is a greater demand for food and housing. Meeting these demands has increased the effects we have had on our environment.

15.1. *Human Communities*

The structure of human communities has changed considerably over the years.

The early hunter-gatherer communities depended on local resources, feeding on animals and plants in the area. Eskimos and African bushmen are present-day examples of such communities.

Some communities have learnt to manage local resources. This is done by replanting crops after harvesting and by only killing a few animals so others remain to breed. These are **pastoral** communities.

Most developed countries have a more complex arrangement of their communities. In these communities agriculture produces more food than is needed to feed the farm workers. The surplus is used to feed people living in **urban** areas (towns and cities). These communities have a **division of labour** with different people doing different jobs but all dependent on each other. This type of community can only survive if a surplus of food is produced by agriculture.

15.2. *Exploitation of Natural Resources*

Land use. There are five main ways in which the land is used:

1. housing
2. agriculture
3. forestry

4. mineral extraction – mining
5. transport – roads and railways.

Water is used in homes and industry. Fish are taken from rivers and seas for food.

Energy. Coal, oil and gas are removed from the ground. These are **finite** sources of energy; they will eventually run out. Energy is also obtained from sun, wind, moving water and nuclear power. These are **infinite** sources of energy.

Renewable resources are those which, if managed properly, can be maintained. Examples are food, vegetation and wildlife.

Non-renewable resources are those which will eventually run out. Examples are fossil fuels and minerals.

15.3. *Conservation of Natural Resources*

If we wish to continue using the natural resources that we exploit, we must be able to conserve them.

Conservation of food resources

Farmers conserve much of our food resources by replanting seeds after harvesting and also by maintaining breeding stocks of food animals.

Other sources of food should be similarly maintained, particularly by the fishing and whaling industries. This can be done by not killing animals faster than they can breed. International fishing agreements help to prevent the overfishing of the species of fish used most commonly for food.

Conservation of trees

Trees are used for their wood and for making paper. Forests are cleared to make space for agriculture. Careful forestry management can maintain forests as a source of wood. Recycling of paper can reduce the use of trees for making paper. Deforestation for agriculture can be reduced by increasing farming efficiency and producing more food from existing agricultural land.

National parks are a way of protecting land from damage. They also provide people with somewhere to go for recreation.

Conservation of wildlife

Many species have become extinct because of the activities of humans

and many more are endangered. There are a number of ways to reduce this problem:
1. Reduce pollution that damages natural habitats.
2. Avoid upsetting the balance of nature.
3. Avoid hunting animals unnecessarily e.g. for sport, furs and ivory.
4. Introduce stricter laws against killing endangered species.
5. Where possible use substitutes for certain animal products e.g. whale oil substitutes and synthetic furs and leather.

Conservation of minerals

We use enormous quantities of metals and the natural supplies of these will eventually run out. This process can be slowed down by recycling as much metal as possible, especially tin cans. The increasing variety of plastics available has reduced the use of metal for some things e.g. car bumpers.

Unfortunately, plastics are made from oil, which is also a non-renewable resource.

Conservation of fossil fuels

Oil, coal and gas are used for making energy. Coal and oil are also used to make fertilizers, dyes, medicines, plastics and many other things. Finding alternative methods of producing electricity will help to reduce the use of fossil fuels. There is a great deal of research into alternative forms of energy and the most promising types of research are:
1. nuclear power
2. solar power
3. wind power
4. water power.

Many countries already have nuclear power stations but there are considerable fears about the safety of these installations.

Recycling of plastics can also help to reduce the demands on fossil fuels.

15.4. *Increasing Food Supply*

An increasing world population requires an increased food supply. There are many ways in which this can be achieved.
1. **Improving soil.** As plants grow they take the minerals from the soil. In

a natural community these minerals would be replaced when the plants died and decayed. On agricultural land the crops are taken away for food and the minerals are not returned to the soil. If the soil is to remain fertile these nutrients must be replaced. This used to be achieved by spreading manure on the land but nowadays it is more usual to use artificial fertilizers. The most important constituents of these fertilizers are **nitrates**, **phosphates** and **sulphates**.

2. **Reducing pests.** It is common in agriculture for large areas of land to be used for growing just one crop. Although this makes harvesting easier it also makes life easier for the pests that feed on these crops. It has therefore become necessary to control these pests, which may be fungi, bacteria, viruses, insects or mites.

Pesticides (chemicals which kill pests) are the commonest way of controlling pest numbers but they have certain disadvantages:

(a) Most pesticides are capable of killing a wide range of species, not just the pest species.

(b) Many pests have developed resistance to certain pesticides and so it becomes increasingly difficult to control them.

(c) Pesticides can cause pollution when they are carried away from the fields by wind or rain.

(d) Pesticides are expensive to develop.

In some areas it has been possible to introduce natural enemies of some pests to control their numbers. This is called *biological control*.

As well as controlling the pests that feed on our crops it is also important to control weeds. Weeds are plants that grow very quickly and in doing so they remove nutrients from the soil for their own use. This means that there are fewer nutrients available for the crop plants. Weeds that grow tall may also prevent light from reaching the crops so they are unable to carry out photosynthesis.

Weeds are controlled by spraying with herbicides before and after the crops are planted.

3. **Improved machinery** can increase the efficiency of ploughing and harvesting.

4. **Artificial selection.** By careful breeding it is possible to improve certain characteristics of animals and plants. For example, some plants can be bred to make them more tolerant to lack of water or resistant to certain viral diseases. Cows may be bred to produce more lean meat and less fat or to produce more milk.

Genetic engineering techniques have allowed certain characteristics to be introduced to the cells of plants without the need for lengthy breeding experiments.

5. **Factory farming.** Grazing animals use a lot of energy in movement and in maintaining their body temperature. In factory farms their movement is restricted and the temperature of their surroundings is controlled. This means that they do not need to eat so much to produce the same amount of meat.
6. **Educating farmers.** As farming methods are improved, farmers must be made aware of the new techniques available to them. This is especially important in underdeveloped countries.
7. **Reclamation of land.** In some areas it is possible to change the nature of the land to make it suitable for agriculture. For example, desert land can be irrigated to moisten it and swamp land can be drained to make it drier.
8. **Culling wild animals.** Domestic food animals are unable to survive in some parts of the world. In certain parts of Africa, for example, domestic cattle are killed by sleeping sickness while the wild animals such as antelopes are resistant to the disease. It is therefore more sensible to cull the wild game in these areas than to try and introduce domestic breeds. These animals are also better suited to the natural vegetation.
9. **Culturing algae and yeast.** These organisms are rich in nutrients and in recent years have been cultured to make food, mainly for animals. This makes more land available for growing crops to feed humans.
10. **Fish farming.** Fish are reared in artificial lakes and in sea inlets. They grow fast as they are fed well. When they reach an optimum size they are harvested.
11. **Changing feeding habits.** Energy is lost at each step in a food chain. Only a small proportion of the energy stored in plants is used in building the muscles of animals that eat them. It is therefore more efficient to 'miss out the middle man' and eat plants. Most people in developed countries eat far more meat than they need or is good for them. A change in eating habits to reduce the amount of meat eaten would make more efficient use of the land.

15.5. *Pollution*

A substance which enters the biosphere and harms living things is called a **pollutant**. Human activities produce many pollutants.

Air pollution

1. **Burning fossil fuels**. Most air pollution is a result of burning coal, oil and gas, either in homes, factories or vehicles. Several pollutants are released when fossil fuels are burnt:

(a) **Soot** on leaves reduces the amount of light reaching the chlorophyll and limits photosynthesis. It also blocks the pores, or stomata, in the leaves, reducing gas exchange and water loss from the leaves.

The Clean Air Act of 1956 established smokeless zones in certain areas. This considerably reduced the amount of soot released into the atmosphere.

(b) **Sulphur dioxide** reacts with water vapour in the air to form sulphuric acid. This produces **acid rain** which damages trees, plants, fish and buildings. Damage to the lungs from breathing sulphur dioxide increases the risk of lung disease.

Most sulphur dioxide comes from power stations and could be reduced by the installation of filters in the chimneys of these buildings.

(c) **Carbon monoxide** from exhaust fumes combines with haemoglobin in the blood, reducing its capacity to carry oxygen. It is possible to instal filters in the exhaust pipes of cars which change the carbon monoxide to carbon dioxide.

(d) **Lead** from exhaust fumes accumulates in the body and can damage the brain, particularly in children. Many countries are now introducing lead-free petrol and car manufacturers are modifying their engines accordingly.

2. **Aerosols** release chemicals into the air which reduce the ozone layer and allow more ultra-violet light to reach the earth. It is feared that this could lead to an increase in skin cancer.

The use of pump-action dispensers instead of aerosols would help to alleviate these problems.

3. **Coal dust** from mines can cause a lung disease called **pneumoconiosis**. Coal miners wear masks to reduce the amount of coal dust that enters their lungs.

4. **Asbestos** causes a lung disease called **asbestosis**. Air leaving asbestos factories has to be filtered and workers have to wear protective clothing. Steps are being taken to remove asbestos from buildings in Britain.

The Health and Safety at Work Act requires employers to provide their workforce with protection from such health hazards.

Water pollution

1. **Sewage.** Untreated sewage entering water will provide food for bacteria. These bacteria will multiply, removing oxygen from the water and killing aquatic animals.

2. **Fertilizers** used on fields may drain into nearby rivers and streams.

Nitrates in these fertilizers allow algae in the water to increase in number rapidly, causing **algal bloom**. This upsets the balance of nature in the water and damages the community of animals and plants.

Nitrates in drinking water can cause stomach cancer.

3. **Pesticides** used on fields may also drain into rivers and streams. Here they may enter food chains and accumulate in predators, particularly fish-eating birds. Fish are also very sensitive to certain pesticides.
4. **Heat.** Many factories take water from rivers and use it as a coolant. The heated water is then returned to the river. Hot water does not contain as much oxygen as cool water so there is less oxygen available to organisms in the river.
5. **Agricultural waste.** Factory farms produce large quantities of manure, usually more than can be used as fertilizer on the land. Excess manure is discharged into rivers, where it reduces the oxygen levels in the same way as untreated sewage.
6. **Industrial waste** may contain chemicals which are harmful in small quantities (e.g. lead, mercury, copper, cyanide). If these are released into rivers they may build up in fish and pass along the food chain.
7. **Oil.** When oil is discharged into the sea it floats on the water where it can damage birds and other organisms. Detergents used to break up the oil slicks are also harmful to marine life.

Pollution from pest control

The effects of pesticides in water have already been mentioned. Pesticides can also cause damage on land. Some years ago crops were sprayed with DDT to kill insect pests. DDT does not break down very quickly so it entered food chains and accumulated in the bodies of certain animals, slowly poisoning them. Other pesticides have had the same effects.

DDT is now banned in Britain and most modern pesticides are broken down quickly in the soil.

Radiation

Low levels of radiation are natural and do not cause any harm. Very high levels of radiation from exploded nuclear weapons have lethal effects as well as causing cancer and mutations in embryos. Accidental leaks of radiation from nuclear power stations may also cause harmful effects on humans, animals and plants in the area.

Noise

This can be a form of pollution when there is too much of it. Loud noise can cause partial deafness and depression. It has also been found to make people work less efficiently. People working close to noisy machinery are required to wear ear protectors. Double glazing can help to reduce noise levels in houses near airports and motorways.

Key Words

Environment	Acid rain	Sulphur dioxide
Community	Urban	Carbon monoxide
Fossil fuel	Refuse	Pastoral
Conservation	Fertilizer	Resources
Pesticide	Artificial selection	Radiation
Pollution	Herbicide	

Questions

1. The graph below shows the levels of nitrates in a river over a period of 30 years.
(a) In what year were nitrate levels the highest?

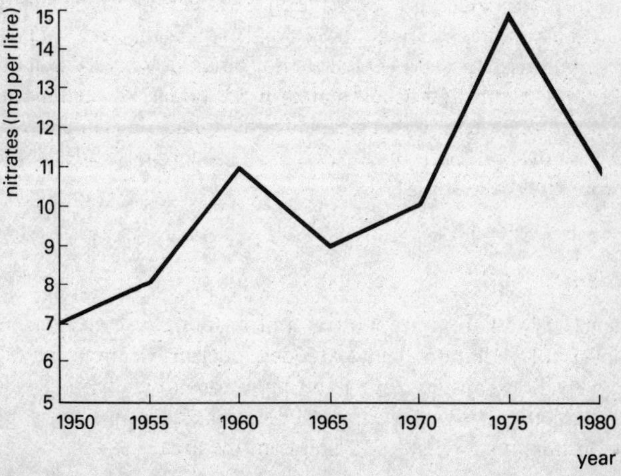

(*b*) *What are the effects of high nitrate levels on the organisms living in the water?*
(*c*) *Suggest a possible cause for the increase in nitrate levels.*
(*d*) *How has factory farming increased the pollution of rivers?*

2. *The table below gives the levels of sulphur dioxide in air and the incidence of bronchitis at different distances from a city centre.*

Miles from city centre	*Levels of sulphur dioxide in air (μg/m³)*	*Percentage of population suffering from bronchitis*
0	85	16
2	62	13
4	53	9
6	25	5
8	18	3
10	4	1

(*a*) *Draw a graph of the results.*
(*b*) *How does sulphur dioxide damage the respiratory system?*
(*c*) *What relationship do you notice between the percentage of people suffering from bronchitis and distance from the city centre?*
(*d*) *What explanation would you offer for this relationship?*
(*e*) *Name one other cause of bronchitis.*

16. Health and Disease

In a healthy body the organs and systems work efficiently and the person feels well, both physically and mentally. There are many things that affect our health and these will be discussed in this chapter.

Most of the things that damage our health are known as **diseases**. These fall into two major categories, **non-transmissible** and **transmissible** diseases.

16.1. *Non-transmissible Diseases*

These are diseases which are not passed from one person to another.

A. **Nutritional deficiency.** Some diseases are caused when the body does not receive the proper nutrients in the diet. A lack of protein, usually caused by starvation, results in a disease called **kwashiorkor**. A deficiency of the correct vitamins and minerals can cause a variety of diseases; these are described in Tables 7.2 and 7.3.

A diet that does not contain the proper nutrients also makes the body susceptible to other diseases because the body is less able to defend itself against them.

B. **Metabolic disorders.** The health of the body depends on thousands of chemical reactions working properly. If one of these reactions goes wrong it can lead to serious problems. For example, in one type of diabetes the hormone insulin (see Chapter 11) is not produced by the body and sugar is excreted in the urine. Consequently, there is less sugar available to the body and fats are used to make protein. As a result the person loses weight and becomes weak and tired. Using fats for respiration can also cause coma. These diabetics are given regular doses of insulin; they also need to eat sugar at regular intervals. In another type of diabetes, blood sugar levels can be controlled by diet alone and insulin is not required.

C. **Cancer** describes a group of diseases caused when some cells behave abnormally. Such a group of cells is called **tumour** and deprives the surrounding cells of food and oxygen. It is generally believed that cancer is caused by a change in the structure of a gene. A gene that causes cancer is called an **oncogene**.

Carcinogens are substances that cause a cell to become cancerous. Many chemicals can do this, as can radiation.

D. **Degenerative diseases** are caused by general wear and tear on the body, resulting from ageing and the way in which the body is treated.

One such disease is **atherosclerosis** ('hardening of the arteries'), caused by a build up of deposits in the arteries. This reduces the diameter of the arteries and blood pressure increases. Atherosclerosis is perhaps influenced by diet and can be prevented by regular exercise.

E. **Inherited diseases** are those caused by genetic defects which are passed on to children. **Phenylketonuria** is an example which was described in section 13.8.

The tests carried out during pregnancy are important for the early diagnosis and treatment of inherited diseases.

F. **Mental disorders** may be caused by an identifiable physical condition, **mental handicap**, or by a general breakdown of mental health, **Mental illness**.

1. **Mental handicap.** The nervous system is very delicate and can be damaged during pregnancy or birth. Damage to the nerves connecting the brain to the limbs may prevent proper movement of the limbs. If the limbs cannot be moved at all they are **paralysed**.

In Down's syndrome, a genetic disorder, there is also a variable degree of mental handicap.

2. **Mental illness** can be divided into several categories:

(a) **Stress.** Life presents all of us with pressures and worries. Most of us cope reasonably well with these but some people are unable to cope and become mentally ill.

(b) **Neuroses** are disorders of the emotions but the person is always in touch with reality. The effects of a neurosis usually are milder than those of a psychosis. Here are several types of neuroses:

(i) Depression. A person suffering from depression feels that they cannot cope with life and stops caring about him- or herself.

(ii) Anxiety. We all suffer mild anxiety at times. In some people this becomes intense panic and these people can no longer lead a normal life.

(iii) Phobias. A phobia is an intense fear of something, such as heights, open spaces or spiders. People can develop phobias about almost anything.

(c) **Psychoses** are major disorders of the mind. There are several types, e.g.:

(i) Dementia. The type of dementia found in some old people is caused by deterioration of the brain cells, usually as a result of reduced blood supply to the brain. It can also be caused by misuse of alcohol and drugs. Another type of dementia which can occur is Alzheimer's disease, the cause of which is not yet known.

(ii) Schizophrenia. Schizophrenics lose touch with reality and live in an imaginary world.

G. **Drug misuse**. There are many drugs that can cause damage to the body when used wrongly. Only those specified in the syllabuses are described here.

(a) **Prescribed drugs.** When used properly most of these do not damage the body. Some have side-effects but may still be used if the side-effects are less harmful than the disorder being treated. Drugs used in chemotherapy treatment for cancer cause weakening and hair loss but by curing cancer may prevent death.

Sedatives are commonly prescribed to relieve anxiety. These can cause drowsiness so should not be taken when driving or working with machinery. Sedatives may also be addictive and should not be taken over long periods of time.

Aspirin is commonly used to relieve pain but in some people it causes internal bleeding.

Penicillin is often used as an antibiotic but some people are allergic to it and can become seriously ill when given penicillin.

(b) **Heroin** produces a good feeling when first used. This encourages people to continue taking it and they eventually become addicted. Long term use of heroin causes vomiting, constipation, nausea and depression. The body becomes weakened and open to secondary infection such as septicaemia (blood poisoning) and jaundice.

Re-using needles produces a risk of cross-infection by diseases carried in the blood e.g. hepatitis and A.I.D.S.

(c) **Solvents**, such as the fumes from certain types of glue, can produce hallucinations. While hallucinating, people are not aware of what they are doing and may injure themselves. Long-term solvent misuse leads to skin disorders and eventually brain damage will occur.

(d) **Alcohol** is a socially acceptable drug and when used sensibly need not cause any problems. Most people drink a little, occasionally. Excessive use of alcohol can cause damage in many ways:

1. Muscle control is impaired because messages from the brain to the muscles are interfered with.
2. Speech, hearing and balance are all impaired by alcohol.
3. Alcohol contains many calories so heavy drinking can cause obesity.
4. Alcohol can become addictive.

5. Heavy drinking over a long period of time can cause permanent brain damage.
6. Cirrhosis of the liver is caused by the liver having to deal with large quantities of alcohol over a long period of time.
7. The kidneys and heart may be damaged by heavy drinking.
8. People behave differently after drinking because alcohol affects the working of the brain. Assaults and vandalism are often associated with drunkenness.
9. Drunk driving can cause injury or death to innocent people as well as to the drunk driver.

(e) **Tobacco** contains several chemicals:

Nicotine enters the blood from the lungs and affects the nervous system. It also increases the heart beat and makes the arteries narrower. This puts an extra strain on the heart. Nicotine is the chemical in tobacco that causes addiction.

Tar in smoke causes cancer of the lungs, mouth, throat and bladder. It also damages the breathing tubes.

Carbon monoxide combines with haemoglobin in the red blood cells so the blood is less able to carry oxygen. Smokers need to breathe more heavily, putting extra strain on the heart and lungs.

There are several illnesses associated with smoking:
1. The lungs are usually cleaned by tiny hairs called cilia. The action of these cilia is prevented by smoking and phlegm builds up in the lungs. This causes coughing which can damage the membranes of the lungs.
2. Bronchitis is an inflammation of the breathing tubes. This results in coughing which damages the membranes and puts a strain on the heart.
3. Emphysema occurs when coughing causes the air sacs (alveoli) to burst. There is then less surface area available for gas exchange to take place.
4. Lung cancer may be caused by carcinogens in smoke.
5. Smoking during pregnancy affects the development of the foetus (see section 13.6).

Preventing drug misuse

There are several ways in which society can help to prevent drug misuse:
1. Education. Most people do not want to deliberately damage their bodies. Widespread publicity about the dangers of drug misuse make it less likely that people will start taking drugs.
2. Legislation. If dangerous drugs are illegal they are harder to obtain and more expensive.

3. Changing the image of drugs. Many cigarette and alcohol advertisers try to establish a glamorous image for their products. This makes people believe that they can improve their own image by smoking or drinking. There are now laws in Britain controlling the ways in which these products can be advertised.

16.2. *Transmissible Diseases*

These are diseases that can be passed from one person to another.

Infectious diseases may be carried in air, water, food or by animals.

Contagious diseases are spread by contact.

The types of transmissible diseases are described in Table 16.1.

16.3. *Control of Disease*

A. **Natural defences**. See section 9.5.

B. **Community hygiene.** The health of individuals within the community depends on the safe preservation and handling of food, a clean water supply and safe refuse disposal. These topics are discussed in detail later in this chapter.

C. **Safe handling of food.** Food poisoning may be caused by consuming food that is infected with microbes. There are several precautions that should be taken when dealing with food:

1. Hands should be washed thoroughly.
2. Cuts should be covered by a plaster.
3. Long hair should be tied back.
4. Utensils and work surfaces should be cleaned thoroughly.
5. Fresh food should be washed before use to remove microbes and chemicals.
6. Microbes are killed by high temperatures so food should be cooked thoroughly.
7. Frozen food should be completely thawed so that every piece of the food gets hot enough to kill microbes. Some convenience foods can be cooked from frozen but it is important to cook for the recommended time.
8. Wash utensils and work surfaces after use.
9. Food should be stored properly. Perishable food must be kept in a refrigerator. The low temperature slows the breeding rate of microbes in the food.

Table 16.1. *Transmissible diseases*

Type of transmission	*Examples*	*Detail*
INFECTIOUS		
(a) Airborne		
(i) Spores in air	Anthrax	Infection occurs when spores are breathed in
(ii) Droplets	Common cold, influenza, pneumonia, tuberculosis, whooping cough	Droplets of moisture containing bacteria or viruses are spread by sneezing, coughing and breathing
(b) Contamination		
(i) Food	Salmonella, typhoid, dysentery	Contaminated food is eaten. Pathogens are transferred to food by dirty hands, utensils, houseflies and other animals
	Tapeworm	Eaten in food. Tapeworm remains in intestine and absorbs food
	Roundworm	Roundworm enters blood and travels to lungs
(ii) Water	Cholera	Water is contaminated by the urine and faeces of infected people
(c) Vectors	Malaria, sleeping sickness	Protozoa passed between people when mosquitoes suck blood
	Rabies	Virus transmitted to person when bitten by infected animal
CONTAGIOUS		
(a) Direct contact	Athlete's foot, ringworm, chickenpox, smallpox, measles, sexually transmitted diseases	Pathogens spread by physical contact between infected people
(b) Indirect	Most diseases that can be spread by direct contact	Objects are contaminated by contact with infected person. Pathogens are then spread when another person touches these objects

10. Cooked and uncooked food should be kept separate.
11. Cooked food should not be rewarmed. If it needs to be reheated it should be done thoroughly so that any microbes are killed.

D. **Personal hygiene.** Personal cleanliness is very important for health. Regular washing can prevent skin infections. It is especially important to wash hands before meals, before handling food and after going to the lavatory. Feet get hot and sweaty, providing a breeding place for pathogens. They should be washed regularly and socks, tights and stockings should be changed every day.

Clothing should be changed regularly. After washing, clothes should be rinsed properly to remove detergents.

Dental hygiene is discussed in section 7.7.

E. **Diet.** Eating the right balance of foods is important to keep the body working properly (see Chapter 7).

F. **Exercise.** Regular exercise keeps the heart healthy and the blood vessels clear of blockage. It also helps to keep the joints working smoothly. Good posture is also important for health (see section 12.8).

G. **Sleep.** Our bodies do a great deal of work during the time we are awake. We need sleep to recover, both mentally and physically. When we are ill we often sleep more than usual. This allows the body to use its resources to make us well again.

H. **Good mental health.** Our mental state can influence our whole body. If we are mentally healthy we are more likely to be physically healthy as well.

I. **Destroying pathogens.**

(i) **Antiseptics** and **disinfectants** are chemicals that kill germs. Antiseptics are mild and can be used on human tissues. Disinfectants are stronger and are used in sinks, lavatories and drains.

(ii) **Antibiotics** are substances produced by fungi which prevent the growth of bacteria. They are used to treat bacterial infections. Some strains of bacteria have developed resistance to the commonest antibiotics and new antibiotics have to be continually developed. Some people are allergic to antibiotics.

J. **Immunization** is a way of helping the body to develop immunity against a certain disease. The way in which the body produces antibodies was described in section 9.5. Immunization uses a **vaccine** which contains weak antigens. The vaccine is introduced into the blood supply. The antigens are too weak to damage the body but antibodies to it are still produced. If the immunized person is later infected with the disease the antibodies are already in the blood to fight it.

Active immunity is when we make antibodies ourselves, following immunization.

Passive immunity is when active antibodies are taken from another person or an animal and injected into the blood. Babies are born with passive immunity because they acquire antibodies from their mother.

The antibodies that are made after immunization do not last for ever but the information for making them is stored. They can then be made again very quickly if the need arises.

K. **Regular health checks.** It is usually easier to treat an illness if it is diagnosed early. Regular health checks can identify a problem before it becomes serious.

16.4. *Testing for Bacteria*

The commonest way of testing for bacteria is to **culture** them on **agar jelly**. Agar contains the nutrients that bacteria require to grow. The process of culturing bacteria is described in Fig. 16.1.

16.5. *Food Preservation*

When food is harvested it is liable to decay by bacteria and fungi. Food preservation allows the storage and transport of food that is so necessary to our way of life. The length of time for which the food may be preserved varies with the method used.

1. **Cooking** raises the temperature of food to a level where bacteria and fungi are killed. If the food is not eaten at once other preservative methods must be used.
2. **Chilling** slows down the growth of microbes. It can be used for the short-term preservation of most foods.
3. **Canning.** Air is driven from the can by heating before the can is sealed. Microbes are deprived of oxygen and die. Suitable for most foods.
4. **Bottling.** Food is sealed in a jar or bottle and heated slowly. Microbes are killed by high temperature and pressure.
5. **Curing.** Meat and fish are hung over wood or charcoal fires. Bacteria are killed by chemicals in the smoke.
6. **Freezing.** Food is cooled to $-20°C$ or below. This prevents the reproduction of microbes. Some bacteria remain dormant, however, so the food must be eaten or cooked soon after thawing.

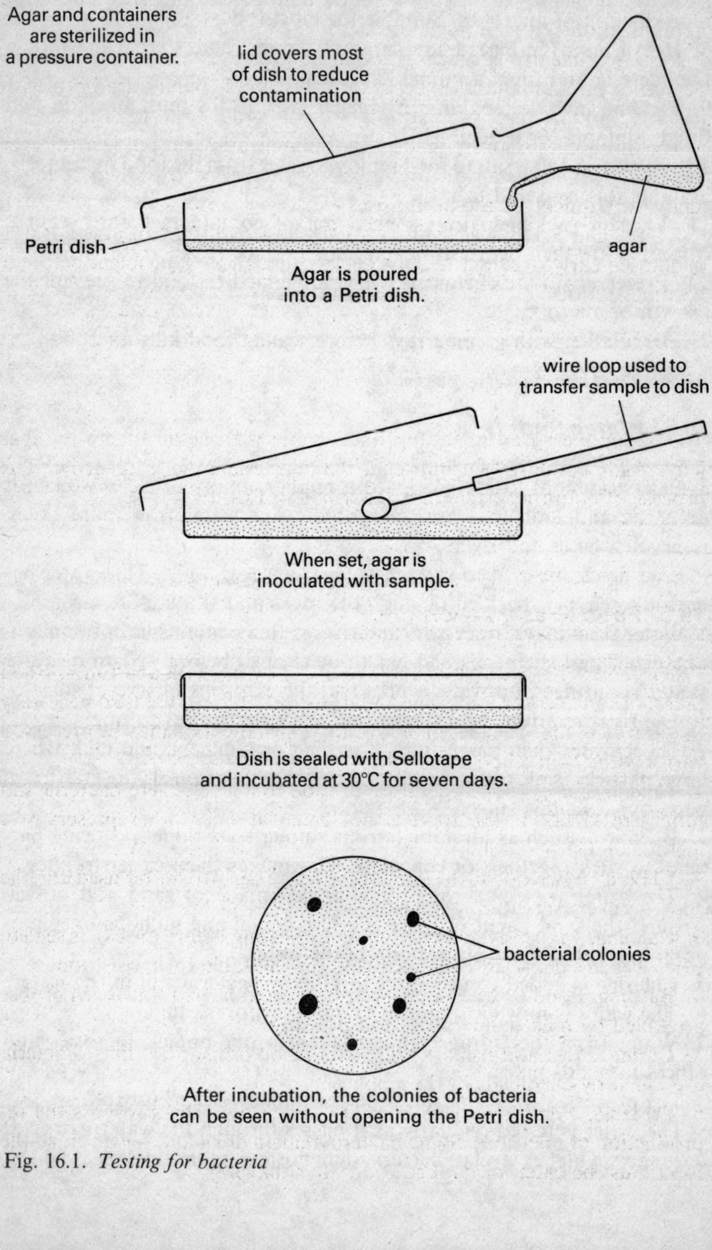

Fig. 16.1. *Testing for bacteria*

7. **Freeze-drying.** Water is removed at low temperature to prevent the reproduction of microbes. Suitable for most foods.
8. **Dehydration (drying)** removes water from the foods so that enzymes in the bacteria and fungi are unable to function.
9. **Pickling** involves soaking in vinegar which kills most bacteria and fungi. Suitable for vegetables.
10. **Salting.** Adding salt to food removes water from the food by osmosis. Suitable for meat and fish.
11. **Vacuum packing.** Air is sucked out of containers before sealing. Microbes are then deprived of oxygen.
12. **Preservatives** are chemicals which are added to food to prevent the growth of microbes.
13. **Irradiation** with gamma rays before sealing food kills microbes.

16.6. *Water Supply*

Water is essential to life. We need a regular supply of clean water for domestic and industrial uses. We obtain our water from bore holes, reservoirs, lakes and rivers.

Bore holes are used to extract water from deep wells. This water has been filtered as it trickled through the rocks and is therefore clean.

Water from lakes, reservoirs and rivers often contains harmful micro-organisms and chemicals and has to be cleaned before we can drink it. Water is purified at a water works and this happens in several stages:

1. Debris is removed by a **screen** that the water passes through.
2. River water then passes into a **settling** or **sedimentation tank** where large particles sink to the bottom. Cleaner water from lakes and reservoirs bypasses this stage.
3. Chemicals such as alum or ferrous sulphate are added, causing particles to stick together, or **coagulate**. This makes them easier to filter.
4. The water trickles through a filter bed made of sand and gravel. Around the sand particles there is a film containing millions of micro-organisms which feed on bacteria in the water.
5. **Chlorine** is added to the water to kill any bacteria still in the water.
6. The water is now clean and is taken to a storage tank.
7. Water from the storage tank is taken to our homes, factories and offices in mains pipes.

The process of water purification is summarized in Fig. 16.2.

The water is tested regularly as it passes through the water works. If tests show a higher level of bacteria than normal, more chlorine is added.

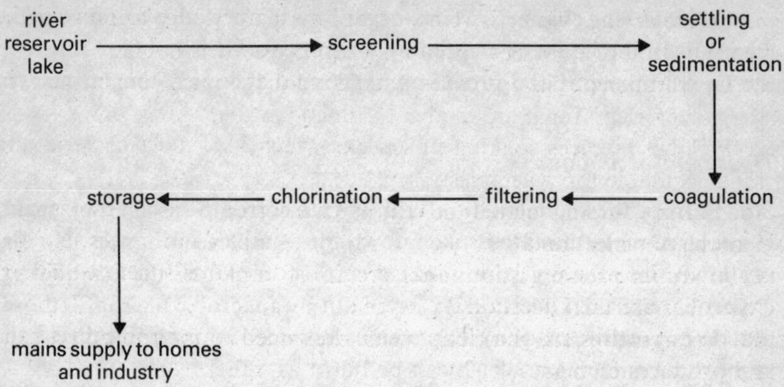

Fig. 16.2. *Purification of water*

Most of the chlorine is used up as it kills the bacteria but a small amount remains to kill any bacteria that infect the water after treatment.

16.7. *Sewage Disposal*

Sewage contains a great many chemical compounds that provide food for bacteria. If sewage were poured straight into a river bacteria in the river would be able to multiply rapidly. Large numbers of bacteria would use up the oxygen in the water and fish would die. The level of organic materials in sewage must therefore be reduced before the sewage reaches the river. Sewage treatment also kills any harmful bacteria.

The first stage is **screening** to remove large objects. The sewage then goes to a **sedimentation tank** where large particles settle out to form a **sludge** at the bottom of the tank. The liquid left in the sedimentation tank is called **liquor** and may be treated in one of two ways.

1. *Biological filtration*

This is the older method of the two. The liquor is sprinkled over a filter bed of stones or coke. This filter bed contains protozoa and bacteria which feed on organic materials in the liquor as it trickles through the filter bed. At the end of filtration the liquid is emptied into a river.

2. *Activated sludge process*

The liquor from the sedimentation tank is mixed with a little sludge and pumped into long channels. Micro-organisms in the sludge digest organic materials in the liquor. To speed up the process air is bubbled through the liquid, mixing it and providing oxygen for the micro-organisms.

Treatment of sludge

Sludge from the sedimentation tank is transferred to a **digestion tank**. Here, large molecules are broken down into simpler substances. No air is allowed into the digestion tank so aerobic microbes (those requiring oxygen) are killed. Digestion is carried out by anaerobic microbes (those that do not require oxygen). This creates less smell than aerobic digestion and produces methane which can be burnt as a fuel.

After digestion the sludge is dried on beds of sand and gravel. During this time the anaerobic bacteria in the sludge do not function as they are in contact with oxygen.

Once dry, the sludge may be used as fertilizer. In some areas it is fermented with bacteria to produce more methane for use as fuel.

The process of sewage treatment is summarized in Fig. 16.3.

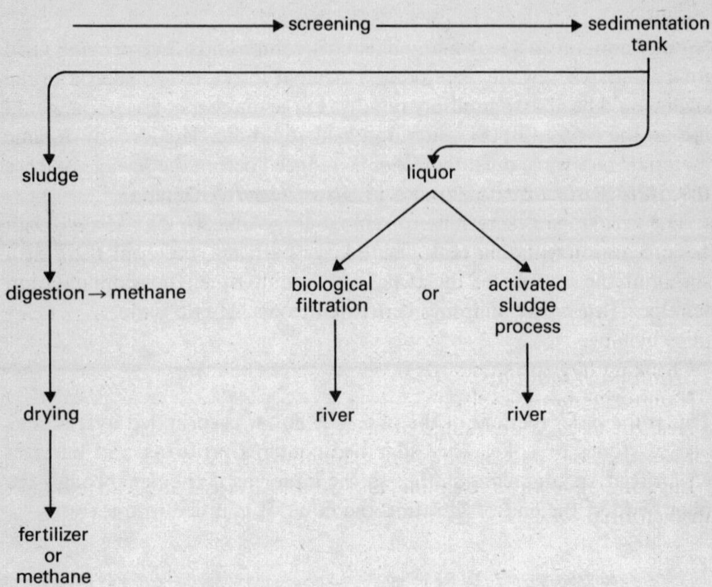

Fig. 16.3. *Sewage treatment*

16.8. *Refuse Disposal*

Solid waste from homes and industry is a potential source of disease and great care must be taken in disposing of it.

Prior to collection refuse should be stored in containers with a lid, such as dustbins, or in plastic sacks which are sealed. These precautions prevent flies entering the rubbish and establishing breeding sites.

After collection the ways in which refuse is dealt with vary from area to area.

Some local authorities put the rubbish on conveyor belts and remove any material that can be **recycled**.

Inflammable refuse may then be **incinerated**. This is the safest way to deal with potentially infectious material such as used dressings from hospitals.

Remaining refuse is taken to waste ground where it is sprayed with disinfectant and covered with a layer of soil. Micro-organisms in the soil help to decompose the refuse. Each layer of refuse should not be more than two metres thick or decay will be too slow. These tips should be sprayed with insecticide to prevent flies breeding.

Sometimes burning or tipping is not possible. In these cases the refuse is packed tightly by heavy machinery and left to decompose slowly.

16.9. *The Role of the Environmental Health Officer*

The precautions that have to be taken to ensure the health of the community are controlled by laws. To ensure that these laws are obeyed each local authority employs Environmental Health Officers. Their duties include:

1. Checking hygiene standards in shops and restaurants.
2. Monitoring noise levels.
3. Health checks at docks and airports.
4. Ensuring housing standards are maintained.
5. Ensuring that street cleaning and refuse disposal are carried out satisfactorily.

Key Words

Environmental health
Refuse disposal
Sedimentation
Filtration
Sludge
Chlorination
Metabolic disorders
Carcinogen
Disease
Neurosis
Water supply
Sewage
Screening
Coagulation
Liquor
Hygiene
Infection
Pathogen
Psychosis

Questions

1. Which of the following is suitable for the long-term preservation of food?
A. chilling
B. pasteurization
C. freezing
D. cooking

2. The figure below summarizes one method of treating sewage. Name the missing stages.

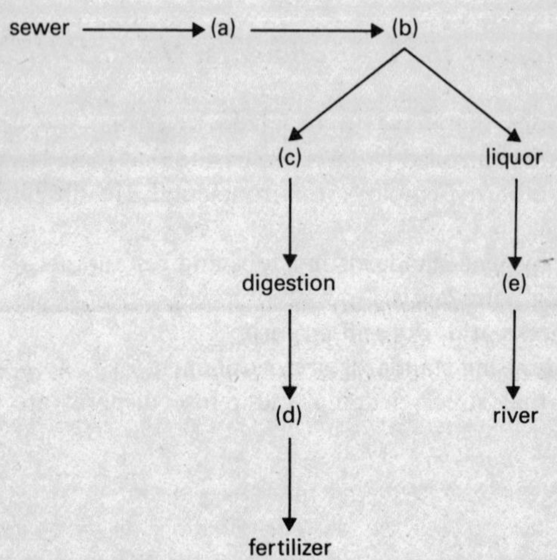

3. It has been suggested that lead from car exhausts which is washed into drains ends up in sewage sludge. What dangers might there be if this sludge were then spread on fields as fertilizer?

4. Which of the following processes is responsible for killing bacteria in the purification of water?
A. screening
B. chlorination
C. digestion
D. filtration

5. Processes A–D are methods of food preservation.
A. Pickling
B. Canning
C. Chilling
D. Salting
From the list A–D choose which process:
(a) slows the growth of bacteria but does not kill them;
(b) deprives micro-organisms of oxygen;
(c) relies on osmosis;
(d) uses acid to kill microbes.

6. Look at the figures in the table below

Time from drinking (hours)	0.0	0.5	1.0	1.5	2.0	2.5	3.0	3.5	4.0
Alcohol in blood (per cent)	0.00	0.04	0.12	0.13	0.11	0.08	0.05	0.04	0.03

(a) Draw a graph of the results shown in the table.
(b) What is the percentage of alcohol in the blood 3 hours after drinking it?
(c) How long after drinking are the alcohol levels the highest?
(d) What effects does alcohol have on the body?
(e) What damage can be done to the body by long-term drinking?

7. The table below gives the numbers of bacteria in frozen meat at different intervals after slaughter.
(a) Which temperature is better for storing meat?
(b) What is the effect of the lower temperature on the bacteria?
(c) Name two *other ways of storing meat for long periods of time.*

Months after slaughter	*Numbers of bacteria per 100 g of meat* *Storage at −15°C*	*Storage at −30°C*
1	8	7
2	15	11
3	27	16
4	42	21
5	59	30
6	73	38

8. (a) Distinguish between neurosis and psychosis.
(b) Give two examples of each.

17. In the Exam

If you followed the advice and instructions in Chapter 2 during your revision, you should now be familiar with the different types of question set by your board and should know how to tackle them. In any case, read over Chapter 2 once more.

Get plenty of sleep the night before your exam. Do *not* stay up all night revising. Get up in good time for the exam, allowing extra time for travel in case of unforeseen delays (traffic jams, train cancellations, a bicycle puncture, etc.). Turn up to the exam in good time and come fully equipped with pens (at least one spare), pencils, pencil sharpener, eraser and ruler.

Now is the time to put all your effort to good use. Remember, what counts is what you put down on the exam paper. This is your only contact with the examiner. Marks can only be given for what you write on the paper – not for what remains in your head.

1. Read carefully the instructions at the head of the exam paper and follow them absolutely.
2. Work out a time allocation for the questions according to the marks they carry. Throughout the exam, check on the time and stick to your allocation – do not overrun.
3. Answer all compulsory questions.
4. If the paper is divided into sections make sure you answer the correct number of questions in each section.
5. Always answer the correct number of questions overall. If you are required to do four long-answer questions, and you only answer three, it is almost impossible to make up the marks for the missing fourth question. On any one question, the first 50 per cent of marks are the easiest to gain. To get 60 marks out of 100, it is easier to gain 15 out of 25 on each of four questions, than to gain 20 out of 25 on each of three.
6. If given a choice of longer-answer questions, narrow down the best questions to answer. You can do this by estimating the number of marks you will get for a question *before* you attempt to answer it.
7. *Understand* what the question asks *before* you attempt to answer it. Do *not* twist the question into an unintended meaning. *No* marks are

awarded for irrelevant information and the answer should include *only* points demanded by the question. Do not write down *all* you know on a particular topic unless it is asked for.

8. Examiners prefer concise answers written in good English. Set out work neatly. The examiner is only human. Draw a single straight line across any work which you do not wish to be marked (an essay plan for example).

9. Plan your longer answers before writing them (see page 9).

10. Use large labelled diagrams if they make your answer clearer and save time and words.

11. If you are running out of time in a question, complete your answer in note form, putting in all the key points. You will gain at least some marks.

12. If any time is left at the end, read through your answers and correct any mistakes.

The exam is the final furlong in a long, possibly hard road. Keep a cool head and do yourself justice.

Index

Italicised page numbers indicate that the reference is to the diagram on that page. Where a sequence of pages is shown (e.g. 142–7), diagrams may be included.

(eq) after a page reference denotes examination question.

PENGUIN REFERENCE BOOKS

The Penguin English Dictionary

Over 1,000 pages long and with over 68,000 definitions, this cheap, compact and totally up-to-date book is ideal for today's needs. It includes many technical and colloquial terms, guides to pronunciation and common abbreviations.

The Penguin Concise Columbia Encyclopedia

The most complete, convenient and authoritative desk encyclopedia for home, school and office. Prepared under the guidance of a distinguished panel of scholars, *The Penguin Concise Columbia Encyclopedia* is a marvel of clarity, convenience and completeness.

The Penguin English Thesaurus Ed. Betty Kirkpatrick

This new edition of Roget's classic work, now brought up to date for the nineties, will increase anyone's command of the English language. Fully cross-referenced, it includes synonyms of every kind (formal or colloquial, idiomatic and figurative) for almost 900 headings. It is a must for writers and utterly fascinating for any English speaker.

The Penguin Dictionary of Quotations

A treasure-trove of over 12,000 new gems and old favourites, from Aesop and Matthew Arnold to Xenophon and Zola.

The Penguin Wordmaster Dictionary Manser and Turton

This dictionary puts the pleasure back into word-seeking. Every time you look at a page you get a bonus – a panel telling you everything about a particular word or expression. It is, therefore, a dictionary to be read as well as used for its concise and up-to-date definitions.

PENGUIN REFERENCE BOOKS

The Penguin Guide to the Law

This acclaimed reference book is designed for everyday use and forms the most comprehensive handbook ever published on the law as it affects the individual.

The Penguin Medical Encyclopedia

Covers the body and mind in sickness and in health, including drugs, surgery, history, institutions, medical vocabulary and many other aspects. 'Highly commendable' – *Journal of the Institute of Health Education*

The Penguin French Dictionary

This invaluable French–English, English–French dictionary includes both the literary and dated vocabulary needed by students, and the up-to-date slang and specialized vocabulary (scientific, legal, sporting, etc) needed in everyday life. As a passport to the French language it is second to none.

A Dictionary of Literary Terms

Defines over 2,000 literary terms (including lesser known, foreign language and technical terms) explained with illustrations from literature past and present.

The Penguin Dictionary of Troublesome Words

A witty, straightforward guide to the pitfalls and hotly disputed issues in standard written English, illustrated with examples and including a glossary of grammatical terms and an appendix on punctuation.

The Concise Cambridge Italian Dictionary

Compiled by Barbara Reynolds, this work is notable for the range of examples provided to illustrate the exact meaning of Italian words and phrases. It also contains a pronunciation guide and a reference grammar.

A CHOICE OF PENGUINS AND PELICANS

Asimov's New Guide to Science Isaac Asimov

A fully updated edition of a classic work – far and away the best one-volume survey of all the physical and biological sciences.

Relativity for the Layman James A. Coleman

Of this book Albert Einstein said: 'Gives a really clear idea of the problem, especially the development of our knowledge concerning the propagation of light and the difficulties which arose from the apparently inevitable introduction of the ether.'

The Double Helix James D. Watson

Watson's vivid and outspoken account of how he and Crick discovered the structure of DNA (and won themselves a Nobel Prize) – one of the greatest scientific achievements of the century.

Ever Since Darwin Stephen Jay Gould

'Stephen Gould's writing is elegant, erudite, witty, coherent and forceful' – Richard Dawkins in *Nature*

Mathematical Magic Show Martin Gardner

A further mind-bending collection of puzzles, games and diversions by the undisputed master of recreational mathematics.

Silent Spring Rachel Carson

The brilliant book which provided the impetus for the ecological movement – and has retained its supreme power to this day.

FOR THE BEST IN PAPERBACKS, LOOK FOR THE

A CHOICE OF PENGUINS AND PELICANS

Adieux Simone de Beauvoir

This 'farewell to Sartre' by his life-long companion is a 'true labour of love' (the *Listener*) and 'an extraordinary achievement' (*New Statesman*).

British Society 1914–45 John Stevenson

A major contribution to the Pelican Social History of Britain, which 'will undoubtedly be the standard work for students of modern Britain for many years to come' – *The Times Educational Supplement*

The Pelican History of Greek Literature Peter Levi

A remarkable survey covering all the major writers from Homer to Plutarch, with brilliant translations by the author, one of the leading poets of today.

Art and Literature Sigmund Freud

Volume 14 of the Pelican Freud Library contains Freud's major essays on Leonardo, Michelangelo and Dostoyevsky, plus shorter pieces on Shakespeare, the nature of creativity and much more.

A History of the Crusades Sir Steven Runciman

This three-volume history of the events which transferred world power to Western Europe – and founded Modern History – has been universally acclaimed as a masterpiece.

A Night to Remember Walter Lord

The classic account of the sinking of the *Titanic*. 'A stunning book, incomparably the best on its subject and one of the most exciting books of this or any year' – *The New York Times*

FOR THE BEST IN PAPERBACKS, LOOK FOR THE

A CHOICE OF PENGUINS AND PELICANS

A Question of Economics Peter Donaldson

Twenty key issues – the City, trade unions, 'free market forces' and many others – are presented clearly and fully in this major book based on a television series.

The Economist Economics Rupert Pennant-Rea and Clive Crook

Based on a series of 'briefs' published in the *Economist* in 1984, this important new book makes the key issues of contemporary economic thinking accessible to the general reader.

The Tyranny of the Status Quo Milton and Rose Friedman

Despite the rhetoric, big government has actually *grown* under Reagan and Thatcher. The Friedmans consider why this is – and what we can do now to change it.

Business Wargames Barrie G. James

Successful companies use military strategy to win. Barrie James shows how – and draws some vital lessons for today's manager.

Atlas of Management Thinking Edward de Bono

This fascinating book provides a vital repertoire of non-verbal images – to help activate the right side of any manager's brain.

The Winning Streak Walter Goldsmith and David Clutterbuck

A brilliant analysis of what Britain's best-run and successful companies have in common – a must for all managers.